# The
# Stained Glass
# Appraisal Guide

*First Edition*

2008-2009

Compiled by
Gary M. Gray, Ed. D
and Carrie Crow

*With an Introduction from
Peter Rohlf and Gunar Gruenke*

Church of the Holy Cross, Paris, Texas

# Table of Contents

| | |
|---|---|
| Judges | ii |
| Acknowledgements | iii |
| Introduction | v |
| Chapter I: Preserving an Important Asset | 3 |
| Chapter II: Judging Between Mom And Rembrandt | 9 |
| Chapter III: How To Appraise Stained Glass | 31 |
| Chapter IV: Comparing Apples and Oranges | 39 |
| Chapter V: The Appraisal Research | 59 |
| Section 1: American Stained Glass Over the Decades | 64 |
| Section 2: The Great Stained Glass Studios | 90 |
| Section 3: The Modern Stained Glass Studios | 160 |
| Section 4: Faceted Glass | 178 |
| Afterword: Stained Glass in the New Millennium | 195 |
| About the Artists | 199 |
| Directory: Stained Glass Association of America Members | 220 |
| Index | 227 |

# STAINED GLASS APPRAISAL GUIDE JUDGES

*Steve Wilson*
Art Glass by Wells

*Eric Ascalon*
Ascalon Studios

*Ettore C. Botti*
Botti Studios of
Architectural Arts, Inc.*

*Larry and Ken Casola*
Casola Stained Glass*

*Paul Pickel*
Conrad Pickel
Studio Inc.*

*Gunar Gruenke*
Conrad Schmitt Studios*

*Karen S. Armentrout*
Cottage Glass

*Kirk Reber*
Creative Glassworks*

*Andrew Paremski*
Enterprise Art

*Troy J. Knight*
Glass by Knight

*Pat Haeger*
Haeger Stained Glass*

*Judith and James VanWie*
Hiemer & Co. Stained
Glass Studio*

*Michael Hope*
Hope Stained Glass

*David Gomm*
Imagine Stained Glass

*John Kebrle*
Kebrle Stained Glass*

*Roy Loman*
Loman Studios

*Tim Smith*
Moss Stained Glass

*Jim Perry*
Perry Stained Glass*

*Dale Preston*
Preston Art Glass
Studio

*John M. Raynal*
Raynal Studios*

*Bill Reinarts*
Reinarts Stained Glass*

*Peter and Hans Rohlf*
Rohlf's Studio*

*Susan Louise Firpo*
SLFirpo Design/Craft

*Randall Leever*
The Boulder Stained
Glass Studios*

*Jamie Jones*
The Leaded Glass
Studio*

*Duncan Tooley*
Tooley Art Glass
Studio

*Jack Whitworth*
Whitworth
Stained Glass*

*Reggie Buehrer*
Window Creations*

*Denotes membership in the Stained Glass Association of America

# Acknowledgements

A Stained Glass Appraisal Guide cannot be written by one person. Oh, it could, but it would be essentially incorrect. This guide is built on centuries of history, and its expertise has been gleaned from many.

Our focus has been on the stained glass that exists in America. We have used the collective expertise of the American stained glass studios to provide for church and synagogue leaders, along with the religious insurance industry, a volume which begins a replacement value consensus (in case a stained glass window requires replication).

The guide started at the request of the church insurance industry as executives approached the American Consultation on Stained Glass to create a tool for appropriate stained glass appraisals.

Two giants of the stained glass industry, Peter Rohlf of Rohlf Studios in New York City, and Gunar Gruenke of Conrad Schmitt Studios in Milwaukee, supported the appraisal guide concept and research necessary for valid evaluations. Specific thanks also go to David Judson, Judson Stained Glass, Calif.; Bill Reinarts, Reinarts Stained Glass, Minn.; Jack Whitworth, Whitworth Stained Glass, Texas, and Al Priest, Salem Stained Glass, N.C.

Throughout America, some thirty stained glass studio executives answered an extensive questionnaire to offer an average appraisal price on numerous sample windows. It is their composite expertise that validates the Stained Glass Appraisal Guide.

Cheryl Franks, Fred Lamb and Pedro Velasco were invaluable in the editing and research processes, respectively. The most credit goes to Carrie Crow (researcher and designer) who worked with this jig-saw puzzle of a publication for over a year and nursed it to completion.

Finally, a thank you to all the churches, synagogues and institutions that are pictured in this book. Most seemed genuinely honored that so many experts would be evaluating their windows.

*Introduction*

# THE WIDE-EYED ANGEL PUSHED BACK

Once upon a time, there was a little angel given only one task. She was to guard a little church against all dangers.

The little angel took her job seriously, never once leaving her post, watching with vigilance for anyone or anything that would harm her little church and all the wonderful people of the congregation. She was always cheerful and spoke to everyone who came by to admire her little church by the sea.

But one day the little angel became lonely because no one came and went from the church; not a soul came by to take pictures of the little edifice; even the seagulls ignored her as they flew inland.

Suddenly off in the distance came a dark storm cloud. It appeared mean and foreboding, far more ominous than the little angel had ever witnessed. The waters near the little church became choppy.

Sensing danger, the little angel was determined not to leave her post. She had to stay to protect her building…she had promised everyone the building would be safe under her watch. Now she had no one to tell that too…she was alone! But, she was focused to face the danger.

As the storm hit the beach, she stuck out her hands to push the turmoil away. The winds grew powerful. Blowing sand pierced her face and hands. Water was everywhere.

Once during the night a wave some 13 feet tall came directly toward the little angel. Genuinely terrified now, the little angel cried out for the wave to go

*Left: This little angel statue is the only undamaged item at St. Peter's By the Sea Episcopal Church, Gulfport, Miss. It seems to still be trying to push the storm away.*

back to the sea, but the wave did not listen. Instead it engulfed the little angel with a fury never before remembered on that beach.

It seemed an eternity but eventually the water subsided and the winds calmed. The little angel had stood her ground. She had not left her post.

But something was not right. She could not move. She tried to look to her left at her little church but her neck would not turn. The little angel tried desperately to look out of the corner of her eyes, but even they would not move. All she could see were her hands directly in front of her. But they wouldn't move either. What had happened? Had she pushed so hard against the storm that she had turned into stone?

Within hours of her terrifying experience, fire and rescue people first made their way down to the beach. She could hear someone talking. Her building was the only one on the beach still standing!! She had done her job.

Sadly, although the church was still standing, a surge of water had swept past the little angel and engulfed the first floor, taking all the walls and windows with it. How sad! What would the church do? Would they ask that she be assigned elsewhere? She had failed in her job and now she had turned to stone.

Then someone came along to take her picture. She heard him say as he walked away. "No one, not even little angels could hold that storm away. The little church will have to start over."

While we are saddened by the plight of the little angel and all the churches that have encountered tragedies through the years, such as Hurricane Katrina, this book isn't about angels.

This book is designed to be a stained glass information source for churches, synagogues, the church insurance industry, and stained glass professionals. It is our hope that THE 2008-2009 STAINED GLASS APPRAISAL GUIDE will serve as a bridge that calms the waters for worried clergy and laypersons across America.

*St. Peter's by the Sea Episcopal Church, Gulfport, Miss. was overwhelmed by Hurricane Katrina's storm surge that effectively obliterated the nave's lower level.*

Throughout America, and the world, there are stained glass windows in imminent danger of fire, accidents, burglary, and, of course, weather. We, of the stained glass industry, have always felt that a replacement value consensus was needed. In retrospect, we were too competitive with each other to dare to conduct a joint attempt at replication costs in case a window was destroyed and the congregation wanted it re-created "exactly" as before.

Left to our industry alone, this consensus would never have happened.

It took the church insurance industry to request a detailed and comprehensive stained glass appraisal guide. The church insurance industry, it turns out, is under extreme pressure from the local religious institutions to help them set the value of their stained glass.

Pastors and church lay leaders had simply heard too many horror stories of church naves burning (or being destroyed in other ways) to find their priceless stained glass had only token amounts of insurance coverage. Further, they rarely had the records necessary to begin the process of replication. They needed a way to compile this knowledge.

It took executives of all three of the large church insurance companies to speak with the American Consultation on Stained Glass to urge some form of consensus and information to begin to be assembled, researched, "judged," and reported.

When the ACSG approached our two studios, we both immediately saw the value of such a project and have supported the effort from the beginning. Not everyone in our profession was ready to risk divulging information in the interest of consensus, but enough have for the initial STAINED GLASS APPRAISAL GUIDE to serve the call of the local religious institutions and those of the church insurance industry.

We now know that little stone angels cannot stop a hurricane as it devours a city like Gulfport, nor can they quench the flames as stained glass artistry melts before terrified parishioners. Little stone angels can't even stop little boys with slingshots who find stained glass to have wonderful bull's eyes for target practice.

**Right: Hurricane Katrina's storm surge destroyed First Presbyterian Church, Gulfport, Miss. These two flags, one Christian, the other American, stood guard at the devastated entrance.**

Therefore, we must deal with our stained glass in other ways. We need to protect our stained glass from the moment it is installed. When stained glass begins to deteriorate, it needs to be refurbished, possibly restored or even re-leaded.

Finally, stained glass needs to be appraised at its proper current replacement value, so that if disaster does strike, little angels do not feel like failures at their posts. It is for that last significant reason this book has been prepared for you.

Peter Rohlf
Rohlf Stained Glass Studios

Gunar Gruenke
Conrad Schmitt Studios

**Right: Dome at First United Methodist Church, Gulfport, Miss.**

Basilica of the Sacred Heart, Notre Dame, Ind.
Produced (1870-1880's) at the Carmelite Sisters' Le Mans Glass Works
(France), under artistic and archaeological director Eugène Hucher.

# The Stained Glass Appraisal Guide

*Zettler window at St. Edmund Parish, Oak Park, Ill.*

## *Chapter I*

# Preserving an Important Asset

There is nothing more beautiful than God's light shining through a stained glass window. The vibrant colors and intricate designs warm our sanctuaries and recount the stories of Christ. These artistic expressions of God's love serve as a comfort and a treasure to worshippers worldwide.

However, when an historic church or cathedral falls into disrepair or suffers the ravages of storms or fires, our hearts break at the thought of losing the stained glass.

Here's the good news. In many cases, with careful attention to detail and craftsmanship, these works of art can be preserved and restored for generations to come. It all begins with a better understanding of stained glass and its properties – and that is the purpose of our book.

## *Why is your stained glass important?*

First and foremost, stained glass windows are a unique part of your historic structure and are inviting to all who see them.

## *Story Tellers*

Stained glass windows tell a story to all comers. Whether stained glass graces a small community church in an underprivileged area or a robust congregation of 5,000 people, its symbols, designs, lead flows, and pictorials create am ambience in which we can worship and communicate with God.

At some extremely important point in the history of most congregations, both Christian and Jewish, there was a time of prayer about what messages their stained glass should portray or represent. If the congregation completed their tasks thoughtfully and in excellent communication with the design artist, an almost permanent and stunningly beautiful set of stories was created.

4

*Cathedral of St. Helena, Helena, Mont.*

Stained glass became, in essence, God's first slide show. Throughout America, ministers used their windows to preach a series of sermons. Likewise, congregations proud of their windows' messages conduct tours, offering yet another opportunity to tell a story.

## *Inspiration*

In 1912, F. X. Zettler began installing at the remote, but massive Cathedral of St. Helena in Helena, Montana, a staggering 11,000 square feet of intricate pictorials. This beautiful stained glass tells the story of the Bible and the history of the Catholic Church.

Nearly one hundred years later, tourists are still drawn to see this cathedral. The stained glass is so beautifully balanced, in story and design, and so delightfully impacted by the flow of light, that tourists often just sit down to stare. Others fall immediately into prayer, while others slowly stroll from one window to another. Their visual senses have become overwhelmed to their great pleasure. Their understanding of the magnificence of the Creator is heightened with awe and inspiration.

It does not take magnificent Zettler (or Tiffany) stained glass to evoke awe. Even the most simple colored glass has a way of allowing God's light to uniquely pour into a sanctuary…adding to the mystery and holiness of this sacred place.

## *Perpetuation*

Probably half of the stained glass in American churches and synagogues are memorials of loved ones, often from many decades earlier.

Perpetuation, the memory of one's own life or that of loved one's, is among the most powerful of human needs. When that perpetuation can be complete in a memorial that people will see for generations, especially if it tells a story and inspires, it also becomes a significant fund raising tool.

*Left: St. Xavier Parish, Missoula, Mont.*
*Right: First Presbyterian Church, Raleigh, N.C.*

Fund raising can make stained glass affordable for churches and synagogues of all sizes. In fact, once these opportunities are made known, there is generally a waiting list of families lining up to fund a new window.

The same motivation exists for replicating destroyed stained glass, or for restoring/repairing deteriorating masterpieces. People have a strong human need to perpetuate memory. Stained glass is almost magical in its capacity to raise funds.

## *Artistic Masterpiece*

There are probably three to four thousand congregations in America today whose artistic stained glass exceeds one million dollars per site. High quality pictorial stained glass created in the first decade of the new millennium is often commissioned at between $800 and $1,000 per square foot. Thus, using the $1,000 per square foot figure, it takes only 1,000 square feet of stained glass to reach a million dollars in artwork. Looking at it in a different way, if a congregation has 200 square feet of other priceless stained glass, the value soars to the million figure easily.

Yet churches, synagogues and insurance companies are unaware of the extraordinary value of the artwork in the local congregation until they face the consequences of destruction—that of a hail storm, fire or a vandal.

The 2008-2009 Stained Glass Appraisal Guide provides the tools for accurate appraisals and restoration, so that churches and synagogues can continue their work—telling stories. It also provides answers for before, when, and after disaster strikes.

*Left: Robbie Head (1889-1893) window at First United Methodist Church, McKinney, Texas*

*Skylight at Anshe Emet Synagogue, Chicago, Ill.*

*Chapter II*

# Judging Between Mom And Rembrandt

My mother learned to paint when she was in her seventies. Every time she had guests in her home, they would use a variety of adjectives to describe her wonderful artistry. "You are becoming the next 'Grandma Moses,'" some would exclaim! But in the end, none of her paintings were ever sold, and they were all distributed among the family members upon her death. Back in those Oklahoma farm days, it was impolite to say anything derogatory.

I still have a number of her paintings in my home and they are proudly displayed, but I have no illusions that I have a Rembrandt or a Da Vinci quality masterpiece in my living room. It is valuable, of course, to me. If the house burned, the paintings could not be replaced, because they wouldn't be repainted by Mom.

With stained glass, the ownership is much more widespread; it is "owned" by a congregation. Usually, the stained glass has inspired generation after generation of worshippers. Should a stained glass window be broken or destroyed, there is usually an overwhelming desire for replacement, restoration or repair.

There are some 400,000 American church buildings in existence today, and the vast majority has some form of inspirational glass (much of which would fit the term of stained glass). Most of that glass is simple, but even elementary glass is expensive and should have special insurance. If it is a window created by Charles Connick in the 1920s, we may be talking $800 per square foot for replacement. Should there be 2,000 square feet of these type of windows in the church, then the fine arts policy needs to have $1,600,000 just for the stained glass (not including the frame and tracery).

## *The General Replacement Value Rules*

Nowhere is it written how to judge the value of a window (this book is among the first to try). It takes years and hundreds of hours inspecting different sets of windows to become an "expert," but there are some elementary rules of thumb to follow. All of these rules interplay with one another, eventually shaping the replacement value.

## *Small > Large*

All things being equal, the smaller the stained glass pieces the greater the value. Stained glass is labor intensive. Smaller pieces require more glass cutting and lead. Windows with small pieces of glass were most prominent during the period of 1885-1899, when "jewels" (many no larger than one inch in diameter) were utilized in the design.

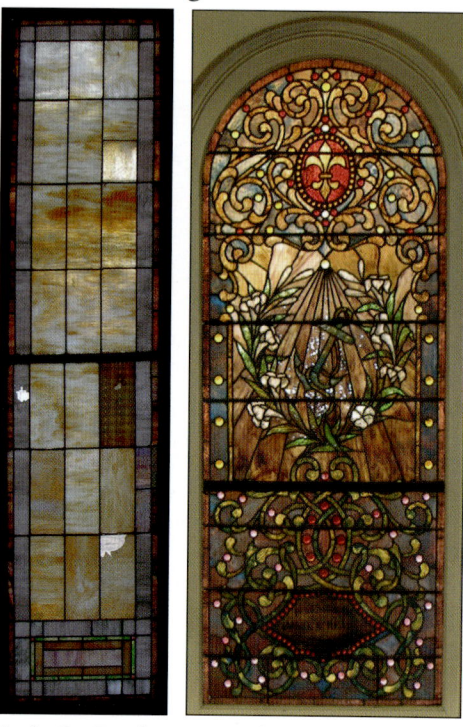

*Large vs. Small*

*Left: St. Paul Baptist Church, Paris, Texas*
*Right: Jewel window at First Presbyterian Church, Raleigh, N.C.*

## *Older > New*

The older the window (even with the same design), the more difficult it is to replace. There are several reasons. First, is old glass availability. Despite many stained glass inventories in existence, the older sheets of stained glass (necessary for exact replacement) are almost impossible to match. Even when a glass is eventually matched, the research to find that glass is time consuming and therefore, expensive.

Second, artistic styles change. It is often difficult for a designer or painter of the 21st century to match that of one from the 19th or even early 20th centuries.

## *Old vs. New*

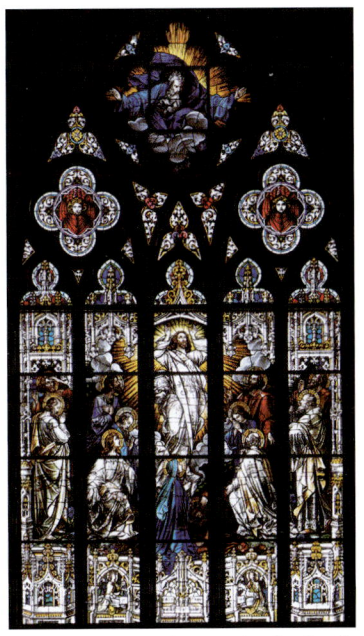 

*Left: Cathedral of St. John the Baptist, Savannah, Ga.*
*(Photo Credit: Don DuBroff)*
**Right: Baylor Baptist Hospital, Plano, Texas** *(Photo courtesy of Shenandoah Studios)*

There are restoration artists who specialize in working with old and broken stained glass. Here the goal is to subordinate one's artistic style to that of the artist of possibly a century before, painstakingly seeking the perfect match. If you will, the restoration artist seeks to become one with the compatriot painter of decades prior.

A final reason is fade. If only a piece or two are broken by hail, for example, an artist should not replace the broken ones with a painted/fired piece of glass that looks new—it will stick out like a sore thumb. Instead, the artist must build in a "fade" so that no one is able to see where the "new" piece is located. The replacement artist is a success when his or her work is not noticeable, and that takes additional attention (and money).

## Painted/fired > Stained

Some pieces of "stained glass" have simply been cut from a sheet of colored glass and leaded into a stained glass window, while another set of glass pieces have each had paint applied. It sometimes takes as many as four or five firings before these are placed and leaded into a carefully designed window.

Even painted/fired pieces with simple shadings or a stencil design are more expensive than straight colored glass. It is more labor and time intensive, not to mention the cost for the designer to create the image. Some pictorial designed windows full of painted/fired pieces of glass are valued as much as ten times more than those of colored glass. In general, however, the ratio is more often two-to-one or three-to-one in replacement value.

**Painted vs. Stained**

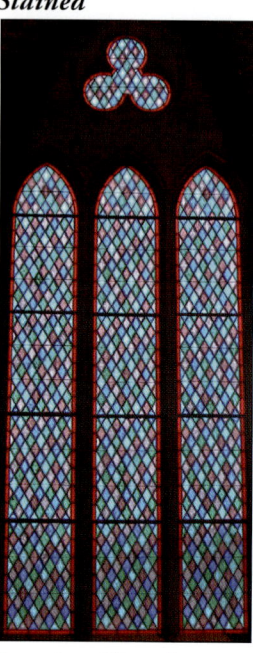

*Left: Myers Park Presbyterian Church, Charlotte, N.C.   Right: Trinity United Methodist Church, Huntsville, Ala.*

## Varied lines > Straight lines

There is certainly value in a horizontal or diamond shaped window but, in essence, the window fabricator has cut a sheet of colored glass into numerous exact-same-size pieces, and then leaded them. With relative ease, borders with different sizes and colors can be added.

Those same sheets of glass can be transformed into a design, but it requires an artisan envisioning a creative flow or image made simply with the use of colors or the rhythmic movement of the lead lines. The cost of the design, plus the labor to do specialized glass cutting, all contribute to the higher cost of this window when compared to that of the straight line.

***Varied vs. Straight***

**Left: River Terrace Church, East Lansing, Mich., by Conrad Schmitt Studios**
*(Photo courtesy of Conrad Schmitt Studios)*
**Right: First Presbyterian Church, McKenzie, Tenn.**

## *Multi-layers > Single layer*

Many of the great artisans of the past (and a few in the present) utilized a second layer of leaded opalescent stained glass (and as many as four) to accomplish the exact color or shading they desired. The great American artists John La Farge and Louis Comfort Tiffany prominently double-layered their scenes while featuring custom designed "drapery" glass on robes. These features make signed La Farge and Tiffany windows at least a 25 to 1 replacement value increase over simple leaded glass.

***Multi-layered vs. Single-layer***

**North Avenue Presbyterian Church, Atlanta, Ga.
Left: Tiffany    Right: Willet**

Some modern studios use the double-layered approach on important areas of their design. This method is relatively rare, however, as it appears in no more than one or two percent of custom designed windows. The most common location is in the robe areas of figures or in the memorial nameplate. A modern full-multi-layer stained glass window would be at least double or triple in price, compared with a similar single glazed one, but these are almost non-existent. The targeted multi-layered window is only slightly more expensive for replication than its single glazed counterpart.

## Design > No design

Whenever an artist deliberately sets out to create a specific message or mood with stained glass, a design is required. Beyond the leaded glass with a series of straight lines, the artist may use a the rhythmic flow, along with a careful choice of colors, to inspire the illusion of "creation," "sunrise," or numerous forms of landscape.

Traditionally, stained glass has been used to either inspire (with light streaming through colors into the interior), and/or to tell a story. The designer moves to a second level (beyond rhythmic flow) when the story needs to be told, possibly with the use of scripture or symbols.

 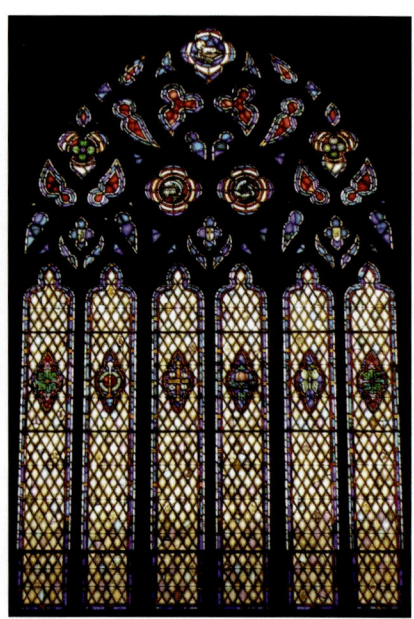

*Left: Greendale Community Church, Greendale, Wis.,
by Conrad Schmitt Studios (Photo courtesy of Conrad Schmitt Studios)
Right: Idlewild Presbyterian Church, Memphis, Tenn.*

*Custom Window by Salem Stained Glass*

A significant variety of designs exist ranging from abstract to literal, and from flows to scenes to human figures. Because of this range, assigning the correct replacement costs becomes more difficult as well. An intricate custom painted design may have a 10 to 1 replacement value ratio when compared to a leaded (non-painted) window with simple leadlines.

*Catalog Window by Salem Stained Glass*

## *Custom > Catalog*

It is not generally known, but the stained glass industry has stained glass that can be purchased via catalog and the Internet. While the liturgy committees of some elite churches may reject such a choice, there is some distinctive value tied to the custom stained glass window. For example, it is possible to choose from a variety of simple designs and basic colors.

Thus if a church desires design D and color 16 in the main field and colors 28 and 73 for the borders, all fitted to window frames that are 36 inches wide and 72 inches tall, the process for both the committee and the stained glass company is simplified.

Let's also assume that the church wanted to tell the story of the Old Testament on the east side of the nave and the New Testament on the west side. No problem, as the committee can pick from possibly 50 different ready-made scenes (usually in the form of 12 inches circular pictorial symbols). Therefore, within the span of one committee session, twenty-four different Biblical depictions can be chosen, starting with Adam and Eve, Noah, Abraham, and

Moses, and ending with the exploits of the Apostle Paul. All of these scenes are multi-produced, bringing the costs down considerably.

The quality of the "catalog" window is sometimes equal to that of the custom window. The problem is that the catalog window is not unique. Someone visiting a church in Chattanooga, Tenn., one day, might be in a church in Charlotte, N.C., the next, and see almost identical stained glass. That would bother some churches, while others could care less.

Custom design is ultimate in stained glass ownership. A custom design utilizes a combination of artistry with lead line flow, antique glass, colors, and/or paint. The most difficult, are the attempts to paint lifelike faces and other body parts.

During the period of 1880 through World War I, faces often went through extensive phases of paint and fire and paint and fire, until the ultimate level of perfection was achieved. The great Munich, Germany companies of Franz Mayer and F. X. Zettler set the standard for the magnificent Catholic stained glass of that period. Because of the tremendous demand for stained glass in America, many of the great artists immigrated to America to establish studios in New York, Boston, Chicago, and St. Louis.

After the 1920s, and through recent years, only a handful of the leading studios retained the skills or the patience to maintain this pre-1917 level of artistry. There is little likelihood that this detail will ever be sought again, but many of the modern studios are researching the methods of those great artisans, to replicate to a degree that quality of facial integrity.

As one might expect, the level of custom design varies with each individual designer or artist, not just with the standards of the local stained glass company. Some faces are, for example, left blank, with the congregant assigned the responsibility of supplying the facial image. Others, like the artisans of the 19th century, use great detail to illustrate facial expression. Some designs are best in the abstract—and thus the debate about replacement value is ever so difficult.

In general, the custom stained glass window is from two to five times as valuable as its catalog counterpart.

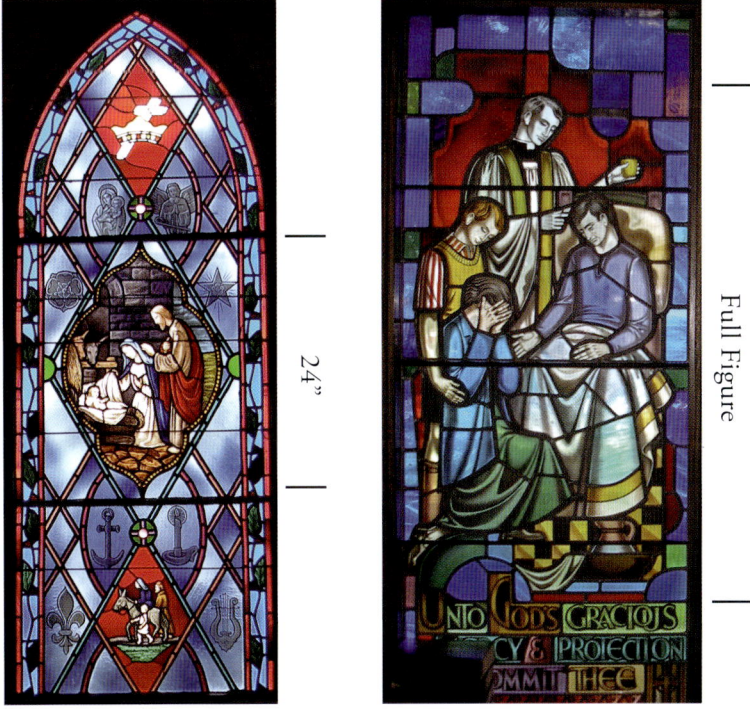

*Left: Medallion at Palm Valley Lutheran Church, Round Rock, Texas*
*Right: Figure at Church of the Incarnation, Dallas, Texas*

## *Figures > Medallions > Symbols*

The Biblical story through stained glass is usually told in one of three ways. The simplest is a single piece of glass with a painted scene. This is most often a symbol in a 12" painted/fired pictorial.

A medallion is more complex. Medallions tend to be larger than symbols, and with multiple pieces of leaded glass formed into a unique design within a larger, simpler design. The size and complexity make it generally more valuable than a symbol.

*Symbol by Salem Stained Glass*

The most complex, and therefore expensive, is the figure design. The figure normally is larger than a medallion, either taking up a significant portion of a window lancet, or possibly taking up the bulk of the entire window. As the pictorial portion of the window increases, so does its replacement value.

## National firm > Local artist

Most local stained glass companies, and there are probably 3,500 of them throughout America, have someone on staff with an artistic flair—or they would be in the accounting business instead. These "Ma and Pa" artists, hopefully, have no illusions of being the next Louis Comfort Tiffany. Instead they must specialize in leaded transoms for new houses and offices, and occasionally for the neighborhood church or synagogue. They are quickly over their heads with a large, complex commission, and are of little use with a restoration or replication assignment.

Even among the national firms, there is significant specialization that will be detailed elsewhere in this book. Needless to say, the design artists in the national firms have been recruited to their positions and are normally of the very best in the nation. The demand allows them to specialize, and therefore to be paid according to their skills.

*Tiffany window at North Avenue Presbyterian Church, Atlanta, Ga.*

Among restoration specialists, there are two basic kinds. First, are the on-site repair and stabilization artisans, where master craftsmen arrive in a truck and most restoration work is completed at the church or synagogue building.

The second kind is studio restoration specialists. In this case the windows are removed from the frame, cataloged and crated to the studio. They are then taken through an intensive restoration (possibly taken apart and re-leaded). If full replication is required, the work must be conducted at the studio.

Thus the "Ma and Pa" local stained glass company needs to focus on serving only the home, the office and the small church. It is the national, or at least regional firm that should be commissioned for the larger tasks. This is true whether the church wants quality "catalog" stained glass, truly unique and high quality custom stained glass designs, on-site restoration or studio restoration. The sophistication level of artistry and technology required is simply too complex for the small shop.

## *Good > Poor Condition*

This appears to be a stupid issue on the surface (the stained glass surface, that is). The truth is, however, that perspectives change when disaster hits.

For example, perhaps a person wants to own an old automobile, buys one that is in poor condition, then does not provide for that old classic over a period of time. One day that person takes it out for a spin and it catches fire and completely burns into obliteration. Will he go now to the insurance company and expect the car to be replaced at the same level as a mint-condition restored model? Because the public often feels they are owed by insurance companies, many have unrealistic repayment expectations for their losses.

It is certainly true of stained glass. Regardless of the condition of the windows when disaster strikes, many expect the windows to be replaced at full current replication values. This is hardly fair, but is often the expectation.

There is a great amount of replacement difference from a nationally known window in one church that is in mint condition and protected from the elements, than one that has been disrespected and neglected. For example, let's assume two churches next door to each other both used the same nationally known firm in the 1920s to create their biblically symbolic leaded windows. The windows are both the same size, in fact the same artist was utilized on both. Yet one has been cared for on a systematic basis and protected from the elements since installation. The other has not received any attention in over 80 years and has never had protection.

There are two ways to look at the replacement value of these windows. Let's say that a window of this caliber and pedigree has a replacement value of $120,000 (200 square feet of pictorial stained glass x $600 per square foot). The problem is that the neglected window would possibly cost between $20,000 to $80,000 for restoration and protection. Further, the neglected one, even if restored, would probably not have the colors matched exactly.

# Expectations of Stained Glass Conservators and Restorers
*By Peter Rohlf, Rohlf Studios*

## High Quality Materials > Low Quality Materials

Stained Glass Conservators and Restorers who are hired to perform replications and/or restoration of historic stained glass windows have an obligation to both the owners and custodians as a whole. It is imperative that these conservators are knowledgeable and informed of all aspects of stained glass restoration and can provide the client with numerous past historic projects which demonstrate their capabilities.

The Stained Glass Association of America has available *Standards for Professional Conduct and Guidelines for Preservation Techniques* to assist responsible conservators in this field.

Some of the basic concerns which need to be addressed when evaluating the cost to restore either fire or storm damaged stained glass windows are to be sure that the same types of glass and textures are used to replicate the damaged areas. Most European windows were manufactured with mouth-blown antique glass. Early American stained glass windows were fabricated using a combination of opalescent and cathedral glasses and in the early days with colored pot glasses.

Replication of painted flesh, drapery or background glasses should be re-created by studios with professional artists and painters who are experienced in this type of work and can provide the client with pictures and references for their clarification.

The materials that go into a restoration project should be of the highest quality available. Restoration grade leads should always be used, along with 60/40 wire solder, which are available from most lead came companies.

An organic glazing compound with marine and soya oils are recommended for waterproofing the stained glass windows and should be included in the specifications for any new or restoration project.

Proper reinforcing of each stained glass section should also be considered when performing historic restoration and should be properly specified in any proposal, along with installation details and materials being used.

It is imperative that good in-studio before photographs be taken so there is a record of what existed before restoration work commences. This will protect the studio if any previous bad repairs had been done as well as provide a back-up for the craftspeople to look at during the work.

Restoration clients can always contact the SGAA or the Restoration and Preservation Committee for further knowledge and understanding of what should be expected from any bidder involved in this type of work. SGAA Telephone: 1-800-438-9581

*Tiffany window at First United Methodist Church, Colorado Springs, Colo.*

And, unless it was re-leaded, the leading would almost assuredly still be in poor condition when compared with its cared-for counterpart. It would have lost much of its original historical value, and it would not be uncommon for the window (and the building) to simply be abandoned.

The condition of the stained glass is therefore an important discussion point for the church property committee AND the church insurance company BEFORE the disaster. It is critical that window conditions be a factor in the ultimate replacement value assigned to the stained glass in the fine arts section of the church insurance policy.

Just as a mint-condition automobile 80 years old is much more valuable than a similar one almost ready for the junk heap, so stained glass should be appraised accordingly. Probably all churches and synagogues feel they pay mint-condition prices on their stained glass, but they should expect damage repayment on what they deserve, rather than on inflated and unrealistic expectations. If that is clearly desired by the church, and fully understood by both the church and the insurance company, then the appraisal needs to reflect that idealistic replication figure, rather than a more conservative or realistic one.

## *Protected > Unprotected*

If you were a robber trying to gain entrance to a church with two stained glass windows side-by-side, you might note that one is only a single layer of leaded stained glass, while the other has a heavy protective covering. Which would you choose?

If you are a 10-year-old boy armed with a slingshot and you are looking for targets, which would you choose? One window is full of potential targets, while the other has a huge sheet of glass or Lexan covering the surface. One is fun, the other isn't.

*Left: St. Paul United Methodist Church, Louisville, Ky. Right: Unprotected window at Baker Memorial UMC, St. Charles, Ill.*

Or if a hurricane is headed your way, which is more likely to have damage to its stained glass—the unprotected window with its valuable 1/8" thick glass or the one with a heavy-duty protective covering?

The answers to these questions are obvious. It is the protective covering that takes away most of the potential for catastrophic loss. There are still ways the stained glass can be damaged, through fire, for example, but the chances of major loss are greatly reduced if the church or synagogue property committee chooses to protect its valuable artwork.

So, here the question is not so much "How much are the windows worth?" but, "What are our chances (odds) of loss?" Here the insurance company has almost no choice but to charge extra for windows that are not protected from danger. There are a couple of other factors, already touched upon elsewhere. The unprotected window not only deteriorates more quickly, but is almost assuredly going to suffer broken glass over the years. These cannot be replaced exactly (despite promises from the stained glass company). And from that moment on, the windows will never be historically accurate again. It is therefore up to the good will of the insurance company as to whether to pay the costs to make them "new" again.

On the other hand, it must be remembered that the protective covering is an expensive investment. If it is destroyed for some reason, it will also need replacement. The insurance agent should assume a replacement value of about $70.00 per square foot (a premium protective covering set in an aluminum frame) beyond the replication costs of the stained glass itself.

## Signed > Unsigned

There are thousands of churches throughout the nation that think they have a "Tiffany" window. Most of them haven't, even though the style of one is unmistakable. The reason is simple. Louis Comfort Tiffany made unique stained glass and he had a lot of students. The students, plus other stained glass studios, all had access to that glass. Because Tiffany obviously taught the most promising students, the resulting "masterpieces" are 1) beautifully done, 2) in a Tiffany style (he taught them) and 3) used unique glass made by the Tiffany Studios. Does the church have Tiffany windows? Even if you bend the truth a long way, it still doesn't stretch far enough. The windows must be signed "Tiffany Studios" or even better "Louis Comfort Tiffany" or must be authenticated in some other way. Otherwise, the windows should be assigned a replacement value at a fraction of an authenticated Tiffany.

*Left: Frei signature, The Cathedral of Our Lady of Perpetual Help, Oklahoma City, Okla.*
*Right: F. X. Zettler signature, Cathedral of St. Helena, Helena, Mont.*

Signing has always been important in any form of artwork. This is usually found in the lower corners of one, two or all the stained glass windows. The signage is often subtle, so look carefully for it. Otherwise, a good source of authentication is the church history records. If authentication is not found, the resulting value is lessened substantially, perhaps by as much as three-fifths of the price.

This book has sought to help provide replacement values for some of the great historical and modern stained glass companies in which signage is a major factor in replacement value. It has named La Farge and Tiffany at the peak of value, with Zettler and Mayer of Bavaria, Loire of France, and American companies like Connick, Lamb, Payne, and Willet as the giants at the next level. Rohlf, Conrad Schmitt, Rambusch, Judson and Willet Hauser are among the most significant of the modern studios.

If your windows are signed, but not necessarily by a studio mentioned here, it may be because your studio was just as high quality but that its artistic products are famous only in a region, or possibly for a shorter period of time. Further research may determine that the replacement value that your church or synagogue windows should command should be approximately the same cost per square foot for replication as the ones mentioned in this book. On the other hand, it may not. Research is the starting point.

Another key is whether the stained glass studio has been a long-term certified member of the Stained Glass Association of America. Membership (and leadership) in the SGAA speaks volumes about the standards a studio represents in the church stained glass market.

****

Judging stained glass is an incomplete science. This volume will help, but the appraisal process will always be done by humans, with opinions that will vary widely. Opinions, profit margins and stained glass studio location will all play a part. Knowing the factors that go into the appraisal process of stained glass, however, should help churches and synagogues, the insurance industry, and the field of stained glass professionals come together into a more systematic approach to authentic appraisals than it has had in the past.

None of these factors, by itself, is to be the basis of an authentic appraisal; but, taken together as a group, these factors will help bring about a consensus. Therefore, when either the amateur or the professional judges stained glass, consider the following in determining its ultimate value (when everything else is equal).

> Small pieces > Large pieces
> Older stained glass > Newer stained glass
> Painted/fired glass > Stained/Colored glass
> Varied lines > Straight lines
> Multi-layered panels > Single layer panels
> Design > No Design
> Custom Design > Catalog Design
> Figures > Medallions > Symbols
> National firm > Local artist
> Good condition > Poor condition
> Protected > Unprotected
> Signed > Unsigned

Consistency of appraisals should be welcomed by all concerned and gives a feel for their artwork's replication value. This can help them take the proper steps to restore, protect and insure their heritage for future generations.

The church insurance company can cover the stained glass for an appropriate amount and not base its premiums on the stained glass being "priceless." That impossible word has caused havoc for decades. Insurance companies need a point of reference and a proper appraisal gives them a good place to start.

Stained glass companies have raised replication prices exponentially over the years with no national consensus. A national standard brings to the industry a legitimate opportunity for competition. When "apples" can be compared with "oranges," wise decisions are better made.

It is the people who stare upon the masterpieces who gain the most. Stained glass has been God's ultimate slide show for many centuries. Collectively these works of faith have inspired hundreds of millions. It is a heritage, which believers of the past want continued for the future.

# The Five Key Elements Of New Stained Glass

*Your congregation has just voted to build a new sanctuary. One of the most important items, several members say, is to have beautiful stained glass—whatever that means. As the chairperson of the new stained glass sub-committee, you are to lead the process of design selection. Your committee's decision will impact not only those who worship there in the sanctuary's first few years but quite possibly, worshipers for decades to come.*

*Many factors can influence the final decision. The input from the architect or a liturgical consultant is usually valuable. Artistic persons from the congregation can be helpful. In the end, however, you learn that creating the right stained-glass windows for the sanctuary requires careful attention to five critical elements.*

## Theme

*Choosing the theme or subject of a stained-glass design is the central element of your decision. The original stained glass from the twelfth and thirteenth centuries was created to tell the biblical story to the uneducated masses. Biblical scenes continue to dominate the themes chosen in the 21$^{st}$ century. Biblical themes are not, however, the only choice for a committee. Historical, regional and denominational themes have also been popular and appropriate. Even the most abstract windows can display themes such as the creation or a sunrise.*

## Design Style

*Today the excessive costs of painted and fired pictorial glass, plus the changing tastes of consumers, have made the traditional window of the 19$^{th}$ and 20$^{th}$ centuries less popular. Modern artists may use pictorials or medallions to focus their theme. They may also use simple backgrounds in traditional, contemporary or abstract form for the remaining space. Fortunately, for those who do desire the traditional biblical pictorial scene, there are a few modern artists who can paint "flesh" in the same style and manner as those great European and American artists of a century ago. Other options available to stained-glass committees include leaded stained glass and faceted glass (thick one inch, colored glass cemented with epoxy).*

## Shape

A critical element of your design plan is the shape of the windows. This should be considered early in the process, so that shape, where possible, is influenced by the theme and design style, rather than the other way around. A designer can reinforce the theme of the windows through their shape. A full wall of stained glass, for example, evokes a decidedly different feeling for the worshiper than does a series of Gothic or circular windows. Involve the architect early in discussion with the stained-glass committee to ensure the chosen window shape fits the overall building design. Other factors—size, number and placement—should also be considered initially.

## Color

Unlike the colors selected for carpeting, pew cushions and choir robes, the colors chosen for the stained-glass windows cannot be readily changed. The colors in your windows will affect the congregation for as long as that sanctuary is used. Since colors affect our emotions—some colors evoke peace, others strength and power—select your colors carefully. Rule of thumb: Stick with more basic colors, and avoid trendy ones. Also be careful about the depth of colors. Too little color can cause a glare problem; too much color depth can make the sanctuary dark and dreary.

*Photo courtesy of Reinarts Stained Glass Studios*

## Budget

What happens when your committee's aesthetic tastes call for a $620-per-square foot design while your budget has allotted only $120? Compromise will likely be necessary, requiring a simpler design or smaller windows, along with an increase in budget. Many churches have found, however, that funding stained-glass windows is easier than raising funds for most other church items. People respond readily to the inspiring idea of stained-glass windows, and often give monies toward windows as a memorial to a loved one. Suggestion: Determine your budget early in the discussion, so the designer can work within certain constraints and create a design only as intricate as available funds allow.

The creation of new stained glass can be a wonderful adventure, especially if your committee has an early understanding about the five key elements that make up a good stained-glass decision. Your first discussions should center on the themes of the windows—bringing focus to the committee early in the process. The remaining elements of design style, shape, color and budget can then round out the clear guidance your design artist needs to do the job. This process will assure you of acquiring a unique stained-glass design with a specific message for your congregation and your building.

**University Baptist Church, Fort Worth, Texas**
**Designer Leandro Velasco of Rambusch Studios**

29

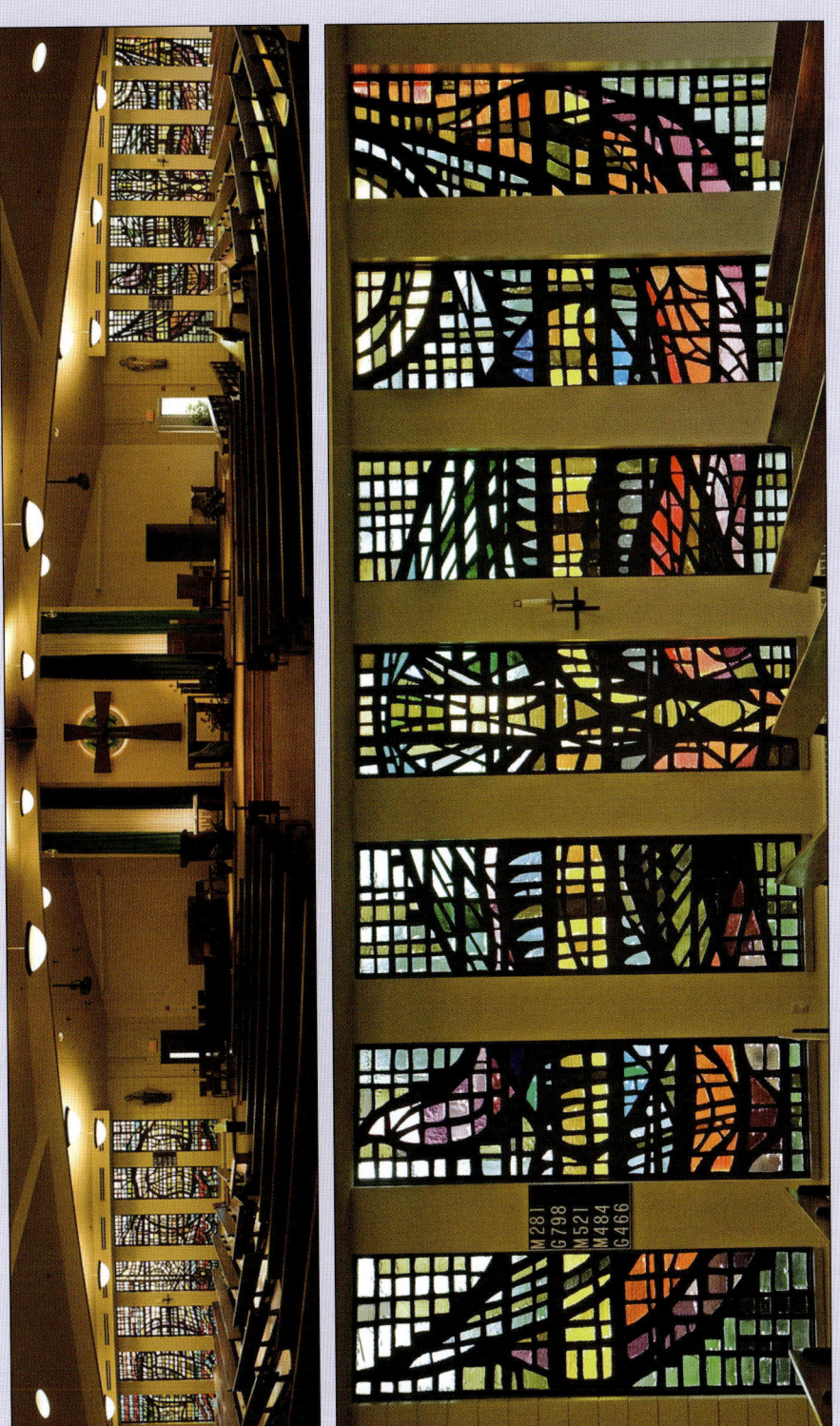

*Pax Christi Catholic, Rochester, Minn., by Reinarts Stained Glass Studios*

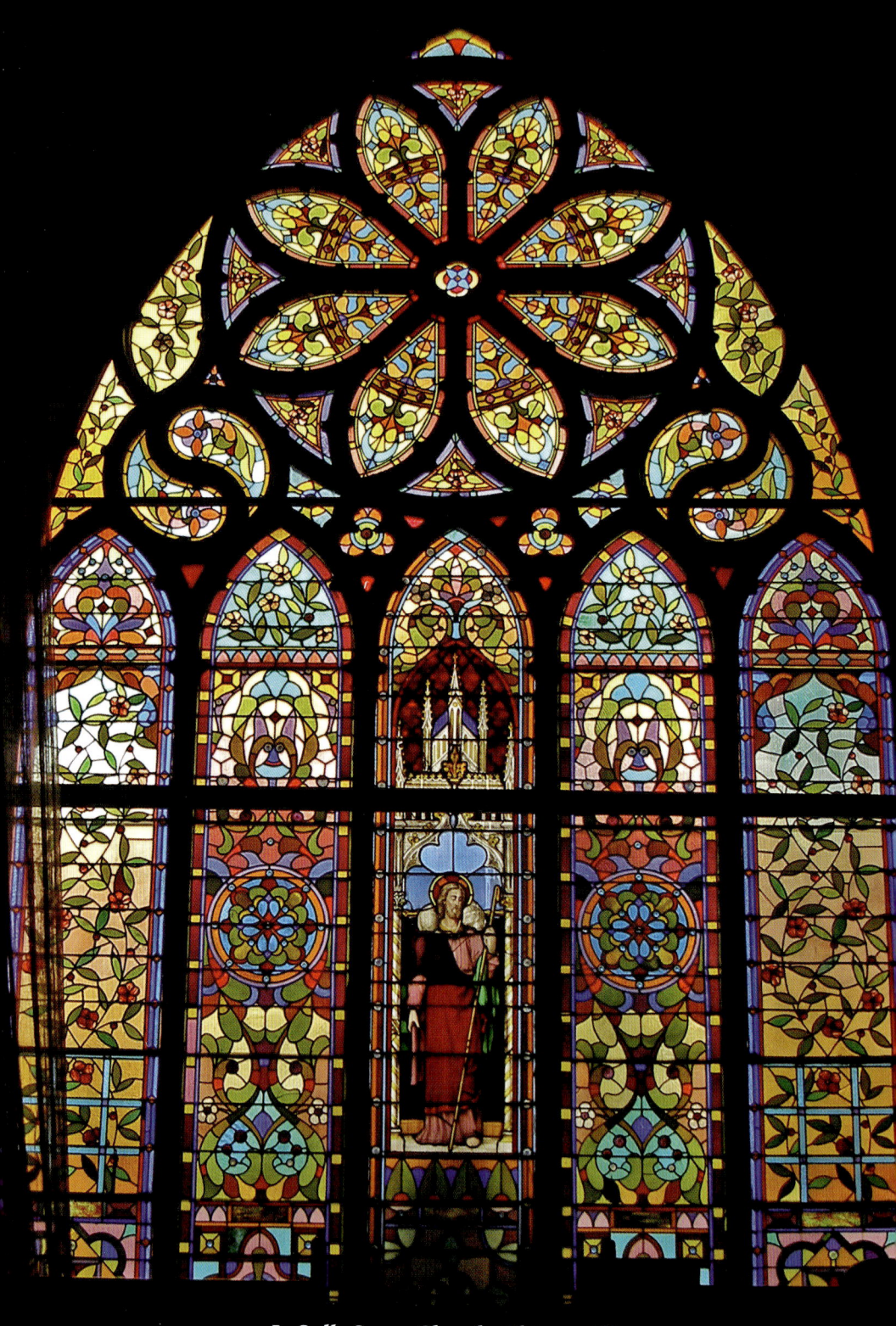

LaSalle Street Church, Chicago, Ill.

# Chapter III

# How To Appraise Stained Glass

"Priceless." That's the most common response of lay leaders when asked the question: "How valuable is the stained glass?"

Except possibly for Tiffany and La Farge designed stained glass, that answer is "nonsense." While replication of stained glass may indeed be expensive, it can be done…at least restoration experts exist who can approximate it.

Therefore, the next question is: "What does a congregation do in case their windows are destroyed?" Again the answer is simple, "Conduct a stained glass appraisal." While it would obviously be best for a professional stained glass appraiser to conduct the work, these are all but nonexistent. This book is designed to aid the amateur appraiser to protect the congregation's greatest physical asset: its stained glass.

Unfortunately, it is usually up to the church insurance executive or the church laity to provide that appraisal. This book is designed to be the central tool for the amateur appraiser. There are other tools necessary before the process can take place.

## *The Appraisal Tools*

- Measuring Tape: Stained glass is appraised by the square foot. Therefore the first step is to know how much stained glass is in a building.

- High Mega-pixel Camera: A careful window-by-window inventory is essential for window replacement in case of disaster. An excellent set of pictures will allow the stained glass restoration artist the most important tool for replication. Further, a complete pictorial inventory of complete windows and specific details will allow stained glass experts to "correct" some appraisal mistakes.

***Early rendering for Baylor Baptist Hospital, Plano, Texas***
*(Photo courtesy of Shenandoah Studios)*

- History of the Stained Glass: Knowledge of the studio that created the stained glass and the installation year are helpful tools for proper replacement value.

*Note: If the stained glass studio still exists, make contact to determine if the original cartoons have been retained on file. If they have, it would be wise to have copies made that can be retained in a secure area (away from the building). This would mean the stained glass studio AND the local congregation would have access to this vital replication tool.*

Further, ask that studio every few years to estimate the current replacement value. This may be the key to the most accurate appraisal value possible.

## *The Appraisal Process*

- Select a Numbering System: Every window needs to be identified for future reference. For example, the lower window in the main nave to the right of the altar would be window number one, followed clockwise by the remaining lower level windows on the right side, then the lower windows on the left side. Then the next window number is the upper window on the right side of the altar, etc. No sequence is necessarily more correct than another. The key to the process is that it be logical; and that the resulting report has clearly stated the location of the window in question.

- Measure Each Window: Unlike many valuable items that need replacement, stained glass is figured by the square footage. Measurement of the width is done first, then the height.

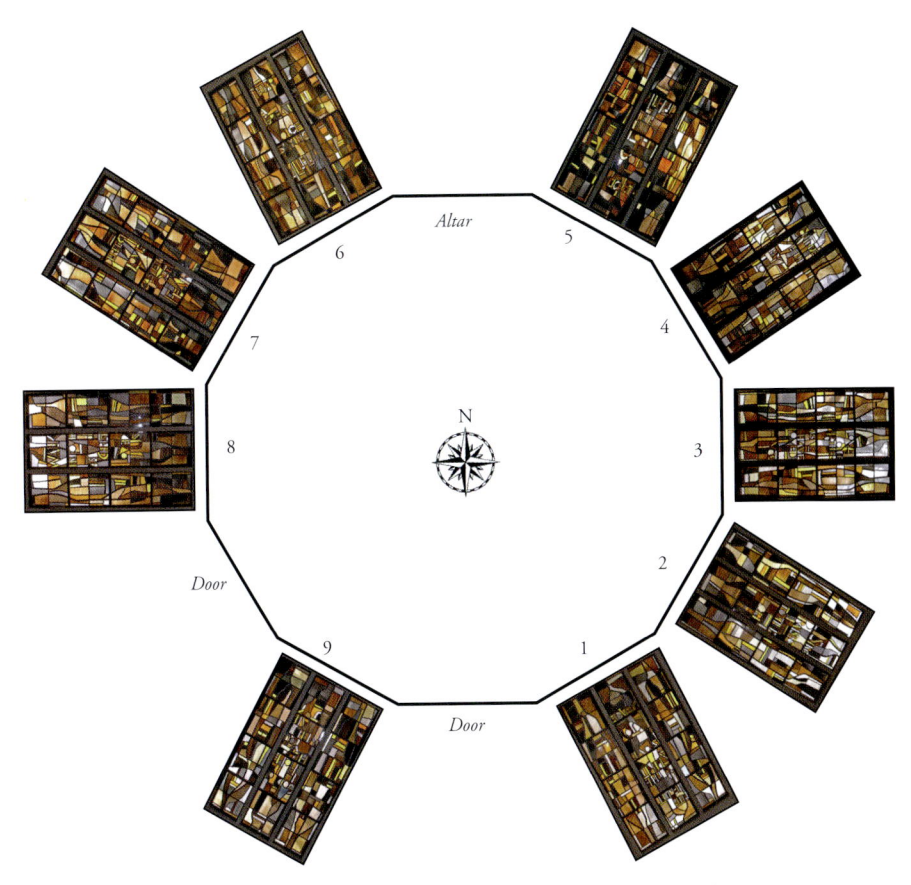

***The Appraisal Process: A Numbering System for***
***Cummins Chapel, St. John's Episcopal Cathedral, Jacksonville, Fla.***

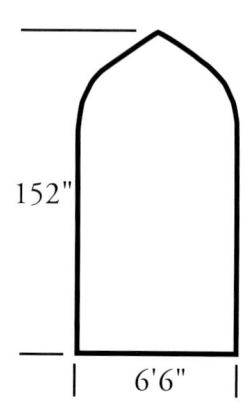

Draw the window to be appraised on a notepad, then measure the width (let's say 6' 6"), by the height 12' 8". It will prove actually easier to measure by inches (thus you have a window 78" x 152" or 83 square feet. Mathematically this is 78" x 152" = 11,856 square inches divided by 144" = 82.33 square feet, rounded upward to 83 square feet.

152"

6'6"

\*\*\*\*

***Note: In measuring the height of a window, measure to the peak of the stained glass (not the stained glass frame). The measurement is to go to the peak regardless of whether the window is pointed at the top (Gothic), rounded (Roman) or is a circle (Rose).***

- Take a Pictorial Inventory: Following the same numbering sequence, take careful interior pictures (and at least one from the exterior) of each unique window. If the window has various features to it, for example multiple symbols and/or medallions, take a careful up-close photo of each one; likewise, take a close-up picture of each figure (not just a sample). This will be critical later for the restoration artist if the window has to be replicated following a fire, hurricane, hailstorm or tornado.

***Gothic, Roman, and Rose Window Shapes***

- Determine the Appraised Value: This is the most important and difficult step. With each unique window in the building, seek to find a similar one in this appraisal guide. This provides a starting appraisal value. For example, if you are examining windows that you know were created by the Willet Studios in 1951; study the various Willet windows in the Stained Glass Appraisal Guide for some sense of what your windows are worth. Compare visually the differences in complexity with those pictures.

Then, utilize the general guidelines of Chapter II to arrive at your final figure. After going through the complete process, let's assume that a replacement value of $525 per square foot has been assigned. Using our earlier example, the window is therefore appraised at $43,575 (83 square feet x $525).

## The Appraisal Report

In a professional appraisal, the church or synagogue should receive:

- a list of the windows
- a map of each window's location
- the name of each window (by scene, by memorial name or both) along with measurements
- a high resolution picture of each unique window (possibly several close-ups of the designs, symbols, medallions and/or figures)
- a history of the window (artist, studio, date commissioned, etc.)
- a replacement value per window = replication cost if destroyed

## The Church Insurance Fine Arts Policy

Each church or synagogue's insurance policy has a fine arts section. Once an appraisal is done, the church insurance carrier is to be notified and the appraisal information is to be added.

By having correct replacement values for windows, both the church and the insurance carrier then insure the proper level of potential replication costs. This dramatically reduces potential surprises for either party when a disaster befalls stained glass.

## The Secure Location for Photographs and Cartoons

There are many horror stories of massive damage to a building where the records needed to restore that building had been held for safe keeping within it—and thus destroyed along with the building.

While it is perfectly okay to keep stained glass replacement records in the main office, it is mandatory that a duplicate set be kept elsewhere, preferably in a safe box away from the building.

Now with the ability to store records easily via computers, an additional method of storage safety might be to provide each trustee a copy of the window appraisal (that includes the detailed pictures) on disc and/or via e-mail attachment. Doing so will give several key leaders immediate access to stained glass pictorial records should a disaster occur.

*Remember, storage in this form is your backup system. Place the original in a secure location, possibly at the local library or historical society, away from the building itself. This is especially true if you have access to the original cartoons themselves.*

## Update the Appraisal Periodically

The costs of stained glass replication (the extremely high quality work to replace a masterpiece) are rising much faster than inflation. As such, an appraisal will be outdated in several years. Therefore, if your windows are considered exceptional, an appraisal should probably be updated at least every five years. Dear church, synagogue leader and even church insurance agent—you may be sitting on a time bomb with your stained glass.

**Cartoon by Reinarts Stained Glass Studios**
*(Photo courtesy of Reinarts Stained Glass Studios)*

That time bomb can be defused with the aid of a pictorial appraisal—even if that attempt is an amateur one that utilizes the expertise of the stained glass industry used to create (judge replication costs) this book. By following these step-by-step procedures, not only will your stained glass most likely be properly insured (in the fine arts section of your church insurance policy), but you will also have the pictorial (and/or cartoon) records safely located when that dreaded time of destruction may arrive.

If you have valuable stained glass, not only will an appraisal help you sleep better before a disaster might occur—you will also sleep better if and when it does happen.

*Right: A replicated 1916 Annunciation stained glass window panel that is unsigned but attributed to Emil Frei Art Glass Co., St. Louis, Mo. Conrad Schmitt Studios created the panel for a client seeking new turn-of-the-century style stained glass.*
*(Photo courtesy of Conrad Schmitt Studios)*

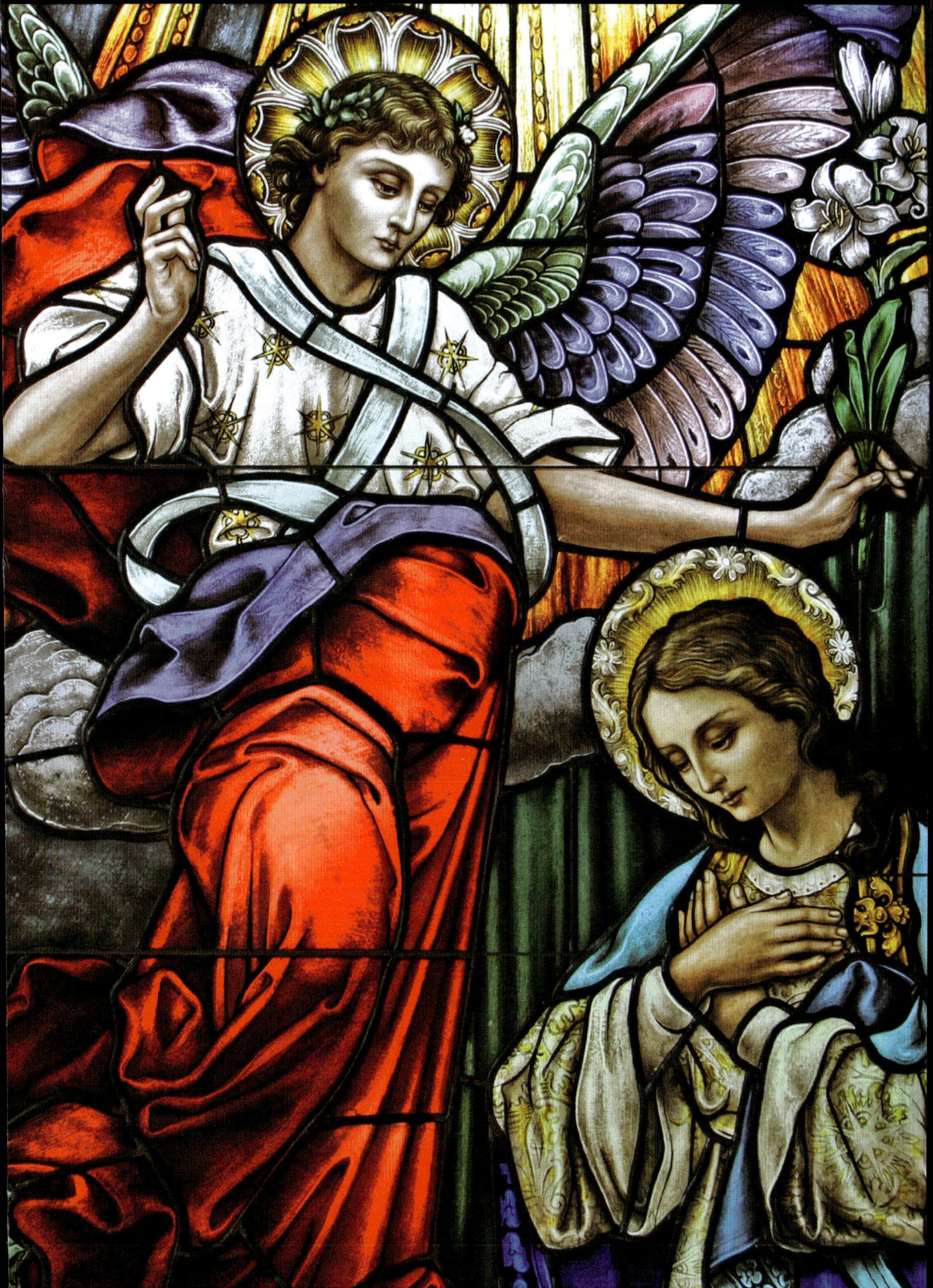

*The Moses Window executed by Charles J. Connick, 1944,
House Of Hope Presbyterian, St. Paul, Minn.*

*Chapter IV*

# COMPARING APPLES AND ORANGES

As with most industries, there are several different varieties of stained glass. Some studios within the industry create only the finest American art, while it is difficult to understand how others manage to stay in business.

When it comes to a disaster, to whom does the church turn and trust to rebuild their precious inspirational art? The same question must be raised by the insurance company. Trust is so very critical.

A start for both the church and for the insurance company is to have an understanding of the four different varieties of stained glass companies. They are referred to here as fruit, so the labels can be later used for comparing "apples and oranges."

### *The Plum*

There are probably 3,500 stained glass companies in America, and most of them are small like a plum and tasty for certain purposes. Most ventured into business because someone in the family loves art and had taken "How to Make Leaded Stained Glass" classes. This was experimented with for a couple of years to the rave review of relatives, friends and neighbors. Finally the little shop was opened and a thriving businesses developed. Small windows were created for the wealthy; transoms were designed for local businesses; and the Trinity Denominational Church ordered a six-foot rose window for its new altar area. Classes were formed within the studio on "How to Make Leaded Stained Glass."

## *The Orange*

Over the decades, primarily since 1885, America has been blessed with a few great studios that have created spectacular and sensitive art for the American religious market. Some of the art is simply inspirational; other pieces magnificently tell the story of the Bible, the denomination or possibly the region.

Those studios which seek to create the finest of artisanship into a window have made up and continue to be the ORANGES of stained glass. They employ professional artists, designers, fabricators and installers to make sure the finished work fits the client's desire for fine art, Biblical storytelling and inspiration—all of which utilize light pouring through the window into the worship areas. Most of these ORANGE studios are family businesses passed down from one generation to the next. Traditionally, they are fully accredited members of the Stained Glass Association of America.

## *The Pear*

While nearly everyone who tours a sanctuary for the first time looks first at the stained glass windows, most cannot tell whether they are looking at a Michelangelo or a Leta Gray (my Mom again!). It's amazing to those who know stained glass that most people 'ooh and aah' about nearly any leaded glass. We seem programmed to do so.

The great masterpiece just doesn't fit with some religious settings. In fact, there is now a movement among evangelical churches to have buildings that can be completely darkened for visual displays. Because many congregations agree this movement has something artificial about it, they still want traditional stained glass, but not at an excessive price.

Enter the PEAR. These studios have created a basic design series for the church to choose at reasonable prices. The studios tell the church:

1. Pick the basic design you want.

2. Choose somewhere between two and four colors desired in each window. Clarify which color is to be dominant and which are the borders.

3. Decide upon a series of symbols (usually 12" round or oval). These symbols can be either shields, swords, crosses, Bibles,

***Series of Salem Stained Glass Symbols***
*(Photos courtesy of Salem Stained Glass Studios)*

etc. or (for a little more) they can be biblical scenes. The committee has maybe 40 designs from which to choose.

4. Provide the exact measurements.

That's it. Basic design, basic colors, basic symbols—everything needed at a low price (compared to ORANGES). Normally the structural quality of a PEAR is as strong as an ORANGE.

Thus, unless the church or synagogue is determined to have a custom made window, totally distinct from any other congregation in America, then the PEAR might at least be considered.

PEARS could be considered a poor church's ORANGE. The old saying, "You get what you pay for," is therefore true. If you want a unique, custom stained glass window, work with an ORANGE (and pay a higher price). If you want a quality stained glass window that tells the story you desire, and uniqueness is not the issue but dollars are, then consider a PEAR.

## *The Apple*

The fourth and final stained glass company is the APPLE—a company that specializes in on-site restoration and protection.

An APPLE does not make a stained glass window, rather it provides that window preventive maintenance and when desired, protection from weather, burglary, accidents, and vandalism.

The APPLE does its work on-site at the church or synagogue. A master crew arrives in a truck with an ample amount of tools and supplies (plus materials shipped directly to the building).

If the stained glass is in relatively good condition, the crew will re-cement the exterior surface of the stained glass for strength and beauty; scrape, prime and paint the exterior stained glass frame, and install a protective covering (normally ¼" float or safety glass or 3/16" LEXAN XL, a nearly unbreakable plastic polycarbonate).

If a window is in seriously deteriorated condition, a stained glass panel can be removed from its frame, laid on a table on-site, be restored and re-braced, and then be reinstalled.

Should a window have several broken pieces of stained glass, research begins immediately for a match. If the broken pieces are painted/fired, those broken pieces are shipped immediately to restoration artists so that replication can be completed before the on-site master crew completes their work.

The same process is true for millwork, which has often rotted over the years. Even the most difficult of wooden tracery can be duplicated by master millwork artisans.

Should a window need re-leading, however, the work is typically taken to the studio, where the vertical jig-saw leaded puzzle is disassembled, cleaned, re-leaded, re-braced and then brought back to the building for installation.

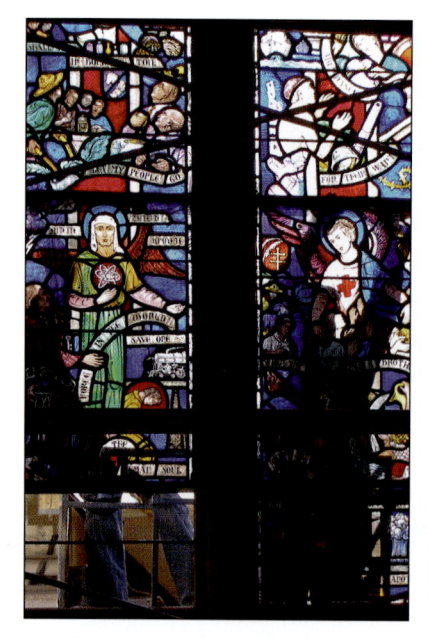

*A crew works at the historic Marshall Building, Northern Oklahoma College, Enid, Okla.* (Photo courtesy of Shenandoah Studios)

APPLES are not designed for the creation of new windows. Rather, they best serve to maintain valuable stained glass starting about 25 years after the initial installation (by an ORANGE, PEAR or possibly a PLUM) until 150 years later when the windows need to be considered candidates for re-leading. If APPLES do their craftsmanship correctly, they need conduct work only every thirty to forty years.

## Which Fruit to Use for New Windows

For new windows, the PLUM is appropriate only for small churches and synagogues. Even then, despite the assumption of an inspirational design, the quality of the lead and the proper placement of braces for strength, are often lacking. Structurally, windows designed and fabricated by PLUMS are relatively weak in comparison to those from the shops of ORANGES and PEARS.

If the church is seeking a masterpiece, the ORANGE is an obvious place to begin. The ORANGE studios have outstanding designers, artists, cartoonists, cutters and fabricators to provide a congregation with a beautiful story of the Bible; or to create an inspirational abstract, utilizing a myriad of complementing colors and lead flows.

When working with an ORANGE, the congregation is paying not only for the custom art and finished product, but also for prestige and tradition. If the desire is for low-end, but beautiful stained glass, an ORANGE can be competitive, but they will rarely be the low bidder on any low-end stained glass commission.

When price is the objective for new stained glass, the PEAR is ideal, because the designs are already created and tend to be simple. This relatively inexpensive product can be produced for a perfect fit into a new structure. PEAR designs and standard biblical scenes are typically well made and will generally last the same number of generations that an ORANGE creation will.

The PEAR has the additional advantage of offering a quicker decision and completion. Even here, the PEAR decision can get bogged down with options for border colors or themes among the symbols.

The APPLE is not appropriate for new windows. Their specialty is in on-site restoration, not the creation of inspirational biblical masterpieces.

## Restoration and Protection

At about the stained glass age of twenty-five, problems begin to develop with leaded stained glass. At that age, leaded stained glass starts to buckle (bulge), and braces are loosened. If the windows are unprotected, broken and mismatched stained glass pieces could become an irritant to the congregation, or water leakage could be found at the base of the windows.

This is the ideal time to use an APPLE, as their expertise is in preventive maintenance for stained glass; and, if not done originally, now is the time for protective covering to be installed.

## Twenty-five Years: Preventive Maintenance

At twenty-five years, the exterior stained glass surface needs a "stained glass oil change" because the cement (holding the glass and the lead together) has begun to cake. Re-cementing is normally suggested. This is a process in which a liquid cementing compound is brushed onto every square inch of the exterior stained glass surface, then buffed. This allows the liquid cement to intermingle with the old caking cement; and when it dries, the resulting window is once again solid and nearly waterproof.

APPLE companies have expertise in the reduction of bulges, installation of additional steel braces, and replacement of broken stained or painted/fired glass. If a panel is in serious or critical condition, the APPLE master craftsman can remove the panel, place it on an on-site work table and conduct the necessary restoration and rebracing before returning the panel to its frame.

If the stained glass wasn't protected at the time of its creation, it is important to consider the process at this first twenty-five year milestone. The deterioration of stained glass is extremely slow, so many property committees have determined that protection is not needed.

Generally this is not a wise decision. One only need inspect the stained glass at ten Protestant churches and ten Catholic churches that are at least a century old. The Catholics, with most of their windows designed and fabricated by German artisans or by immigrants of Germany, tended to place a glass protective covering on stained glass at the time of installation. The Protestants, using English and American stained glass companies, did not. The Catholic windows are, for the most part, in excellent condition (for example, there are very few mismatched pieces of colored glass). The Protestant windows were so deteriorated by the 1950s, an entire industry (the APPLE stained glass companies) developed around their repair/restoration and protective covering process.

So, starting at twenty-five to thirty years of stained glass age, the property committee should conduct preventive maintenance, and install or replace protective covering. If Lexan was used over the exterior frame and was not vented, it is quite possible the wood could have rotted.

ORANGE, PEAR, and PLUM companies are not equipped generally for this type of on-site preventive work.

## *Seventy-five Year Restoration*

At about seventy-five years, stained glass is in a position for major attention (of course, much depends on the preventive maintenance over the years). If the windows have not received much attention and braces have not been installed in all the key places, then severe or possibly even critical bulges may appear in nearly every panel. Sometimes this bulging causes the breakage of glass and the splitting of the lead. Without attention, these windows will only continue to deteriorate.

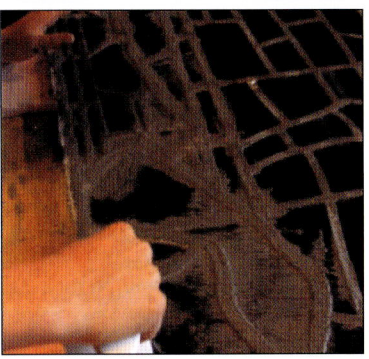

*A crew works at University Baptist Church, Ft. Worth, Texas (Photo courtesy of Shenandoah Studios)*

This level of restoration is certainly open to debate across the stained glass field. The debate is whether the windows would be best served by in-studio restoration rather than on-site repair. The former style is conducted by PLUMS, ORANGES, and PEARS, while the latter is the province of the APPLES.

Which is better? Without question, if a studio has restoration artisans and utilizes the best technology available, the studio restoration is superior to the on-site approach and should help the congregation gain an additional 150 years of life.

That is normally where the PLUM is disqualified. PLUMS by their very nature are small in scope and spend their time creating small, and often relatively simple, projects. They are normally overwhelmed with the restoration of a masterpiece. Project size alone usually eliminates them; if not, then the lack of restoration specialists and technology certainly should.

PLUMS tend to see a window as a jig-saw puzzle, so when it comes to restoration, the only thing they are trained to do is to take the jig-saw puzzle apart and put it back together again. PLUMS, therefore, might be called in to re-lead a damaged window—but unless the window is 150 years old, re-leading is "overkill" (that is, unless the window has been neglected, leading to premature degradation). They might even put braces back in the same place, meaning that within 25 more years, the window will have bulges in the same unbraced sections again.

Re-leading a window is not necessarily smart restoration—and it is the most expensive. Phrased in another way, if you have a problem with the motor, don't you normally seek to have only the one part replaced rather than rebuilding the entire motor?

Both ORANGES and PEARS are normally equipped at the studio for in-house restoration work. In most cases, the church or synagogue will be well served. Most APPLES can also conduct in-studio restoration.

*There is this one caution: There is a tremendous temptation to suggest that windows be re-leaded at this seventy-five year stage. If properly repaired, restored and protected over the years, these windows usually have an additional seventy-five years before the re-leading process is usually necessary. If re-leading is being proposed, obtain several opinions before proceeding with this extremely expensive project.*

## One Hundred Fifty-Year Restoration

Assuming re-leading has not already taken place, the lead in a stained glass window is ready for replacement at about 150 years. ORANGES, PEARS and APPLES are equipped for this ultimate restoration of stained glass work. Indeed, the windows need to be disassembled and all cracked and broken glass replaced. The components' edges need to be glued and the window rebraced (with new vertical and horizontal steel braces as necessary) and then reinstalled.

A significant amount of the stained glass on the eastern half of the United States is nearing (or has surpassed) this critical stained glass birthday. Possibly more than any other reason, this "birthday" will bring about a new era in stained glass, the era of restoration. In fact, already many of the

## *Stained Glass Fruit Comparison Table*

| Fruit | New Windows | Restoration/Protection | Quality | Costs |
|---|---|---|---|---|
| Plum | Small churches only. | Restoration by re-lead. Poor protection technology. | Low to medium | Low to medium |
| Orange | Large, liturgical, artistic churches. | Restoration by re-lead. Average protection technology. | Medium to high | Medium to high |
| Pear | Similar design throughout. | Restoration by re-lead. Average protection technology. | Medium | Low to medium |
| Apple | No | On-site repair, restoration. Protection and insulation. Potentially high protection technology. | Medium to high | Low compared to re-lead |

old, established studios report over fifty percent of their work is now in restoration, rather than in the creation of new glass masterpieces.

## What to Do When Tragedy Hits

Damage, when it comes, comes rapidly. In 1989, stained glass throughout San Francisco was shaken by a massive earthquake. Remarkably, the stained glass of the city had little damage, because it is set in lead and therefore has some flexibility. One mammoth Catholic Church had its spire completely destroyed, but not one crack was discovered amidst the stained glass!

The opposite problem took place with the Oklahoma City bombing. The First United Methodist Church had just installed new LEXAN XL protective covering. The blast completely melted the LEXAN XL and shattered the stained glass into tiny pieces. Everything was gone in an instant.

Unprotected stained glass has no chance in a hurricane. If winds and flying debris don't destroy the windows, it is likely that the storm surge will. In a hurricane, even poorly installed protective covering is likely to be ripped from its frame, exposing the window behind to the wrath of the storm.

But most windows across America are damaged or destroyed by either fire or hail. Horror stories arrive at church insurance and stained glass offices across the nation with regularity.

It is at this moment that the church official panics and realizes that maybe a one-hundred-year heritage has been lost forever. A similar property committee chairperson from across the street is distressed about the loss, but is prepared to handle the replication process.

She is comforted because she knows the stained glass has been professionally appraised and that replacement value is written into the fine arts section of the church property insurance. Less the deductible, she knows she will have the necessary funds available to replicate the windows.

Secondly, she has a complete high mega-pixel pictorial record of each window with close-ups of all symbols, medallions, and figures. This allows a restoration stained glass artisan to match almost exactly the artwork and style of the original artist.

Further, she has researched the studio(s) that originally designed the windows. If they still exist, she knows that at least one studio has in storage the actual full-size cartoons originally used. If the studio is out of business, she has a list of those specializing in restoration.

Returning the stained glass back to normal will still require a two- to twelve-month process, but this property chairperson need not panic. Rather, it is a matter of settling with the insurance company and providing the selected stained glass restoration firm the pictures, and possibly the cartoons needed for quality replication.

## Whom Do You Call?

The scope of the damage is the key to the nature of the stained glass company called to solve the problem.

If the synagogue has sustained only two or three broken pieces of glass from a fallen tree limb, the PLUM down the street may be able to match and replace the pieces.

If the hail, wind or vandal has caused breakage in a number of areas through the nave or chapel, the APPLE company may be best suited. APPLES are adept at on-site repair. With protective covering experts as well, the property committee usually will want protection against this kind of damage in the future, a situation ideal for APPLES.

If several of the broken pieces are sophisticated, the APPLE will remove the fragments and one or two neighboring pieces, to send to an expert restoration artist. These uniquely gifted artists have learned replication art and the styles of different decades and artists. These specialists have even learned to apply a built-in fade so the new painted/fired glass matches the neighboring pieces.

If a major portion of a valuable window is destroyed, the task escalates to ORANGE studio replication. The damaged panel, once in the studio, undergoes a sophisticated process of glass matching, design reproduction, re-leading and re-bracing—whatever is necessary to bring the window back to normal.

*Note: As in all phases of life, there are some stained glass companies ill-equipped to match glass or to artistically redesign painted/fired glass. They will try, but the congregation will not be satisfied with the results. People notice that one badly mismatched piece far more than 1,000 blended ones. Select your ORANGE studio with care.*

*When Hurricane Katrina hit, no one was in St. Michael's Catholic Church located on the ultimate southeast point of Biloxi's coast. It is a good thing, as no one would have survived. Not only was the church dramatically impacted by hurricane level five force winds, but a water surge 130" high simply waltzed through the chapel and nave, taking glass protective covering, multiple tall stained glass panels, the altar, pews and everything else in its path. Are you prepared for such a disaster?*

# Dealing with the Aftermath of Fire

*Conrad Schmitt Studios was first commissioned to conduct an investigation and documentation of the lost decoration that includes notes, tracings and photographs that establish a permanent record of the decorative scheme of Sacred Heart, Indianapolis, Ind., at the time of the 2001 fire. Interestingly, the existing 1936 decorative painting scheme had been created by Alphonse Schmitt, a son of Conrad Schmitt.*

*The Studio was subsequently awarded the work to restore the decorative painting, recreate eleven sanctuary and ceiling murals, replicate four Mayer of Munich stained glass windows that were beyond repair and to conserve fourteen damaged windows in the nave.*

*The restored church was rededicated eighteen months after the fire, with Catholic dignitaries in attendance. Conrad Schmitt Studios won a national award from the Painting and Decorating Contractors of America for the project, which also earned a special Phoenix Rising Award from the Historic Landmarks Foundation of Indiana.*

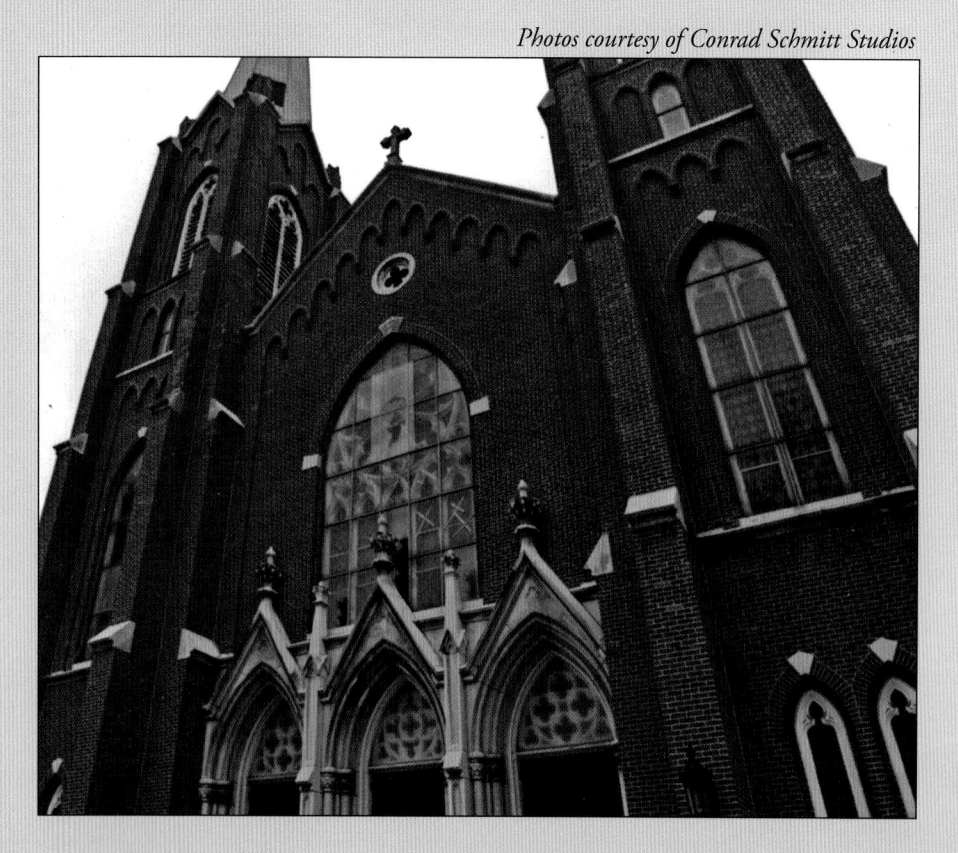

*Photos courtesy of Conrad Schmitt Studios*

51

# Inspecting Stained Glass

*Even simple stained glass designs are subject to degradation and must be inspected every decade or so to insure the continued health of the window for the inspiration of future generations of worshippers. So, how does the minister or property chairperson know whether stained glass needs attention or not? Do a personal inspection tour. Here's what to look for:*

## Lead

If lead has been protected and given preventive maintenance over the years, the lead cames should not need replacement for at least 150 years! Many churches, on the basis of recommendations from stained glass companies—and jittery lay people in fear of losing their windows—have been known to re-lead every couple of decades.

*Look directly at the lead (don't worry about anything else for the time being) and try to determine how often you can find breaks in the lead itself. Multiple breaks throughout a window mean re-leading is probably going to be essential. However, this should be happening only in windows one hundred or more years old or windows that have not had a protective covering (glass or plastic) since they were new. When the windows reach 150 years, the window is ready to re-lead, regardless.*

## Bulge

A bulge can threaten a stained glass panel more than anything else. This bulging effect may extend inward or outward as much as 3" and eventually (when left unattended) the stained glass will simply fall out of the frame. This is caused by the great weight of the stained glass, missing cement, deterioration from weather and poor bracing.

*Observe the window from the interior and look up. Try to determine if the stained glass is vertical, or has one or many locations throughout the window that are forming a rounded curve (or folding effect), either inward or outward. Simply focus on each panel, looking for bulges, then move to the next panel, and so on. If the windows are vertical, that is good. If you see bulges of at least 1" from vertical, the process is already underway to eventually lose the windows.*

## Braces

Steel braces (usually the width/length of the stained glass panel) are used to secure the stained glass panel of lead came, glass and cement and keep it vertical. These braces can be both vertical and horizontal and sometimes other angles. Most modern braces are rectangular, while 100-year-plus windows have rounded braces tightened at the joints by wire. They are soldered at the lead joint areas (or wired tight) and then secured at both ends into the window frame. Bulges do not commence in areas of the stained glass panels where bracing has been properly placed and remains tightly secured.

*From the interior of the stained glass window, take hold of each brace to determine if you can find movement. No movement is good. Check both ends of the brace to see if it is firmly attached to the frame. Also determine if the original solder is holding at the lead joints crossed by the brace. Loosened braces, prior to a bulge developing, can be corrected relatively easily, but must be addressed or other problems with begin to occur.*

## Glass

There are two forms of what is generically called stained glass. Some glass is originally manufactured in sheets with a color and variety of colors built-in. This glass is referred to here as stained glass. Other glass (often clear glass) is painted one layer at a time by an artist, and then fired to a heat level that allows the paint to be absorbed into the glass. This process, referred to here as painted/fired glass, is repeated until the desired appearance is achieved. Small pieces of both stained glass and/or painted/fired glass are then placed into a larger artistic panel via the application of lead came and cement.

Obviously, glass can be broken and poorly painted/fired glass can fade. And nothing bothers a person sitting in the pew more than seeing a broken piece of glass letting gleams of light pour through. A close rival for irritation is a badly mismatched repair, where now a green piece of glass is located where a brown piece was originally.

*Look at each individual piece of glass to see if you can spot cracks, breaks, bullet holes and badly mismatched glass. Caution: Stained glass is very hard to match, even by those who say the match will be perfect, so leave as many pieces as possible with only one crack or two minor ones (to ensure a better match). Those with multiple cracks easily visible from the congregation will need attention.*

## Cement

The first element of stained glass to normally deteriorate is the cement between the lead came and the glass. But, much like the preventive maintenance of an automobile requires changing the oil every 3,000 miles, the cement should be re-cemented every twenty years or so. The re-cementing process is a simple and old fashioned one of applying a cementing compound to the exterior (possibly with a paint brush), and then rubbing the surface with a rag or brush, leaving the new cement to intermingle with the old. The result is a restrengthened (somewhat water-and-air-tight) joint and brilliantly clean exterior windows. Re-cementing is the single most important preventive maintenance step for the continued healthy life of your stained glass.

*While standing on the interior side of the stained glass, press firmly and directly on the center of a lead joint near the middle of a stained glass panel. If you get movement and/or hear a caking sound, re-cementing is needed.*

## After the Inspection

If you have found bulges, soft cement, loosened steel braces, and/or broken glass, contact professionals (three different ones) for their suggestions and costs. If you are one of about seventy-five percent of churches today that have maintained their windows, then rest assured this portion of your church's heritage and ministry has been inspected and is not a concern.

**Right Top: Reinarts Stained Glass Studios restores windows at the University of Illinois Neumann Center** *(Photo courtesy of Reinarts Stained Glass Studios)*
**Right Bottom: Shenandoah Stained Glass Studio removes stained glass panels at Northern Oklahoma College from exterior for restoration.**

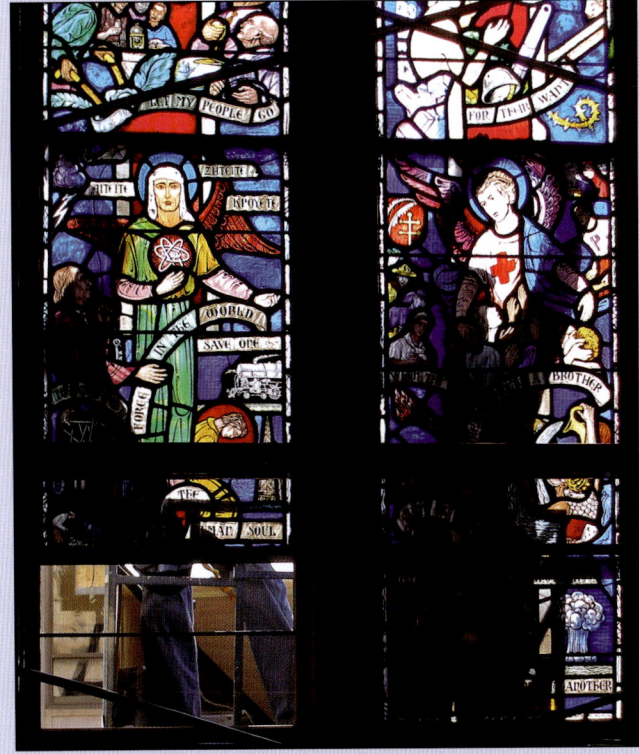

55

# Protecting Stained Glass

*A church or synagogue has several options when considering the protective covering used to shelter their valuable stained glass from weather, vandalism, accidents and robbery. Glass was historically used as a protective covering with the beautiful German windows installed between 1885 and 1917.*

*In the 1960s a polycarbonate plastic (primarily that of Lexan made by General Electric) was the covering of choice, but it has tended to yellow and cloud. In 2008-2009, the four most prominent choices for protective covering are:*

## 3/16" Lexan XL

*Lexan is what churches have been putting on stained glass since the 1960s. It is nearly unbreakable and will remain aesthetically pleasing for about 20 years. The original LEXAN discolored in about six years. The new advanced product with a UV protective coating is much better, but, being a plastic, will get cloudy and dusty, especially on windows that face the sun.*

## ¼" Float Glass

*Float glass is what is used in most business settings and is gaining popularity with churches, because it will look nice for a long time (if not broken). If the float glass protective covering is broken and some of your stained glass is also broken, your stained glass contractor can match most stained glass nearly to perfection. The advantage of float glass is that it will continue to look nice for many years. It will be taken off when repair is needed on the stained glass or if the frame (often, the paint) in which it is set is beginning to deteriorate (this is probably thirty years down the road).*

## ¼" Lexan XL

*¼" LEXAN XL is obviously thicker than 3/16" LEXAN and therefore will remain more firm over the years. It will be only slightly more effective at protection, but since most of the windows can be completed with larger pieces of protective covering, the ¼" LEXAN might look better long-term.*

*Shenandoah Stained Glass Studio is in the early stages of on-site stained glass restoration, protection, and insulation at First Presbyterian Church of River Forest (Chicago), Ill.*

## ¼" Safety Glass

Safety glass offers the benefits of long-term aesthetic appearance of glass, but also protects the stained glass from the extremely heavy blow (that might break ¼" float glass). The safety glass will break as well, but it will not shatter. The reason is that it is made with 1/8" glass, then plastic, then another 1/8" glass layer. Thus, if broken, the plastic layer will not allow it to shatter; and, in most cases, will not damage or destroy the stained glass protected to the inside.

These are the covering materials to protect the stained glass. The one chosen depends mostly on whether it is more important for your church or synagogue to protect valuable windows (without any fear of outside breakage), or to have long-term outside protective covering beauty. If a church has extremely valuable windows or is in a vandalism-prone area, LEXAN or safety glass is the wise choice. If the windows are less valuable, then simple float glass is the best option for long-term appearance.

*Emil Frei Window, 1957, St. Luke's United Methodist Church, Oklahoma City, Okla.*

*Chapter V*

# The Appraisal Research

With 3,500 stained glass studios in America, there were many potential judges. The entire membership of the Stained Glass Association of America was the starting point. Since many of the windows to be "judged" were aged nearly to the crucial 150-year lead lifespan, what better group to provide a sense of history and artisanship to the replication of windows?

With the SGAA as the base group, the appraisal guide researchers picked at random additional studios from the Internet, much as many churches, synagogues and insurance agents do when selecting their stained glass company. A total of 142 questionnaires were originally sent.

Eventually, some thirty studios returned the rather lengthy questionnaire.

## *The Eight Categories*

The appraisal guide researchers compared the results from different perspectives.

1. Overall: The Green O star is the overall average of all 28 studios' estimates of replacement value per square footage.

    *Using the overall totals as the base, or 100%, all the sub-categories were compared to these. The average replacement value (replication costs) for all windows was $602.*

2. The Blue N is the average of studios located in the north and eastern United States. Basically, the dividing lines were all states to the east of the Mississippi River and north of the Ohio River.

    *The North and East regions were expected to be the highest category, and indeed they were at 139.5% of base. The studios in this region tend to have a large segment of multi-generation* studios. They also have much higher-than-average labor costs. In most cases these studios have in-studio artists capable of high quality replication, including "flesh."

3. The Gray S is the average of studios located in the south. Those studios south of the Ohio River and east of the Mississippi River were included.

    *The South is the home of the "Pear" or catalog studio. However, none of the traditional pears (Law, Lynchburg, and Salem) were included among the judges. Regardless, the South had one of the lowest overall percentages (87.7%) against base.*

4. The Teal GP is the average of studios located in the great plains, including Texas, Louisiana, Iowa, Missouri, Oklahoma and Minnesota.

5. The Red W is the average of studios located in the west, including those studios in Washington, California, Oregon and Utah.

6. The Orange SG is the average of studios who are affiliated with the Stained Glass Association of America (SGAA)

    *Possibly the biggest surprise of the entire research was with members of the SGAA which projected replication at a low 97.8% of base. Since this is the group most involved with the high-dollar replacement work, possibly these averages are among the most valid for actual replication.*

7. The Purple N combines the replacement values of non-member SGAA studios.

    *The opposite shocker occurred with the non-SGAA members at 102.8%. While some of these studios undoubtedly have high quality artists, it is doubtful they tend to be large enough for outstanding restoration specialists. Therefore, it is possible that some guessing took place with some of the more intricate historical replacement estimates.*

8. The Yellow L is the average of those with annual stained glass sales of $500,000 or more.

*More parity was found with this large vs. small studio comparison. The large studios estimated at 102.2%. This may be another of the most valid groupings simply because these studios have had more practical experience in coping with church disasters such as hurricanes, burglary, accidents and fire.*

9. The Black S is the replacement value estimates of those with annual sales of less than $500,000.

*At 99.8%, the small studios were also near par.*

## The Appraised Windows

Most of the windows pictured in the appraisal guide were inspected by the American Consultation on Stained Glass. The bulk of the rest were provided by the studios of Rohlf, Conrad Schmitt, Judson, Reinarts and Salem. These windows, overall, represent the cross section of the stained glass in the American church, Catholic, Protestant, and Hebrew.

For easy usage by the church property committee or the church insurance agent, the windows are in four categories.

1. Basic American Leaded Stained Glass—the majority of windows in America were made by unsigned American stained glass studios over the years. This category begins with the most basic and spans the time period of 1870 and continues for one hundred years. The great era of the "Jeweled" window (1880-1900) is included in this category.

2. The "Great" Stained Glass Studios—featuring the greatest artists (studios) of American stained glass, in particular La Farge and Tiffany of America, and Zettler and Mayer of Germany.

3. The Modern Stained Glass Window—some of the recent styles are considered.

4. The Faceted Window—also known as dale de verre, a thick colored glass style form of artistry.

Once within the category, all studios are mentioned in alphabetical order.

All of those institutions whose windows were photographed by the ACSG were informed of the consideration for appraisal and were given the opportunity to object to its use in the book. Any institution objecting to the use of its windows' photographs had those photos immediately removed.

## *The Start of Consensus*

This 2008-2009 issue of the Stained Glass Appraisal Guide is but a start. Synagogues, churches and the church insurance industry will finally have some basis for appraising stained glass and understanding the difference between basic stained glass and historically significant masterpieces of religious art.

# Tiffany and La Farge Replications
*By Peter Rohlf, Rohlf Studios*

The process to replace or replicate a destroyed Tiffany or La Farge window is more than likely beyond the realm of our industry.

The perplexing problem is the replication of the drapery glass and the intensity to have manufactured opalescent glasses in the varying shades and textures which both Tiffany and La Farge were able to achieve. There are a few glass manufacturers; Youghiogheny, Bullseye and Kokomo Glass workers who will attempt to reproduce these glasses. However one would have to order an excessive quantity and there is no guarantee that the exact reproduction will be achieved.

From a technical point of view, there are craftspeople in our industry who have the knowledge and know how to perform edge-gluing and double and triple plating to restore damaged panels, along with re-leading these historic windows.

Any attempt to either replace or restore a Tiffany or La Farge window should be done in strict accordance with the SGAA Technical Manual and Standards and Guidelines for the Preservation of Historic Stained Glass which is available at the SGAA Administrative Offices located at 10009 East 62nd Street, Raytown, MO 64133 (Tel: 1-800-438-9581).

*Left: Tiffany window at North Avenue Presbyterian Church, Atlanta, Ga.*

# Section 1

Stained glass is, in essence, a vertical jig-saw puzzle. The most typical form is leaded stained glass which starts with a lead came and its two channels. Glass fits into each channel and is solidified by cement. Hopefully these windows have been braced and protected so they will continue to inspire generations into the new millennium.

Inspiration has always been important in stained glass, but early American stained glass sought to do so primarily with geometric designs. When artwork was fired into the glass, the resulting figures or medallions were of traditional Hebrew or Christian symbols or famous paintings.

Some stained glass was created for churches and synagogues prior to 1880 (especially in the East), but its significance nationwide was limited. America's most prolific stained glass era was from 1885-1900 when "jeweled" windows were paramount in Protestant edifices. Jewels diminished in popularity and use until about 1917 during America's participation in World War I. Few of these windows were signed.

In the decades since, stained glass companies have come and gone. Other than a few giant stained glass studios (which are featured in the upcoming sections), American leaded stained glass has often sought inspiration at budget prices. The windows that follow are representative of the (unsigned) American leaded stained glass over the 19$^{th}$ and 20$^{th}$ centuries. These windows represent the vast majority of the stained glass found in nearly every American neighborhood, whether downtown, the suburbs or the country.

# American Stained Glass Over the Decades

# Basic American

| | | |
|---|---|---|
| ⭐ O | **$104** per sq. ft. | **Can this window be 100% duplicated? 96% YES** |
| ● N | $126 | *Easy basic design, Wissmach English Muffle glass readily available.* - Glass by Knight Stained Glass Art Studio |
| ● S | $95 | *This window is a simple geometric pattern and can easily be replaced with minimal time and labor.* - Cottage Glass |
| ● GP | $100 | |
| ● W | $91 | *As with most repetitive designs, cost can be decreased with quantity of windows.* - Whitworth Stained Glass |
| ◆ SG | $95 | *While it would be rather simple to replicate this window, one would have to ask why to replicate it. Its loss would serve as an improvement upon the premises.* - Ascalon Studios, Inc. |
| ◆ N | $115 | *Simple design, inexpensive glass.* - Creative Glassworks |
| ▲ L | $97 | *Although the design is simple and the fabrication is easy, the glass is no longer available with that unique texture. Custom making the glass is impractical for this window.* - Tooley Art Glass Studio |
| ▲ S | $112 | |

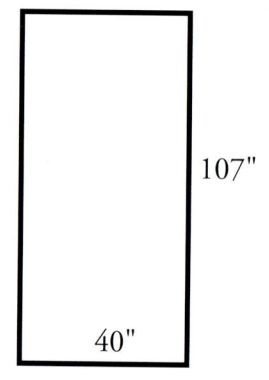

107"

40"

## Cedar Valley Community Church, Waterloo, Iowa

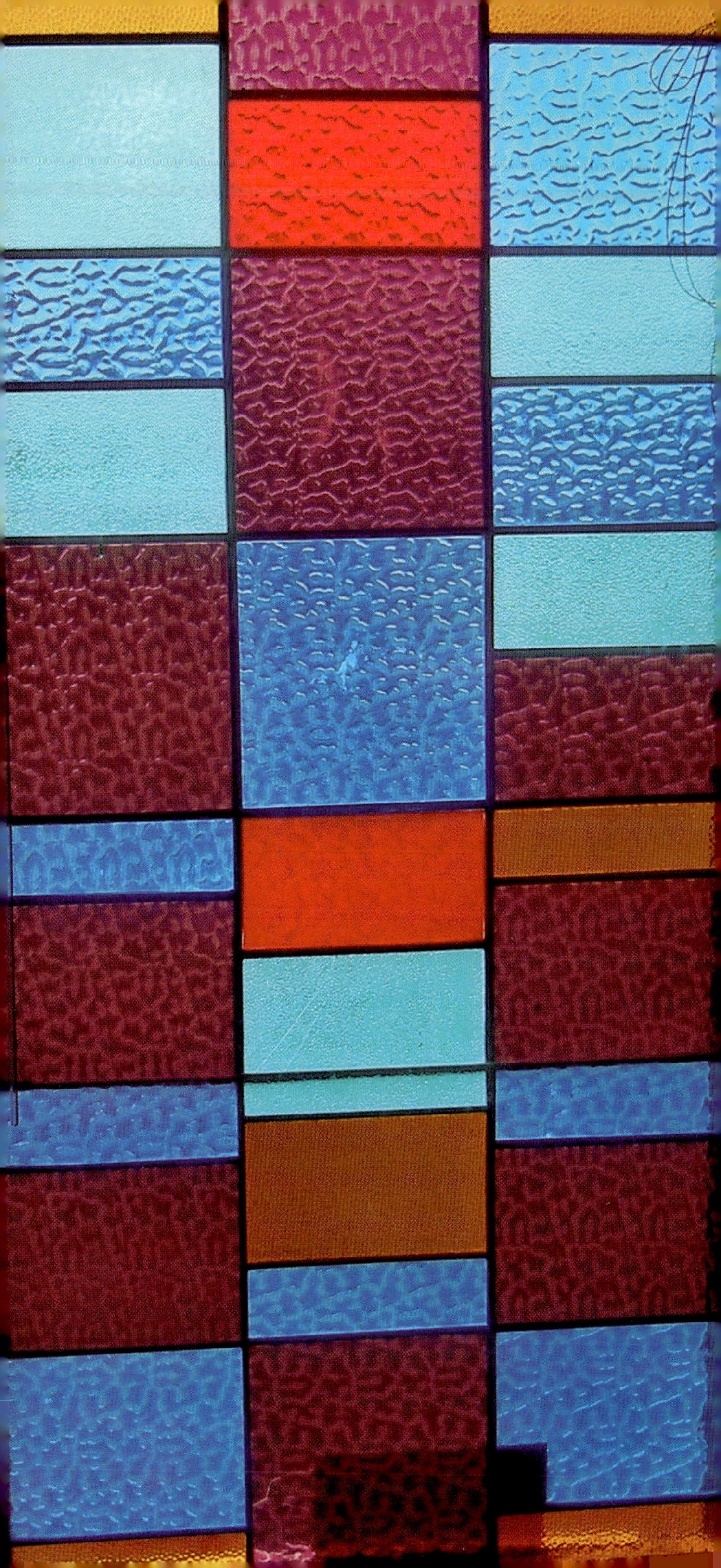

# Basic American

| | |
|---|---|
| O | **$139** per sq. ft. |
| N | $158 |
| S | $137 |
| GP | $136 |
| W | $122 |
| SG | $135 |
| N | $144 |
| L | $134 |
| S | $147 |

Can this window be 100% duplicated?   90% YES

*It appears that all pieces are basic geometric shapes with consistent sizes. I believe it can be replicated.* - Cottage Glass

*Simple geometric design with colored cathedral glass.* - Creative Glassworks

*Although the design is simple and fabrication easy, the glass is no longer available with that unique texture. Custom making the glass is impractical for this window.* - Tooley Art Glass Studio

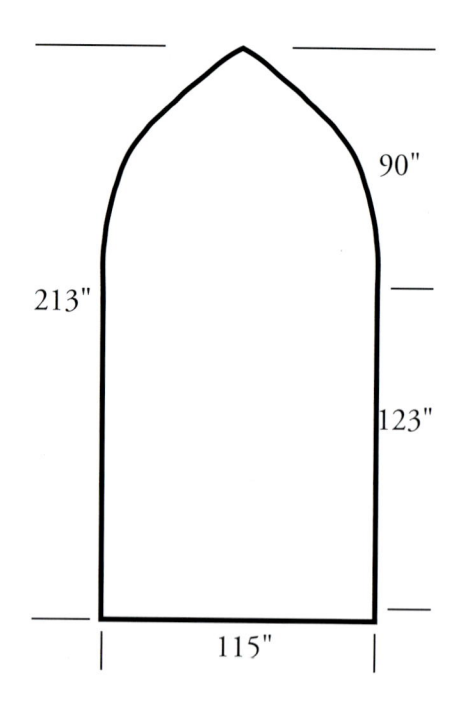

213"

90"

123"

115"

Immanuel Congregational Church, Brush, Colo.

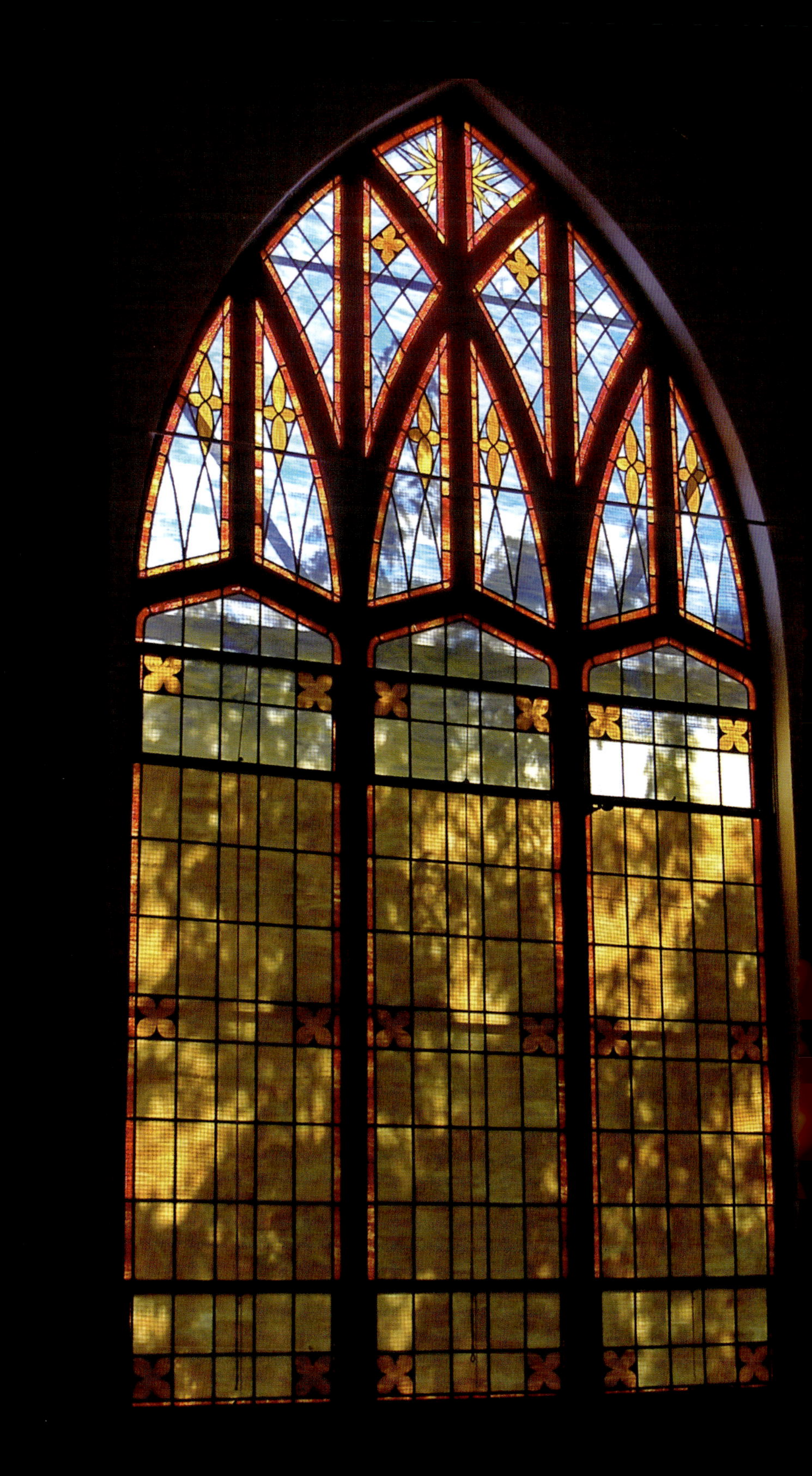

# 19ᵗʰ Century American

| | |
|---|---|
| O | **$255** *per sq. ft.* |
| N | $327 |
| S | $274 |
| GP | $246 |
| W | $147 |
| SG | $230 |
| N | $285 |
| L | $252 |
| S | $267 |

Can this window be 100% duplicated?   86% YES

Despite extensive research, the design, manufacturer and supplier could not be determined. The windows were installed during the original construction phase of the church, probably late 1892.

*This is a very complicated pattern, albeit symmetrical on the grid and basically geometric. The costs of repair would vary on the location of the damaged pieces and the number of pieces to be replaced and reassembled. I believe it can be replicated. This is also likely a signature piece.* - Cottage Glass

*Fairly complex, cathedral glass.*
- Creative Glassworks

*Although the design is simple and fabrication easy, the glass is no longer available with that unique texture. Custom making the glass is impractical for this window.* - Tooley Art Glass Studio

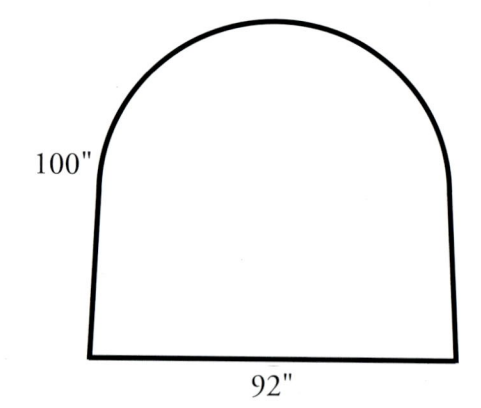

100"

92"

**All Souls Unitarian Universalist Church, Colorado Springs, Colo.**

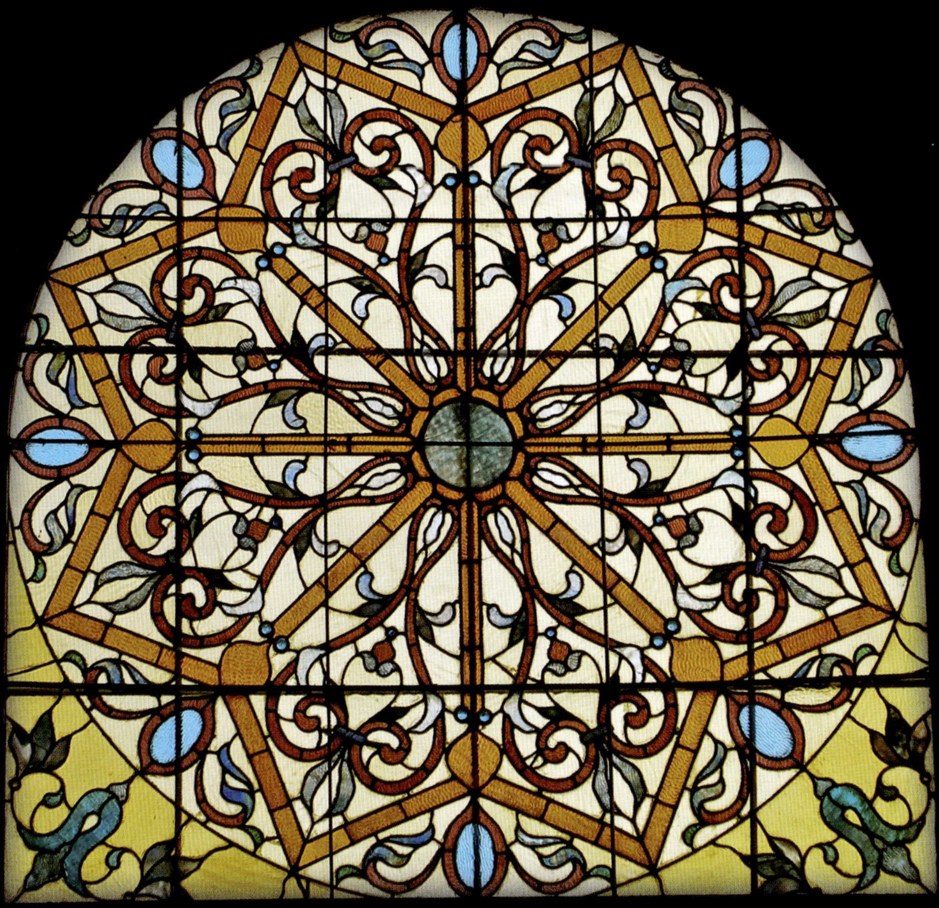

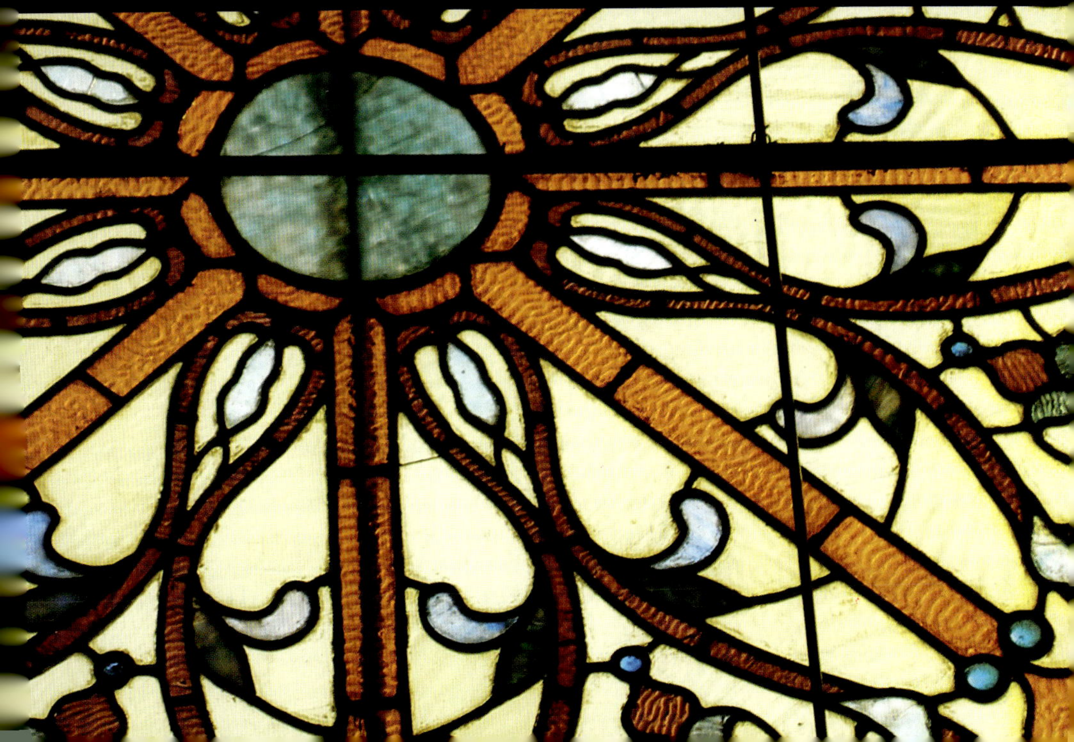

# 19ᵀᴴ Century American

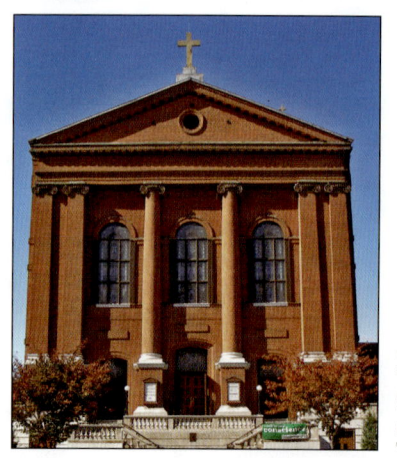

**O** **$312** per sq. ft.

**N** $338

**S** $395

**GP** $269

**W** $254

**SG** $316

**N** $306

**L** $316

**S** $305

Can this window be 100% duplicated?   86% YES

*Hand-rendered painting.* - Creative Glassworks

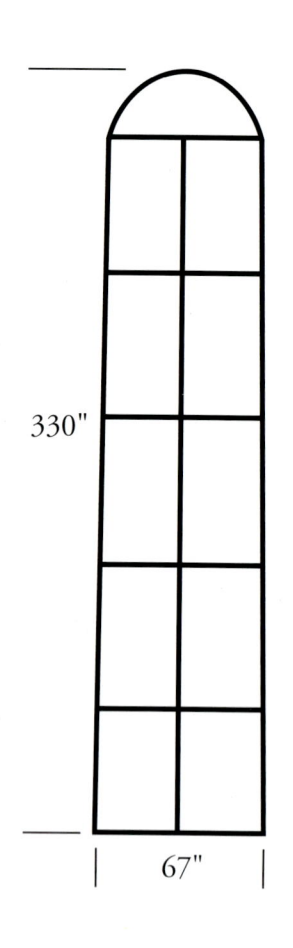

330"

67"

St. Aloysius Church
Gonzaga College High
School, Washington, D.C.

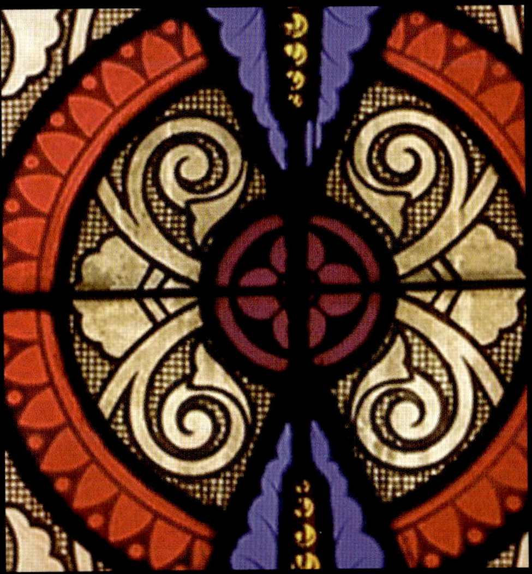
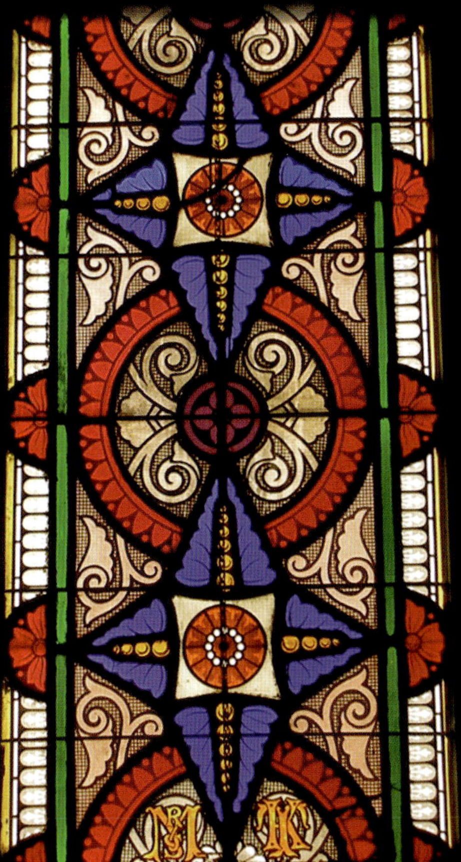
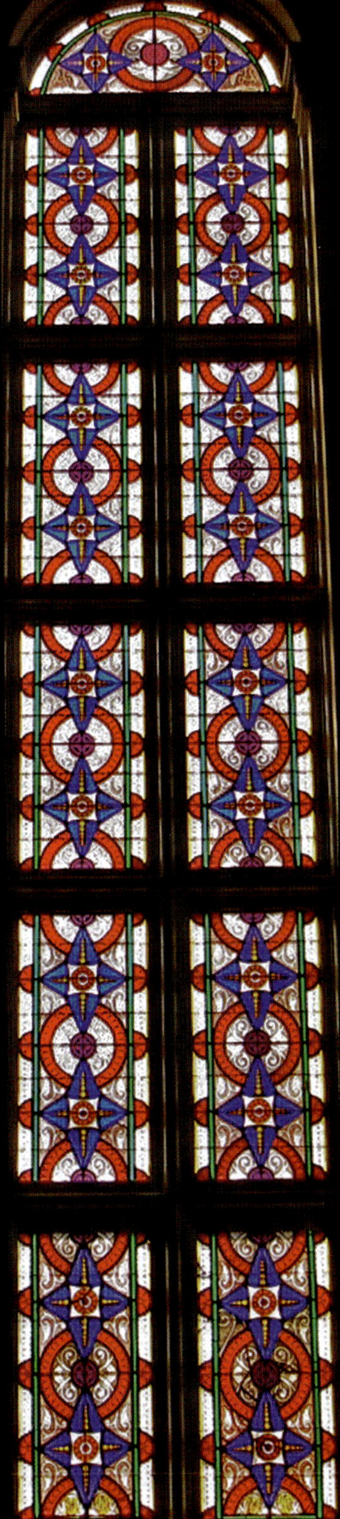

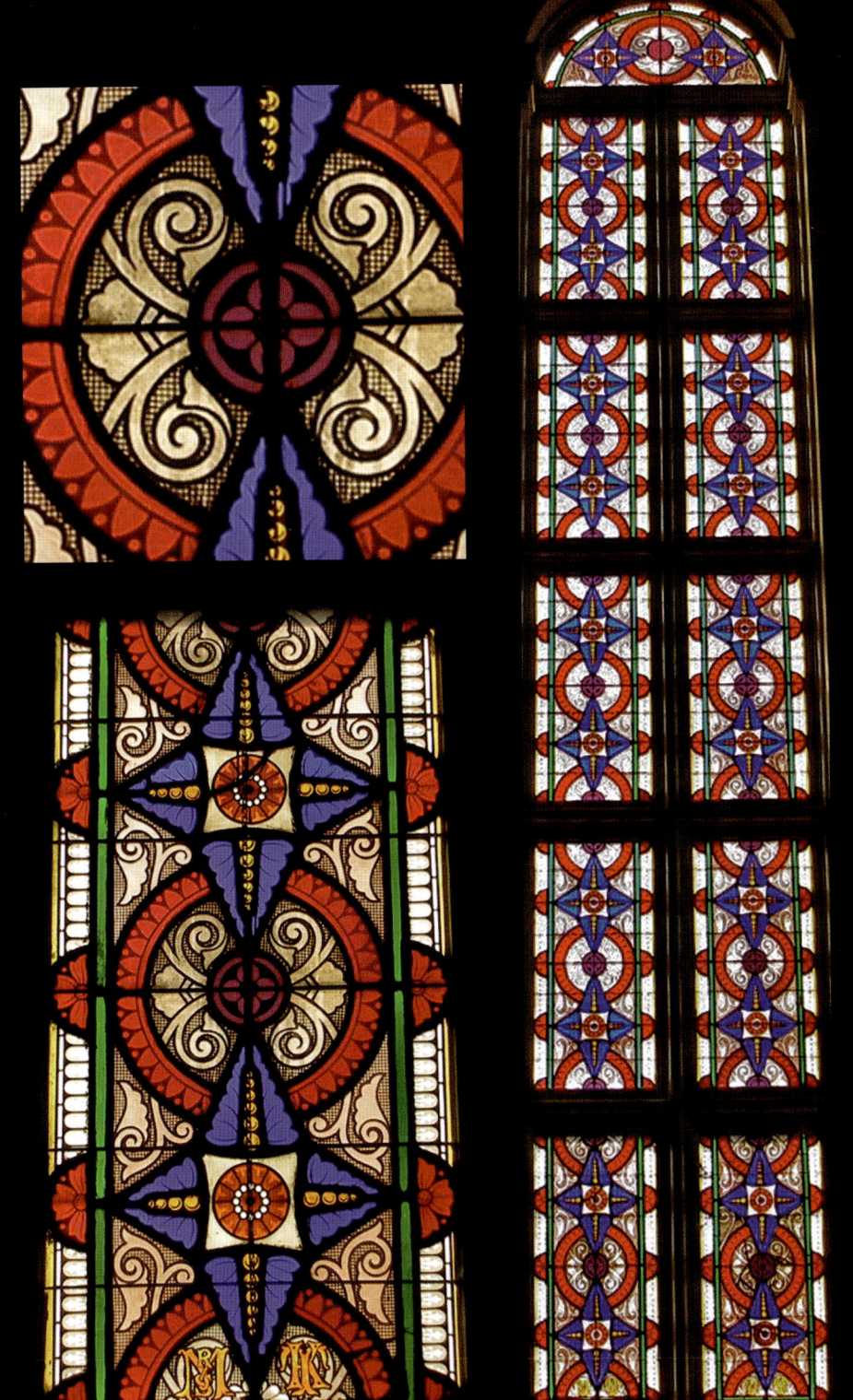

# 19ᵗʰ Century American Jewels
## 1885-1900

| | |
|---|---|
| O | **$385** *per sq. ft.* |
| N | $426 |
| S | $387 |
| GP | $355 |
| W | $383 |
| SG | $342 |
| N | $442 |
| L | $380 |
| S | $388 |

Can this window be 100% duplicated?   85% YES

1894. Includes a snow-white dove for the favor Our Lord enjoyed in God's eyes during His life on earth, the cross, for His sacrifice in atonement for our sins; the crown, symbolizing His eternal majesty; the lily, for His purity and the lily of the valley for His chastity. - *from Incarnation Memorials & Gifts*

*Good design, medium difficulty construction, minimal painting, medium to large pieces.* - Glass by Knight Stained Glass Art Studio

*Nicely painted, moderately complex. Looks like the Rudy Bros.* - Creative Glassworks

*To qualify the square foot prices reflected herein, it might be helpful to understand that the size of the window affects that figure. So, a smaller window might have a higher per square foot than a larger window of similar complexity or style.*
- Hiemer & Company Stained Glass

82"

26"

## Church of the Incarnation
### Episcopal, Dallas, Texas

TO THE SACRED MEMORY OF
EDDIE HUDSON TABOR
DIED JANUARY 3rd, 1894
GIVEN BY THE SUNDAY SCHOOL CHILDREN

# 19ᵗʰ Century American Jewels
## 1885-1900

| | |
|---|---|
| ⭐ O | **$432** per sq. ft. |
| 🔵 N | $669 |
| ⚫ S | $381 |
| 🔵 GP | $358 |
| 🔴 W | $285 |
| 🔶 SG | $394 |
| 🔶 N | $480 |
| 🔺 L | $430 |
| 🔺 S | $446 |

Can this window be 100% duplicated?   76% YES

Begins to show signs of La Farge influence. - Kebrle Stained Glass, Inc.

Difficult to match Rondels and Unique Jewels. - Raynal Studios

Very complicated design, intricate cutting, rare glass. - Enterprise Art Glass Works Inc.

Highly ornate but apparently no painted work. - Creative Glassworks

Though we felt most windows could be replicated, it should be noted that some glass may no longer be available and substitutions be required. - Hiemer & Company Stained Glass

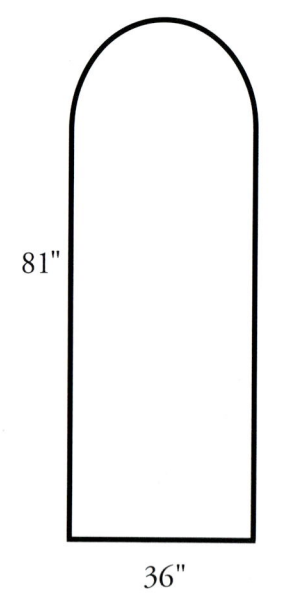

81"

36"

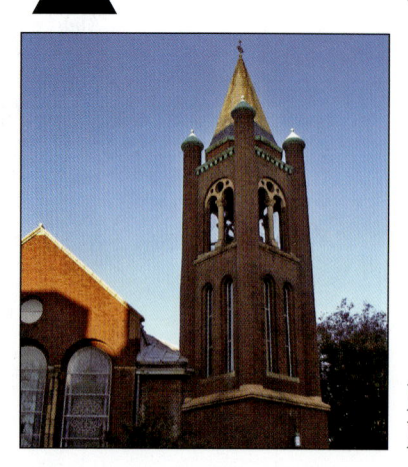

First Presbyterian Church, Raleigh, N.C.

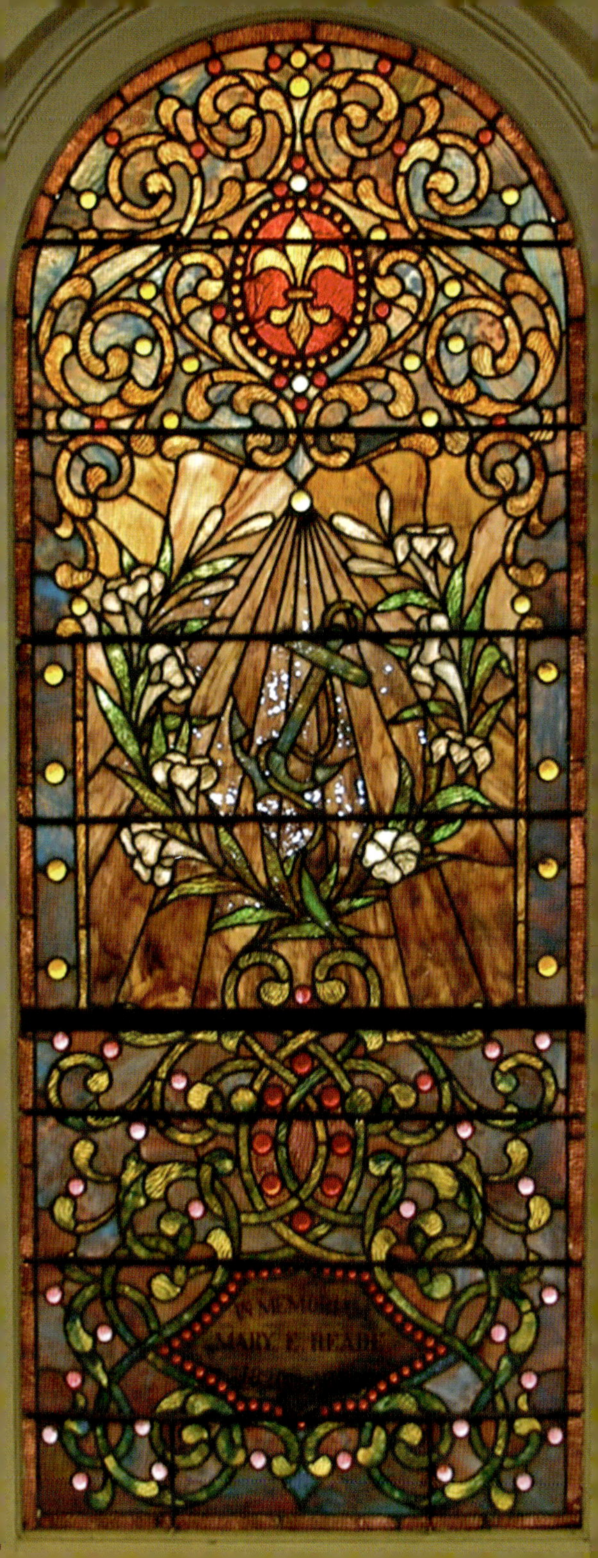

# Early American
## 1895-1910

|   | A.<br>$442<br>per sq. ft. | B.<br>$392<br>per sq. ft. | C.<br>$309<br>per sq. ft. |
|---|---|---|---|
| O | | | |
| N | $504 | $488 | $410 |
| S | $545 | $372 | $275 |
| GP | $355 | $358 | $242 |
| W | $395 | $342 | $335 |
| SG | $467 | $360 | $277 |
| N | $410 | $434 | $352 |
| L | $403 | $413 | $292 |
| S | $489 | $384 | $331 |

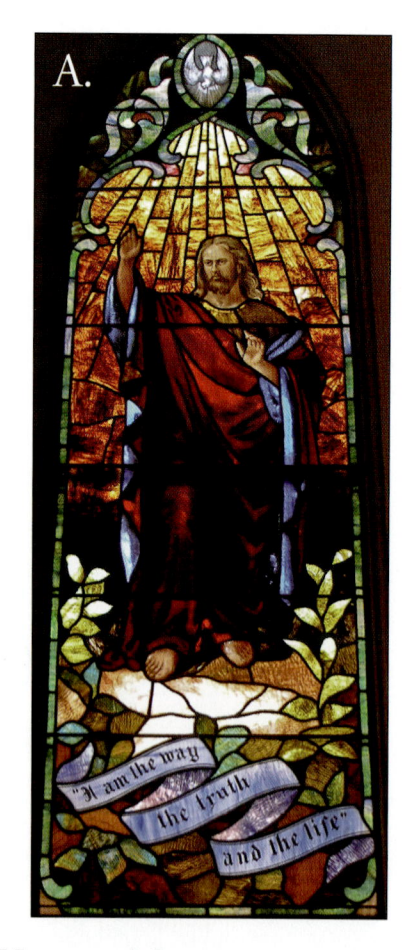

Can this window be 100% duplicated?

A. 73% YES

B. 81% YES

C. 78% YES

A.

First United Methodist Church, Marion, Iowa

C = 88" x 144"

*Good composition and figure painting.*
- Kebrle Stained Glass, Inc.

*These are complicated and dense designs.*
- Cottage Glass

*Robe appears to be drapery glass probably multiple layers – early opalescent is difficult to match.* - Raynal Studios

(Editor's note: the robe is not drapery glass)

A & B = 38" x 155"

# 20ᵀᴴ Century American, Basic

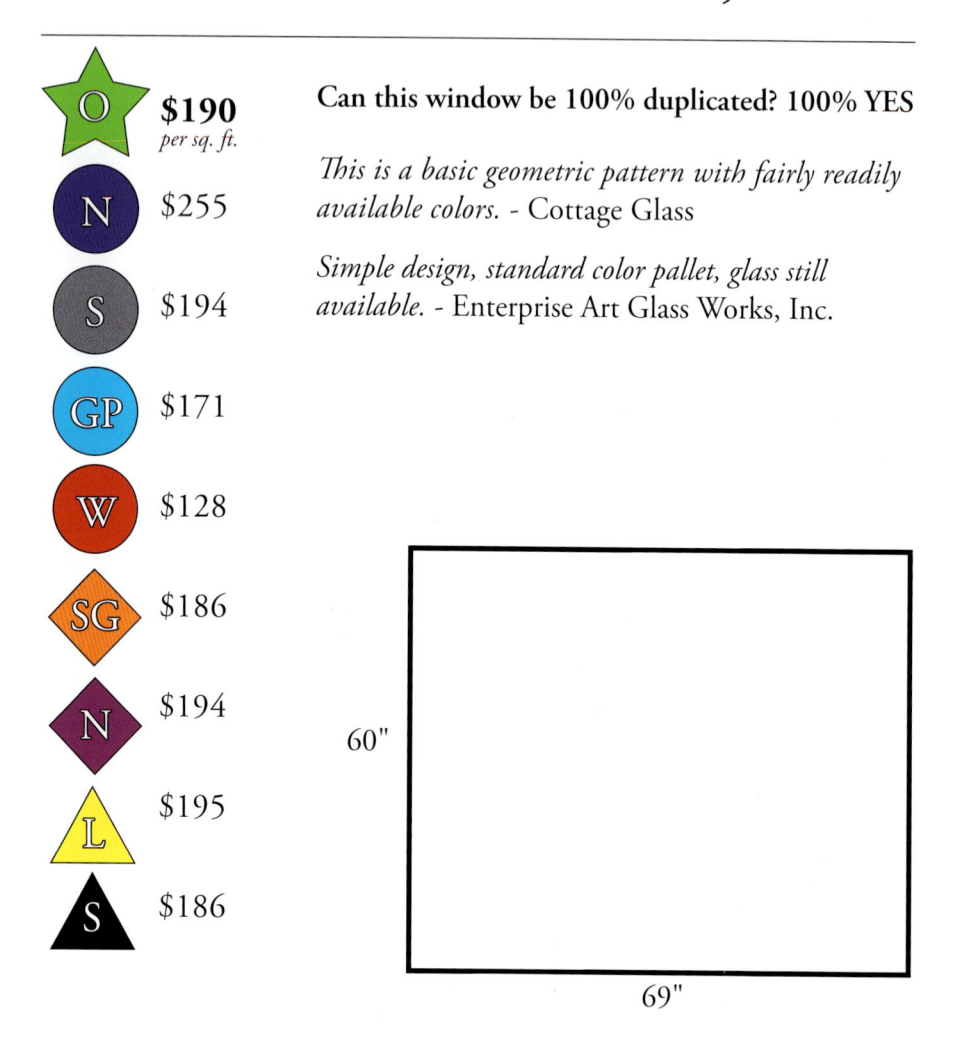

| | | |
|---|---|---|
| O (star) | **$190** per sq. ft. | |
| N | $255 | |
| S | $194 | |
| GP | $171 | |
| W | $128 | |
| SG | $186 | |
| N | $194 | |
| L | $195 | |
| S | $186 | |

Can this window be 100% duplicated? 100% YES

*This is a basic geometric pattern with fairly readily available colors.* - Cottage Glass

*Simple design, standard color pallet, glass still available.* - Enterprise Art Glass Works, Inc.

60"
69"

Central Baptist Church
Winchester, Ky.

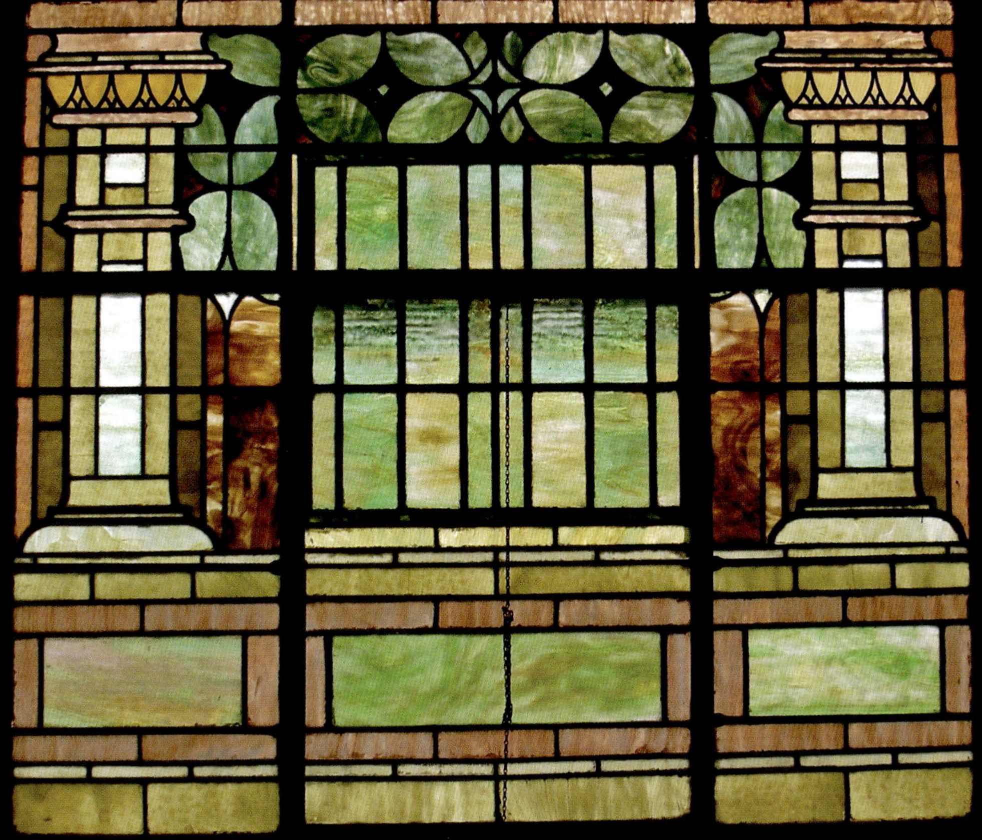

# 20ᵀᴴ Century American
## 1960s

- O — **$298** per sq. ft.
- N — $354
- S — $268
- GP — $322
- W — $198
- SG — $273
- N — $327
- L — $322
- S — $276

Can this window be 100% duplicated?   91% YES

*Although the close-up reveals a fair bit of shading or tracing with glass paints, this is a fairly straightforward design and I believe it can be 100% replicated.* - Cottage Glass

*Fully painted.* - Creative Glassworks

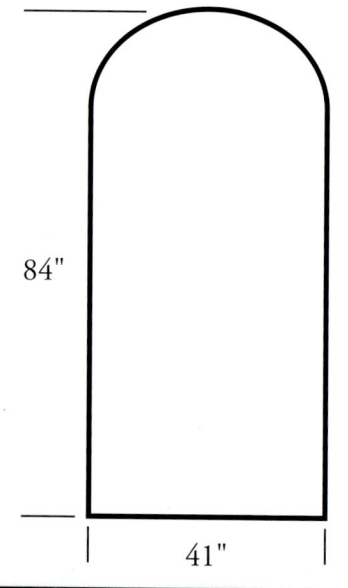

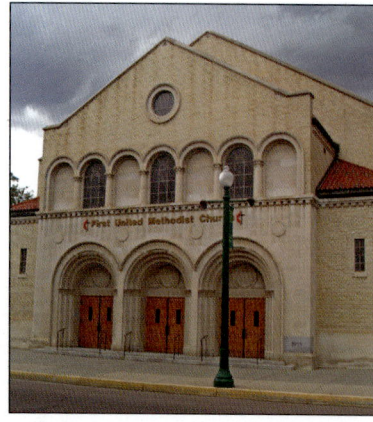

84"

41"

First United Methodist Church, Colorado Springs, Colo.

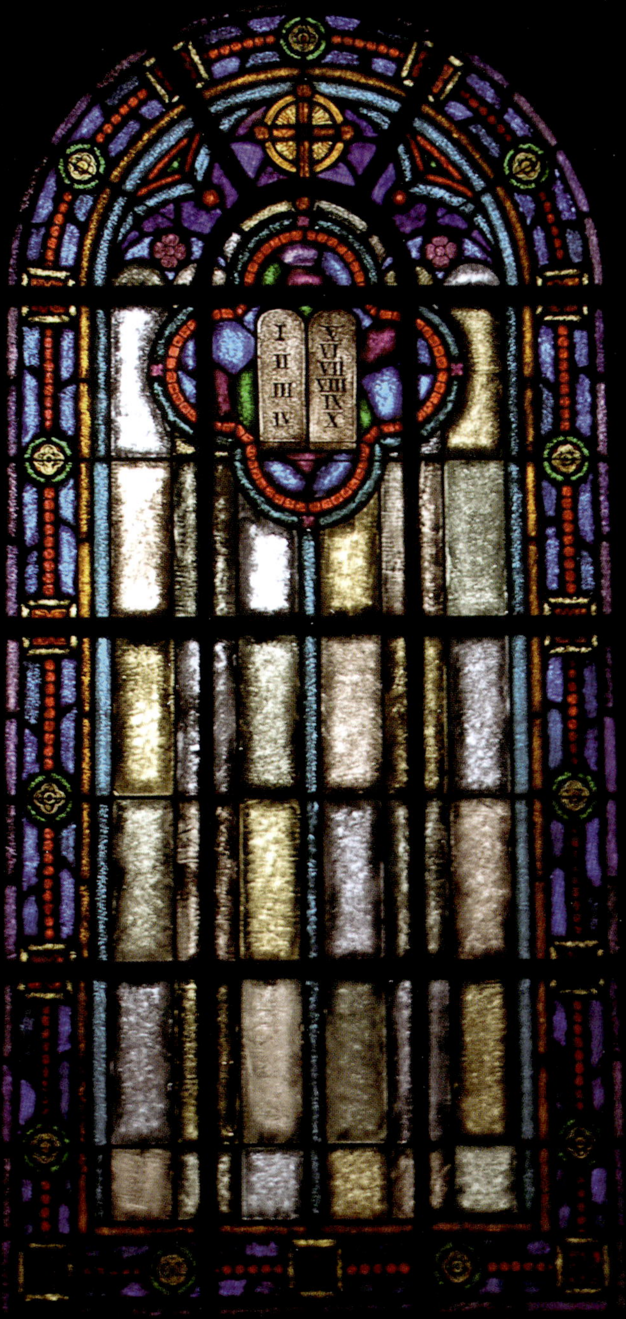
I II III IV
V VI VII VIII IX X

# 20ᵗʰ Century American

| | |
|---|---|
| O | **$197** per sq. ft. |
| N | $219 |
| S | $187 |
| GP | $201 |
| W | $168 |
| SG | $197 |
| N | $197 |
| L | $201 |
| S | $193 |

Can this window be 100% duplicated? 100% YES

*This is a simple, straightforward geometric design with some, but not a great deal of shading or tracing with paints and I believe it can be 100% replicated.* - Cottage Glass

*Simple layout, simple painting.* - Creative Glassworks

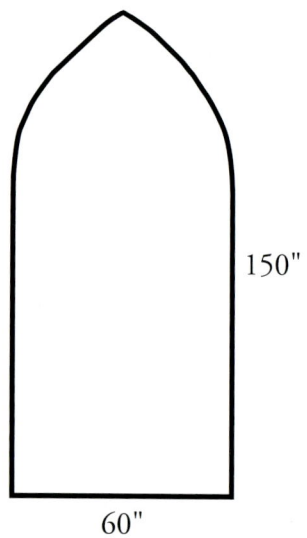

150"

60"

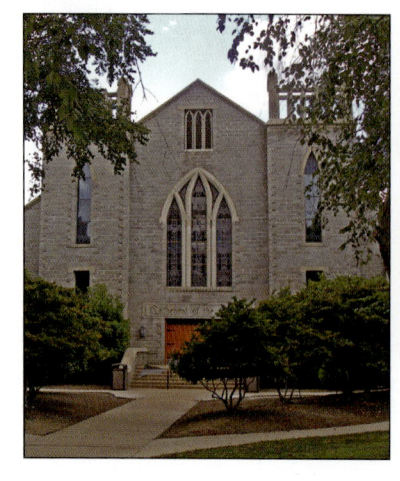

## Cathedral of the Ozarks, Siloam Springs, Ark.

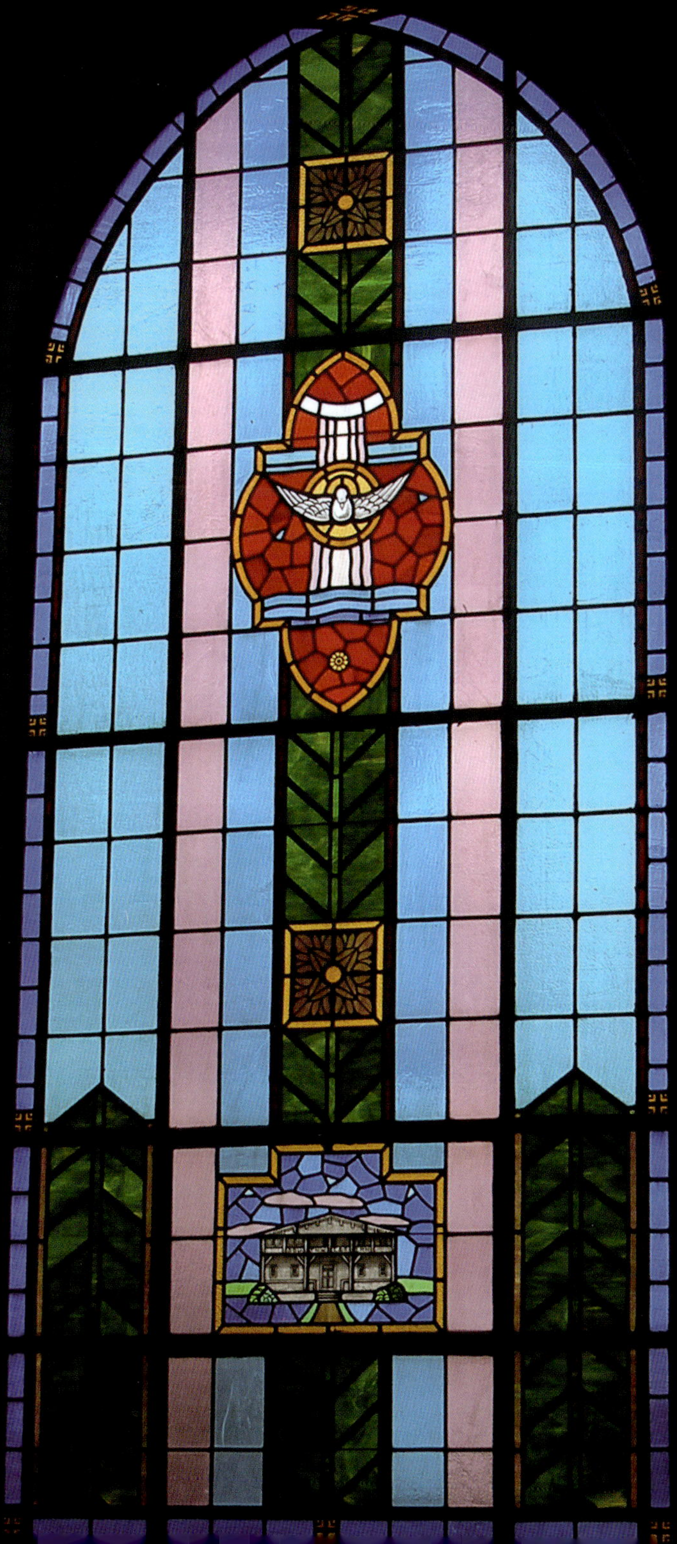

# 20ᵗʜ Century American

| | |
|---|---|
| O | $262 per sq. ft. |
| N | $291 |
| S | $274 |
| GP | $283 |
| W | $154 |
| SG | $270 |
| N | $251 |
| L | $284 |
| S | $249 |

Can this window be 100% duplicated?   95% YES

*Medium to large pieces, glass easily matched.* - Glass by Knight Stained Glass Art Studio

*This is a complex design and dense in the number of pieces per square foot, however, it appears the design is almost entirely glass with little or no painting.* - Cottage Glass

*Cathedral antique glasses.* - Creative Glassworks

*A cluttered redundancy around the figure of Christ.* - Kebrle Stained Glass, Inc.

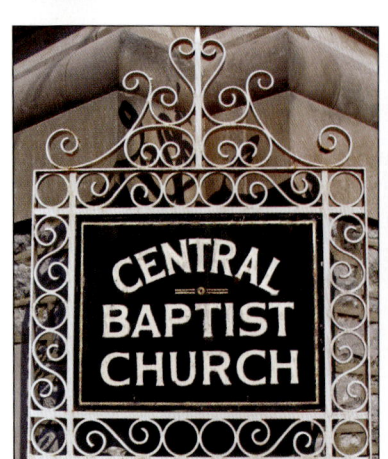

144"

Central Baptist Church
Winchester, Ky.

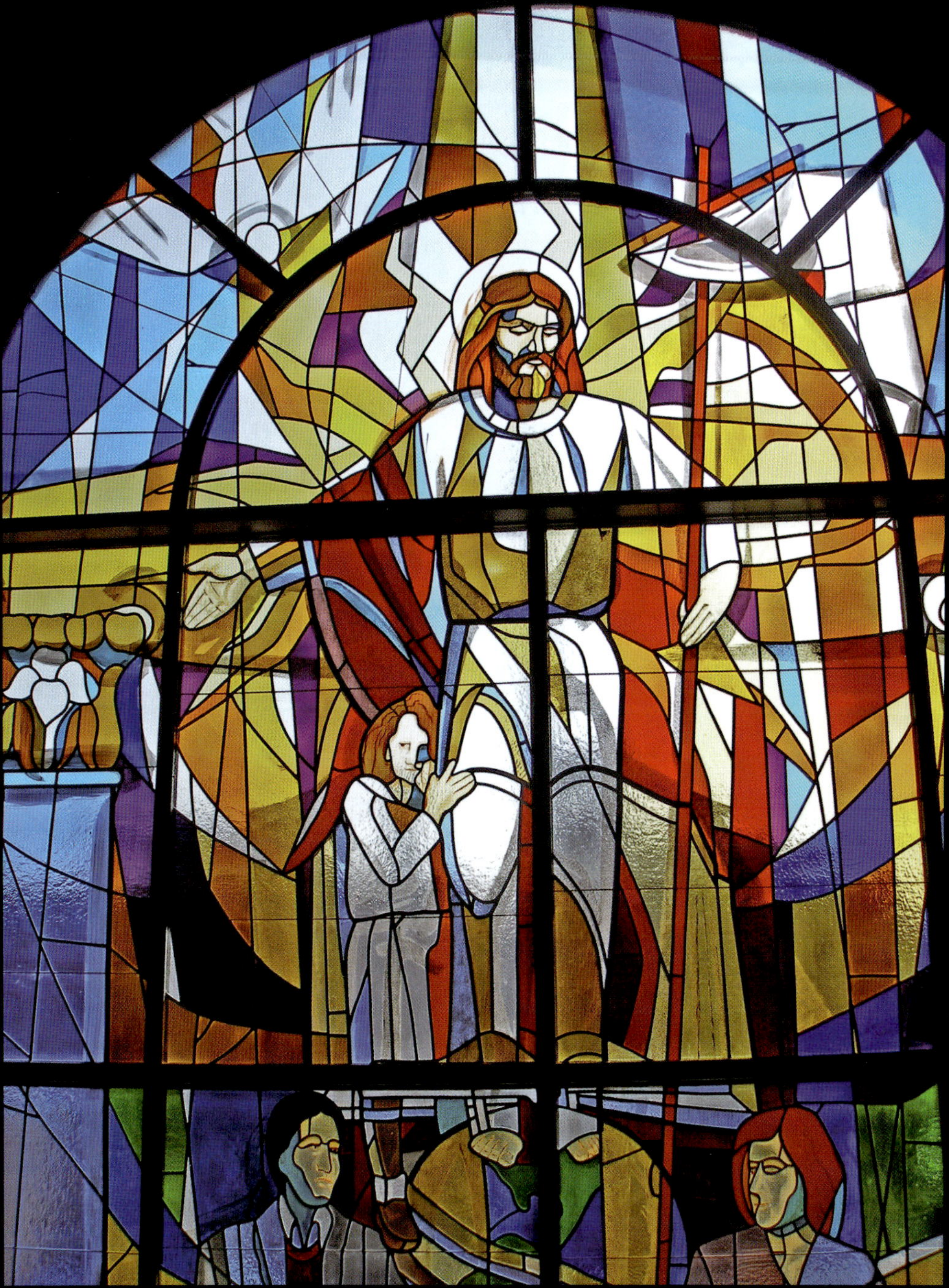

# 20ᵀᴴ Century American

| | | |
|---|---|---|
| O | **$290** per sq. ft. | Can this window be 100% duplicated?   87% YES |
| N | $362 | *Each piece in this window is painted, including the background.* - Whitworth Stained Glass |
| S | $292 | *Repetitive design, all painted, common glass.* - Enterprise Art Glass Works, Inc. |
| GP | $276 | *Fully painted, complex leading.* - Creative Glassworks |
| W | $207 | |
| SG | $299 | |
| N | $278 | 220" |
| L | $310 | |
| S | $262 | 145" |

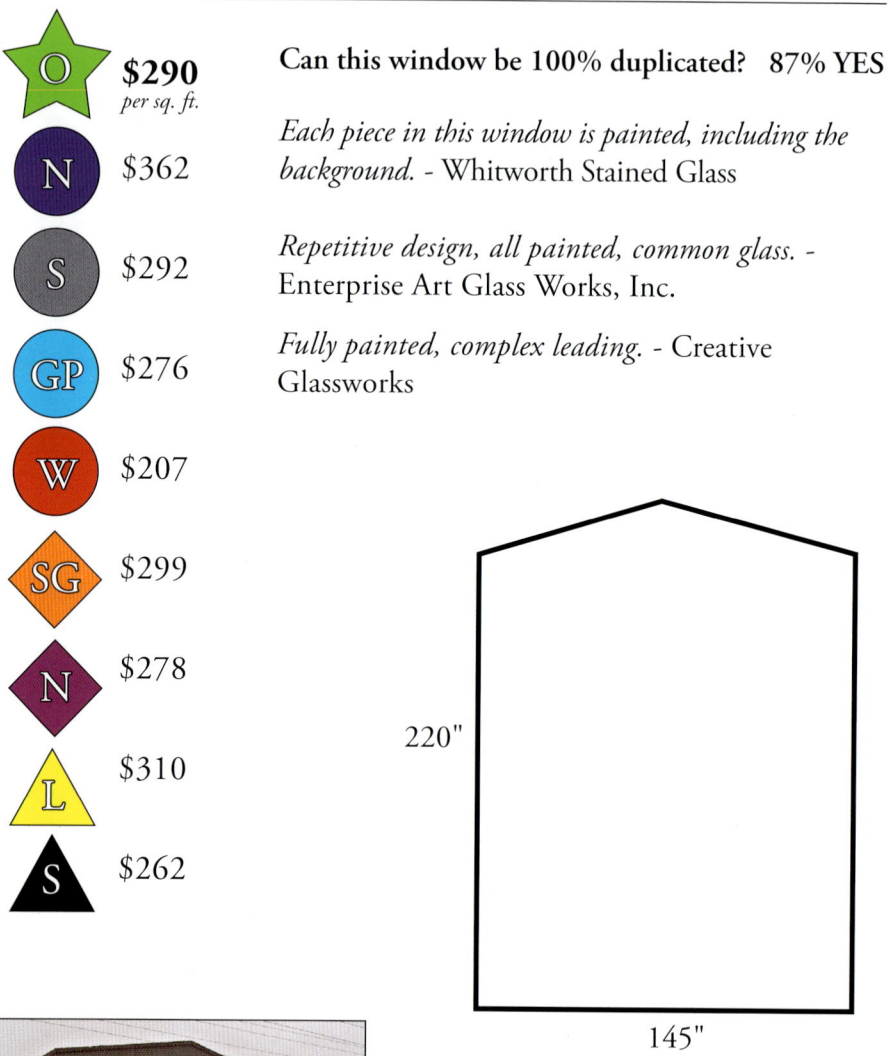

First Baptist Church,
Seymour, Texas

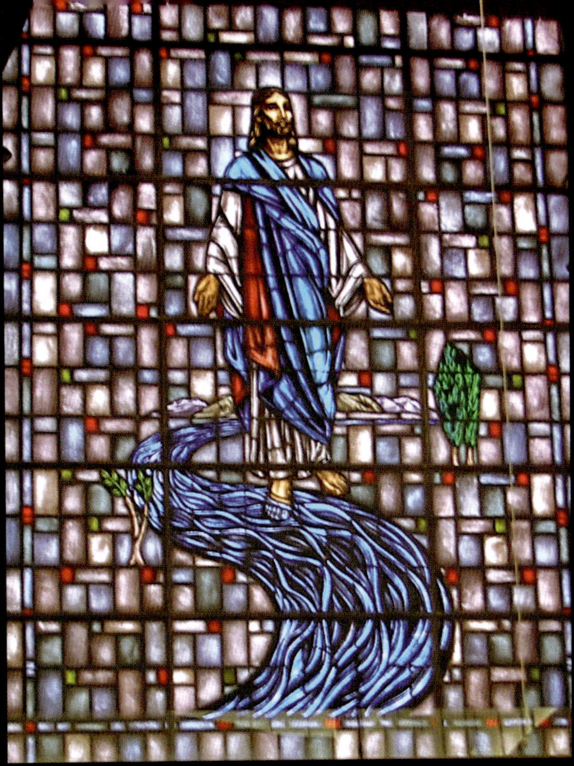

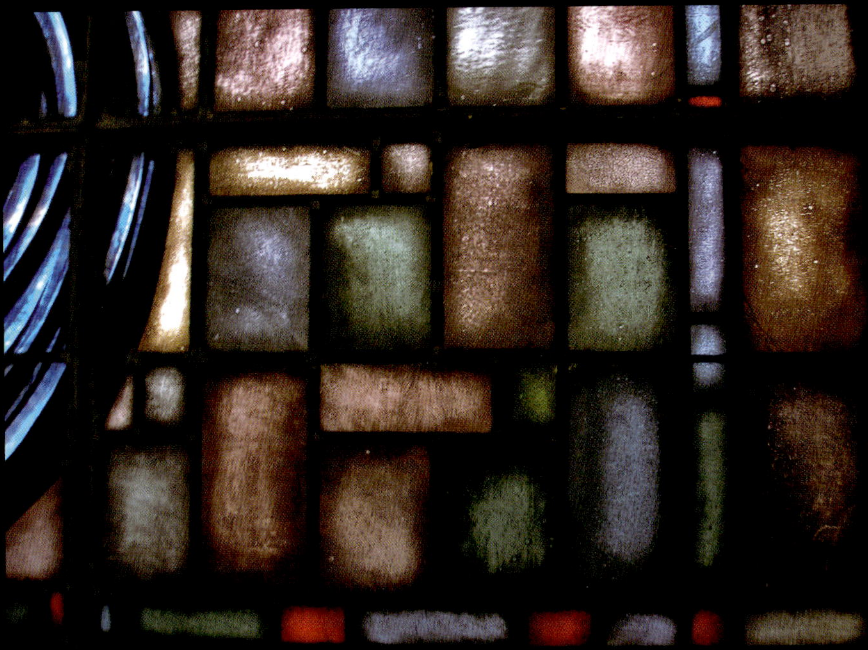

# Section 2

Stained glass emerged primarily as a European art form. Artists and craftsmen could spend lifetimes designing, firing and fabricating a European cathedral's leaded glass masterpieces. Most of America's greatest stained glass during the nineteenth century was made in Germany and Britain, and some came from France and Italy. Typical of these windows were biblical scenes exquisite in detail and color. The painted faces and hands were remarkably lifelike. The stained glass visually told the Christian message to the illiterate masses. Hundreds of artisans were employed in Bavaria alone (Franz Mayer and F. X. Zettler) to meet the overwhelming demand.

At the turn of the twentieth century, American stained glass briefly was the world's finest when Louis Comfort Tiffany, borrowing from the master John La Farge, took the art to new heights. Eccentric, brilliant and wealthy, Tiffany utilized new forms for molding thick, rippled drapery glass using strikingly beautiful pastel colors. Unconcerned about profit, Tiffany sought to create the ultimate stained glass masterpiece—a goal he achieved in window after window.

American stained glass quality remained high during the 1930s and 1940s with the emergence Connick, Willet, Payne, and Lamb. Other studios like Rohlf, Conrad Schmitt, Frei, and Judson have continued to maintain high levels of artisanship from generation-to-generation.

This section features the masters of stained glass found in America who continue to stand tall for their abilities to tell the biblical story through light and with brilliant painted/fired colors designed for the ages.

# The Great Stained Glass Studios

# Connick

| | |
|---|---|
| O | **$673** *per sq. ft.* |
| N | $870 |
| S | $625 |
| GP | $648 |
| W | $484 |
| SG | $710 |
| N | $630 |
| L | $681 |
| S | $687 |

**Can this window be 100% duplicated?   82% YES**

The Transfiguration Window, by Charles J. Connick, is immediately adjacent to the east transept, and was given by the women of the church in memory of those who had passed away. Jesus is the central figure. On His left is Moses with the Tables of the Law and on His right is Elijah with the prophetic scroll. The dove, symbol of the Holy Spirit, appears above a bright cloud in the tracery.

*From "A Journey of Hope: The House of Hope Presbyterian Church 1849-1999, page 117.*

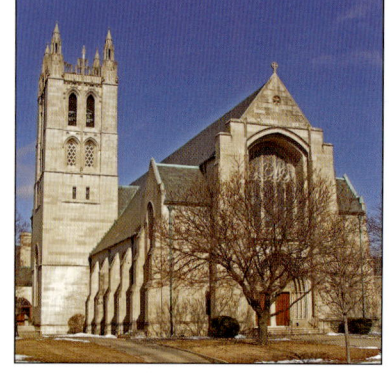

163"

86"

House of Hope Presbyterian
St. Paul, Minn.

Given by the Women of this Church in Loving Memory of Those who have passed away

# Connick Associates

| | |
|---|---|
| O | **$558** *per sq. ft.* |
| N | $767 |
| S | $563 |
| GP | $468 |
| W | $420 |
| SG | $569 |
| N | $544 |
| L | $569 |
| S | $559 |

Can this window be 100% duplicated?   88% YES

"Shepherd Show Me How to Go." In this window we see the love and care Jesus, the Good Shepherd, has for us, the sheep of his flock. The theme is taken from the parable of the sheep, which is recorded by John in chapter 10:14-15: "I am the good shepherd, and know my sheep, and am known of mine. As the Father knoweth me even so I know the Father: and I lay down my life for the sheep." He carries the little lost sheep in his arms close to his heart. The shepherd's crook in his right hand symbolizes the care Christ has for his flock and reminds us of the Bishop's staff which symbolizes the continuing care the church exercises in Christ's name. - *from Stained Glass Windows of Christ and Holy Trinity Church*

*A true masterpiece!* - Kebrle Stained Glass, Inc.

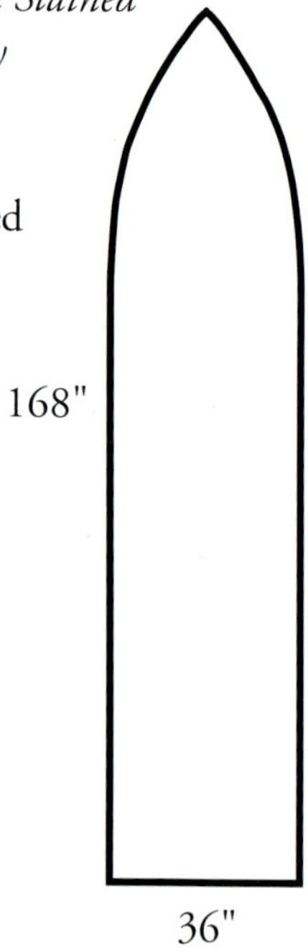

168"

36"

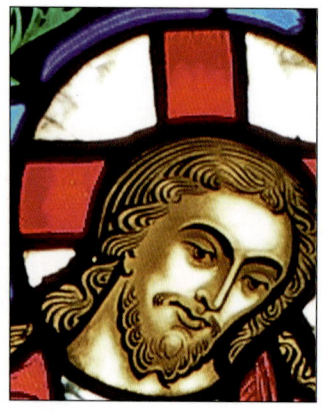

## Christ and Holy Trinity Episcopal Church, Westport, Conn.

SHEPHERD SHOW ME HOW TO GO
IN MEMORY OF
RICHARD LAWRENCE CORDELL

# Conrad Schmitt Studios

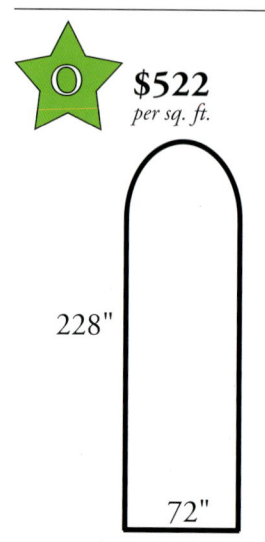

**O** $522 per sq. ft.

Can this window be 100% duplicated? 100% YES

*All antique glass.* - Rohlf's Stained Glass and Leaded Studio, Inc.

228"

72"

*Photos courtesy of Conrad Schmitt Studios*

## St. Ambrose Cathedral, Des Moines, Iowa

BISHOP JOHN CARROLL
ENGLAND 1790
PAULINE JARICOT
1822 FOUNDRESS OF THE SOCIETY FOR THE PROPAGATION OF THE FAITH
FATHER MAZZUCHELLI INDIAN MISSIONARY BUILDER OF FIRST CHURCH IN IOWA
TAKE AWAY THE RUST FROM SILVER AND THERE SHALL COME FORTH A MOST PURE VESSEL
CELEBRATING MASS AT FORT DES MOINES
UNITED STATES

# Conrad Schmitt Studios

**$425**
*per sq. ft.*

Can this window be 100% duplicated? 100% YES

*Large pieces and minimal painting keeps labor costs low on this project. - Church Windows by Tooley Art Glass Studio*

*Photos courtesy of Conrad Schmitt Studios*

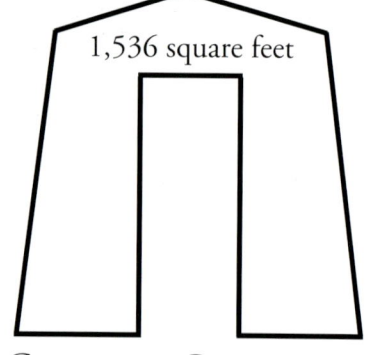

1,536 square feet

## St. Gertrude Catholic Church, Franklin Park, Ill.

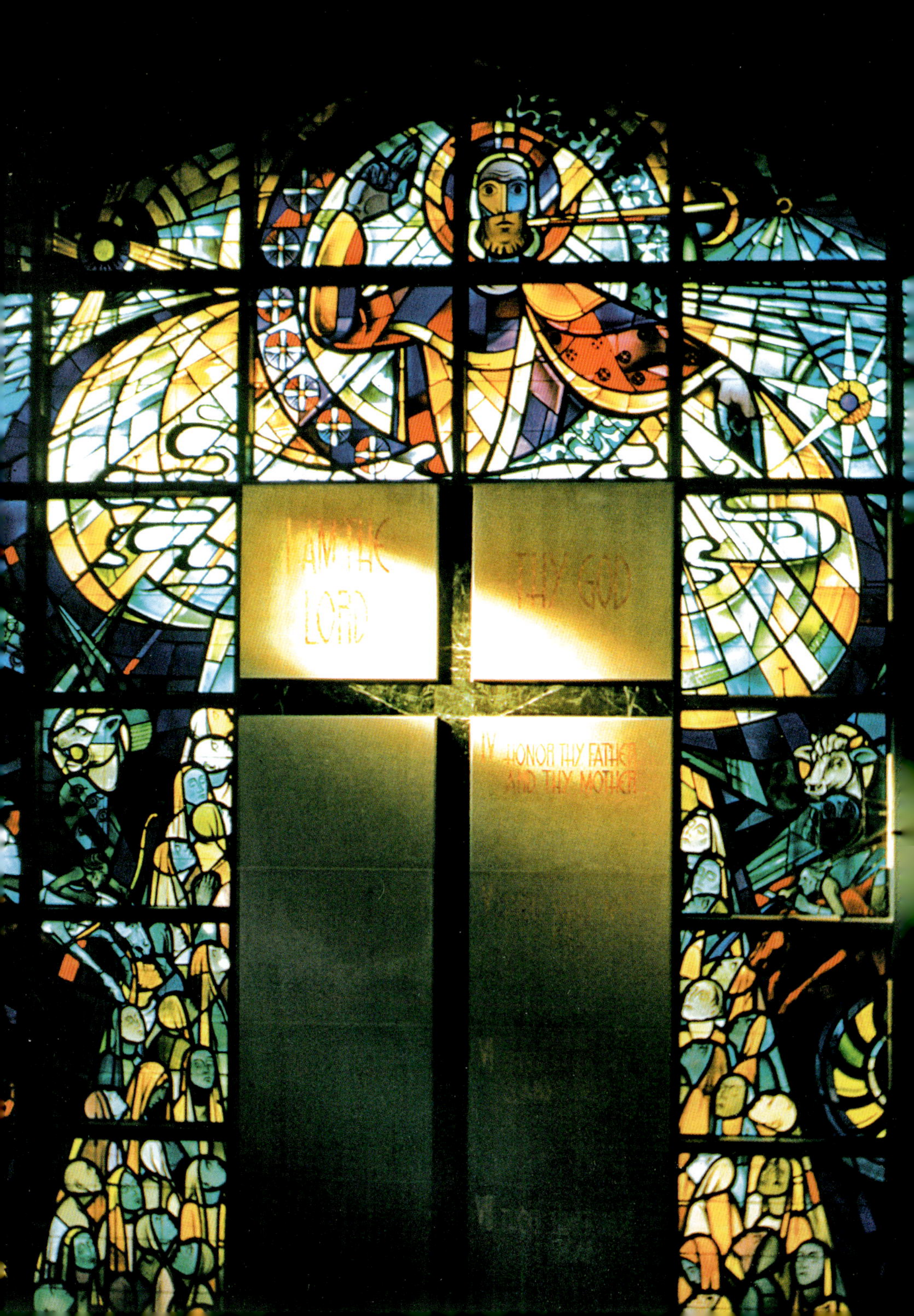
I AM THE
LORD
THY GOD
IV HONOR THY FATHER
AND THY MOTHER

# Conrad Schmitt Studios

| | |
|---|---|
| O | **$444** per sq. ft. |
| N | $467 |
| S | $480 |
| GP | $391 |
| W | $468 |
| SG | $475 |
| N | $402 |
| L | $430 |
| S | $454 |

Can this window be 100% duplicated?   95% YES

The image of the Pantocrator is one of the Greek Orthodox icons incorporated into the stained glass windows at this 1961 Frank Lloyd Wright designed Church.

*Well done in orthodox painted style.* - Anonymous

*Great Schmitt.* - Kebrle Stained Glass Inc.

*Partially painted.* - Creative Glassworks

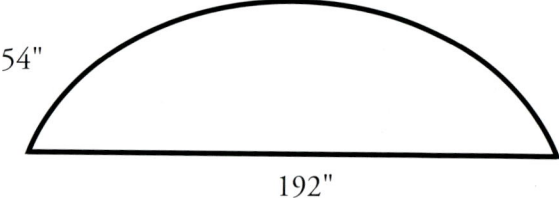

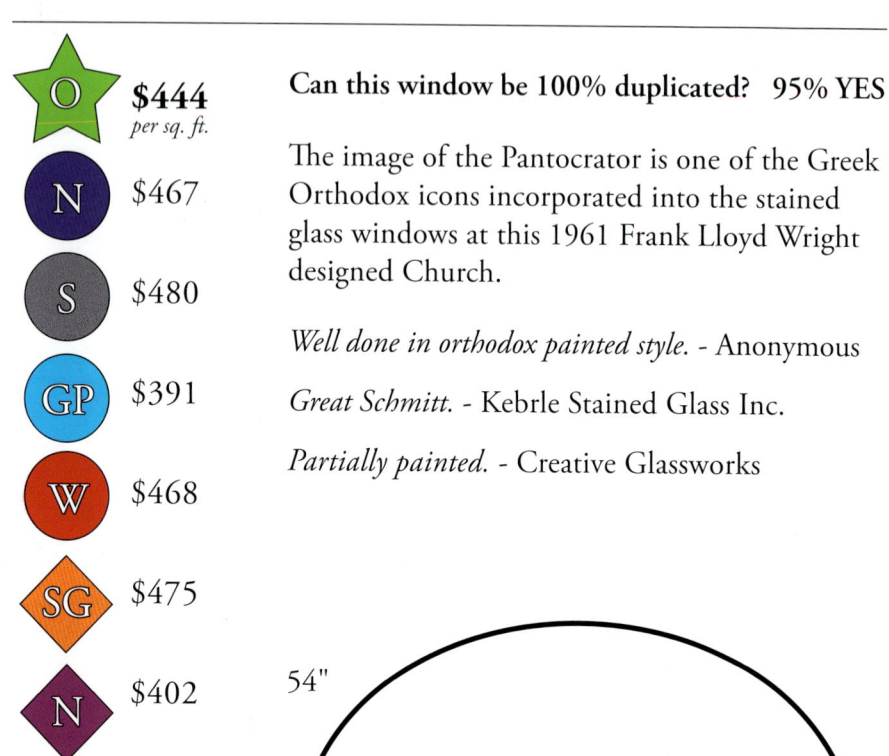

54"

192"

## Annunciation Greek Orthodox Church, Wauwatosa, Wis.
*Photo courtesy of Conrad Schmitt Studios*

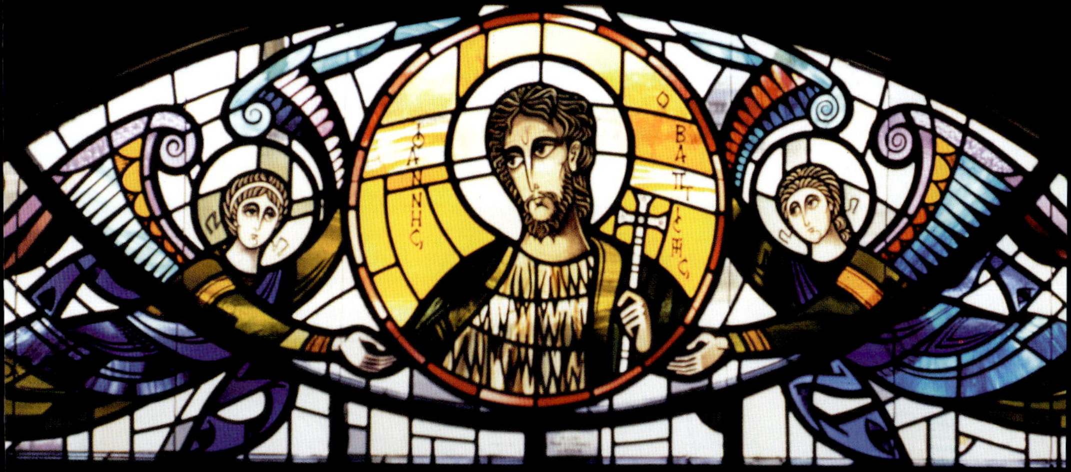
ΙΩΑΝΝΗϹ
Ο ΒΑΠΤΙϹΤΗϹ

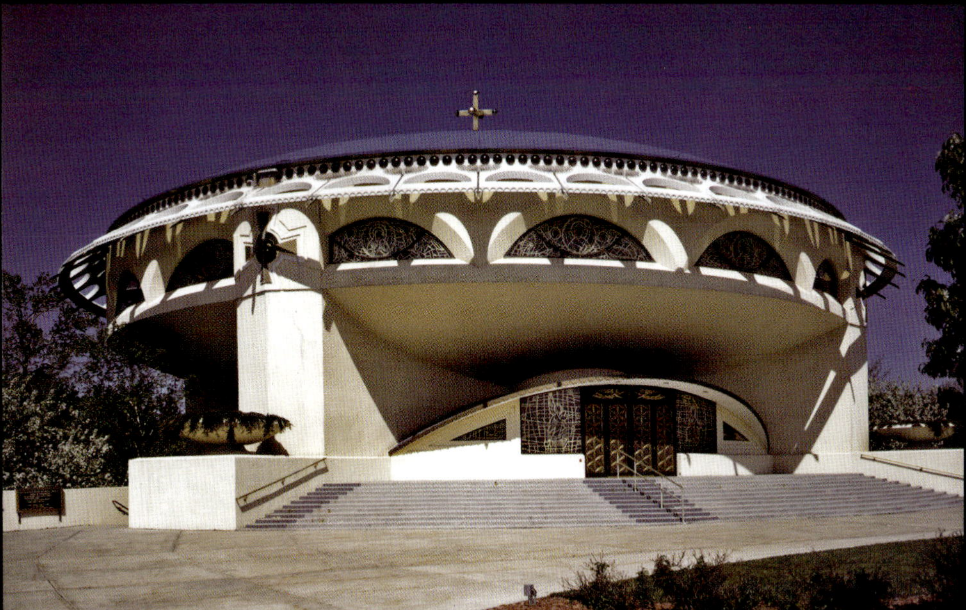

# Cox & Sons
## (Buckley, London, 1889)

| | |
|---|---|
| O | **$752** per sq. ft. |
| N | $1133 |
| S | $575 |
| GP | $656 |
| W | $591 |
| SG | $691 |
| N | $830 |
| L | $680 |
| S | $838 |

Can this window be 100% duplicated?   77% YES

*The flesh work is one of a kind, made with the Masters Eye.* - Enterprise Art Glass Works, Inc.

*High quality painting.* - Creative Glassworks

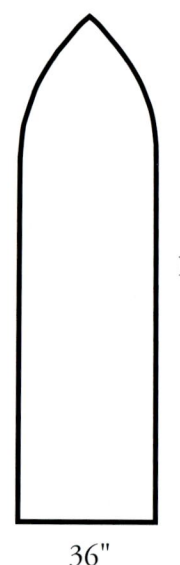

126"

36"

St. Mark's Episcopal Church, Cheyenne, Wyo.

πόθεν οὖν ἔχεις τὸ ὕδωρ τὸ ζῶν;

IN MEMORIAM
JULY 1851 · WELTHA ANITA EMMONS · FEB. 1888

# D'Ascenzo

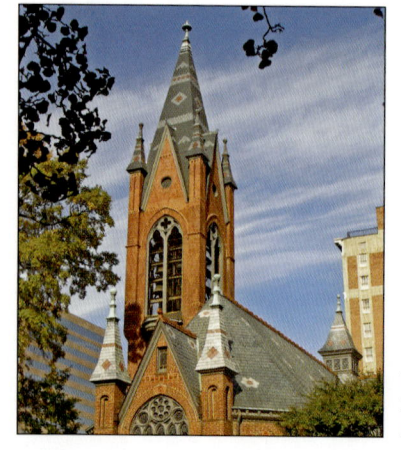

| | |
|---|---|
| O | **$711** per sq. ft. |
| N | $917 |
| S | $685 |
| GP | $622 |
| W | $606 |
| SG | $699 |
| N | $725 |
| L | $711 |
| S | $737 |

Can this window be 100% duplicated?   86% YES

*An American Master.* - Kebrle Stained Glass, Inc.

*Small to medium pieces, heavy painting, lots of detail, unsure of availability of glass.* - Glass by Knight Stained Glass Art Studio

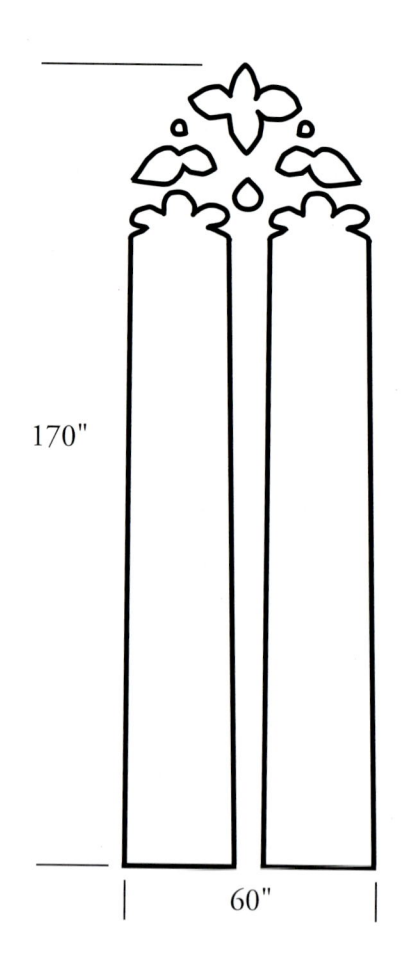

170"

60"

FIRST PRESBYTERIAN CHURCH, BIRMINGHAM, ALA.

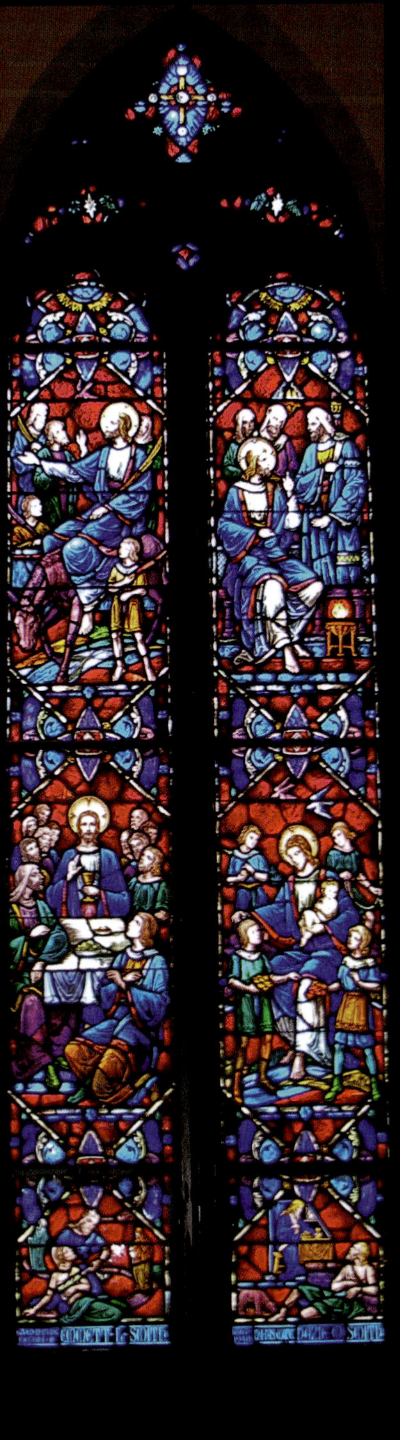

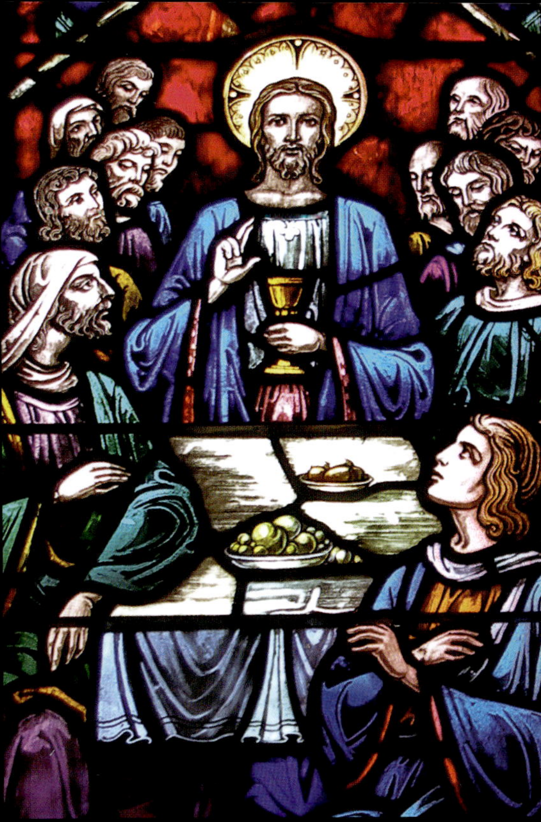

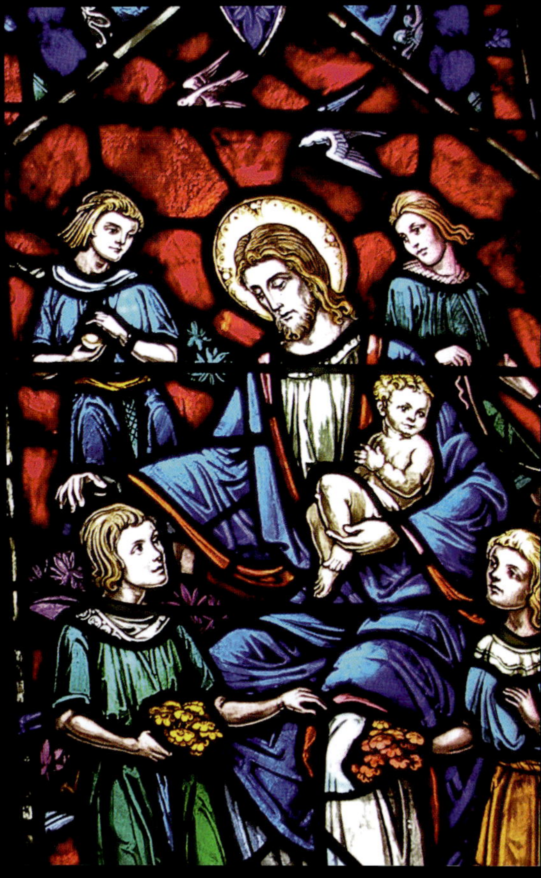

# D'Ascenzo

**$722** *per sq. ft.*

Can this window be 100% duplicated?  86% YES

The window is itself appropriately Italianate in its subdued hues, Gothic style and Renaissance-inspired motifs. The artist Nicola D'Ascenzo, a leading stained glass craftsman, helped to reintroduce the Neo-Gothic style into stained glass production at the turn of the twentieth century. The subject of the central roundel is that of the Italian literary giant Dante Alighieri (1265-1321) and his life-long love Beatrice.
- *taken from the Philbrook Museum plaque*

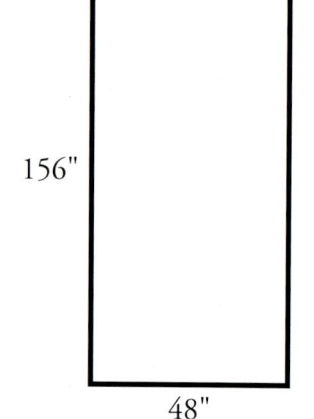

156"
48"

*Extremely delicate painting can theoretically be reproduced, but obtaining an exact match in all areas is practically impossible!* - Church Windows by Tooley Art Glass Studio

*Beautiful enamel work, much character in the fine deail.* - Enterprise Art Glass Works

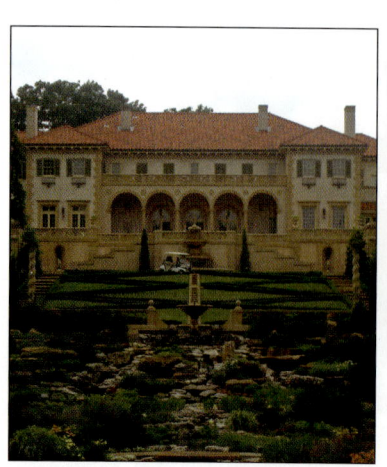

Philbrook Museum, Tulsa, Okla.

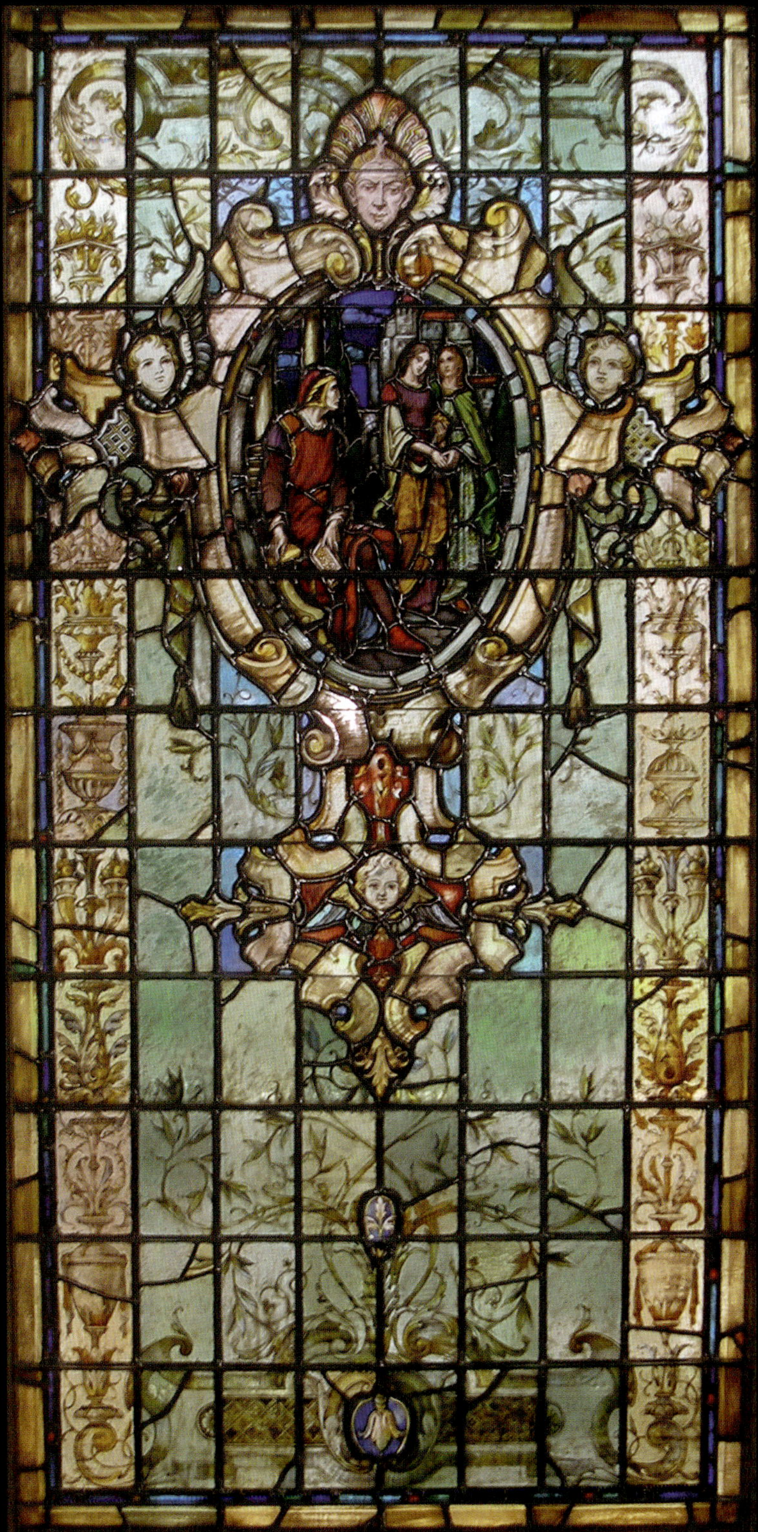

# Emil Frei

- O $658 *per sq. ft.*
- N $768
- S $635
- GP $653
- W $534
- SG $633
- N $692
- L $693
- S $654

Can this window be 100% duplicated?  86% YES

Diameter of 168"

Cathedral of our Lady of Perpetual Help, Oklahoma City, Okla.

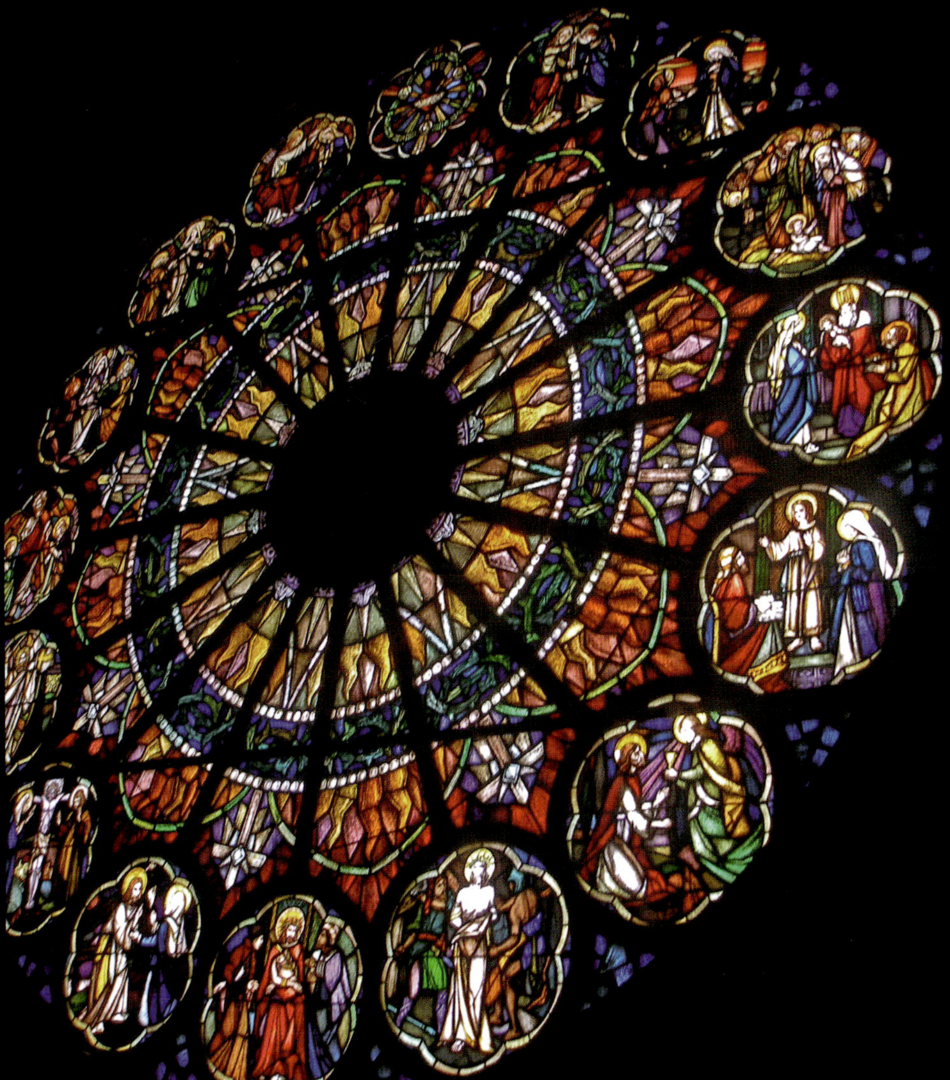

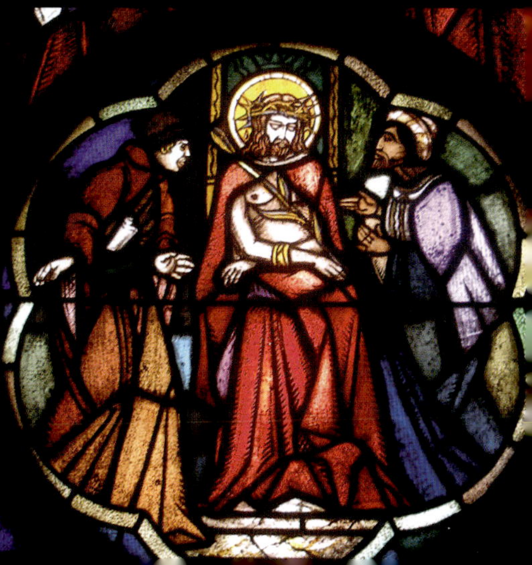

# Franz Mayer, Munich

| | |
|---|---|
| O | **$888** per sq. ft. |
| N | $1376 |
| S | $775 |
| GP | $730 |
| W | $615 |
| SG | $846 |
| N | $943 |
| L | $846 |
| S | $962 |

Can this window be 100% duplicated?   76% YES

*Generally, in all windows, the number of painted heads, silver stain, etc. are major considerations for cost to replicate as well as detail.* - Anonymous

*An inspiration of art and glass. You can fake it but you will not 100% replicate this style.* - Enterprise Art Glass Works, Inc.

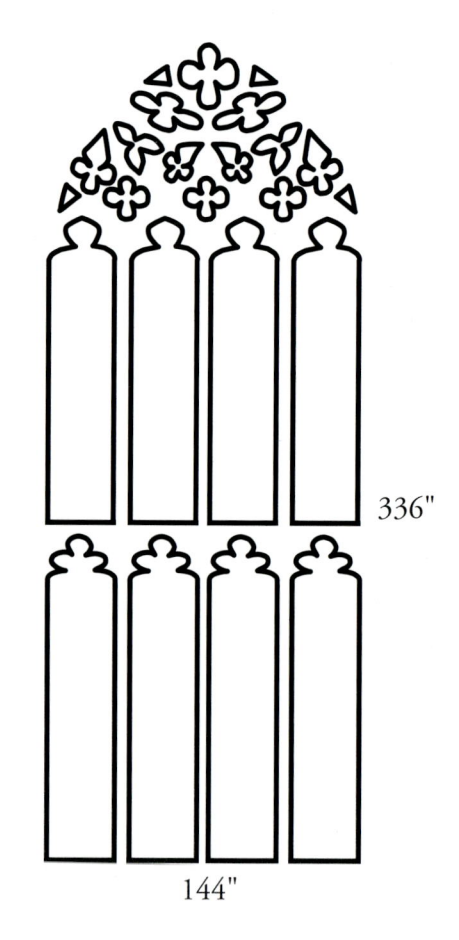

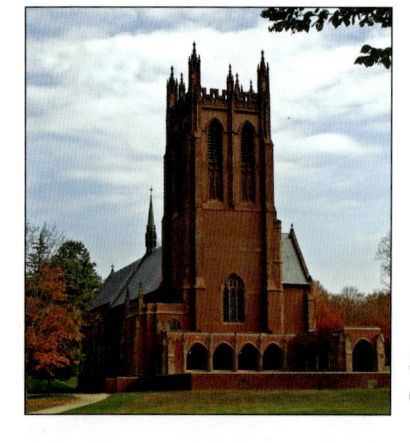

336"

144"

St. Paul School, Concord, N.H.

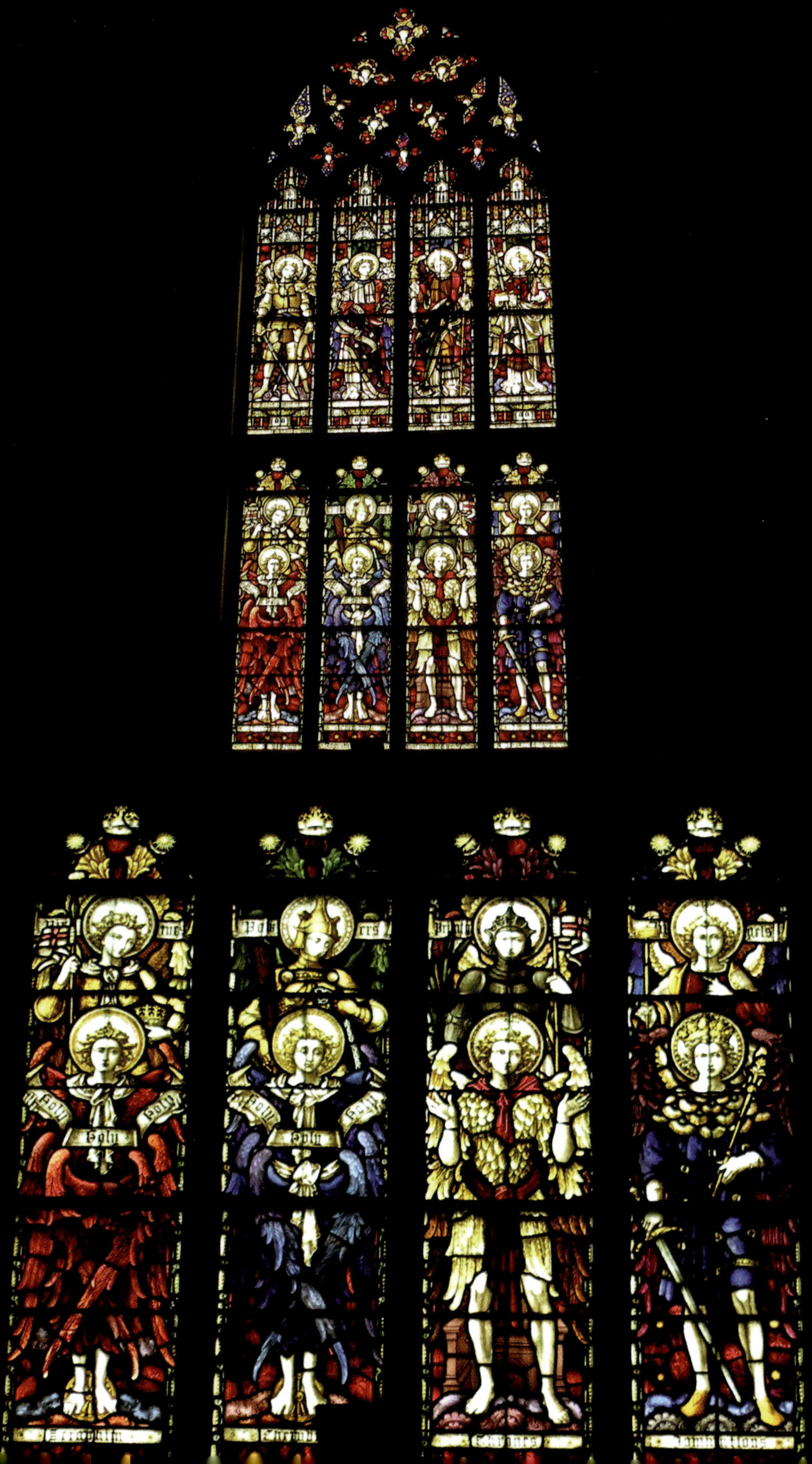

# Franz Mayer, Munich/London

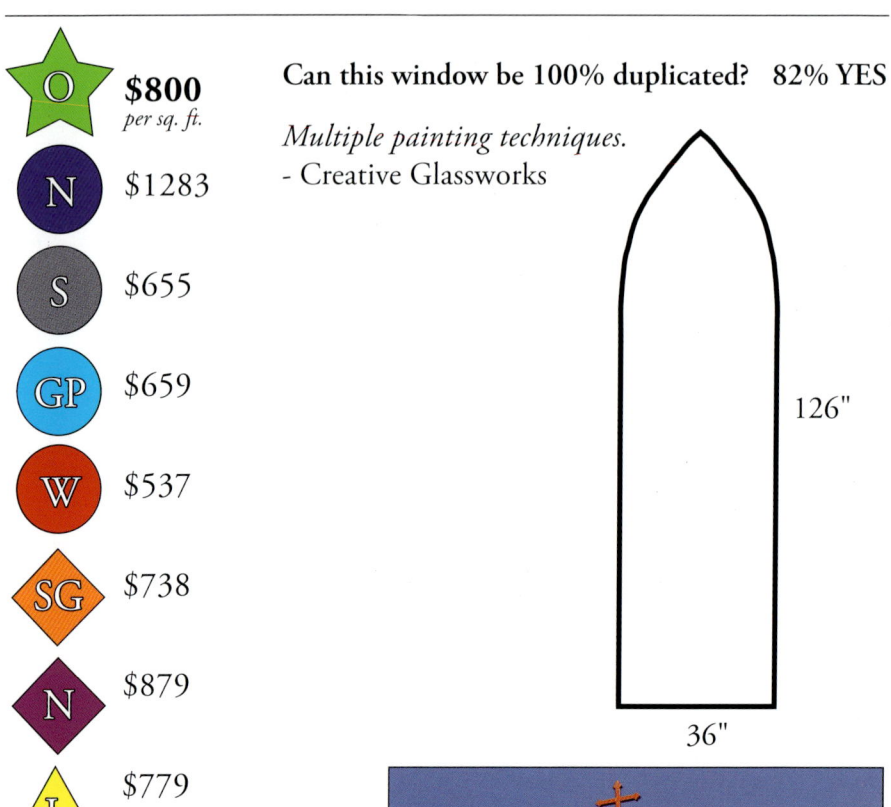

- O — **$800** per sq. ft.
- N — $1283
- S — $655
- GP — $659
- W — $537
- SG — $738
- N — $879
- L — $779
- S — $842

Can this window be 100% duplicated?   82% YES

*Multiple painting techniques.*
*- Creative Glassworks*

126"

36"

St. Mark's Episcopal Church, Cheyenne, Wyo.

Faith

# Heaton

| | |
|---|---|
| O | **$838** per sq. ft. |
| N | $1183 |
| S | $738 |
| GP | $735 |
| W | $648 |
| SG | $828 |
| N | $850 |
| L | $871 |
| S | $838 |

**Can this window be 100% duplicated?   82% YES**

*Salvator Mundi* was created for the chancel of Christ (Episcopal) Church of Grosse Pointe Farms, Mich., in 1935-36 by Clement Heaton (1861-1940). The window was the gift of Mrs. Gustava D. Anderson, to commemorate the fifth anniversary of the church. Heaton commenced design on the Pentecost window in August of 1935, but after numerous design changes that took place during the autumn and winter months, the installation of the window had to be deferred until June of 1936.

*Best English of the time.* - Kebrle Stained Glass, Inc.

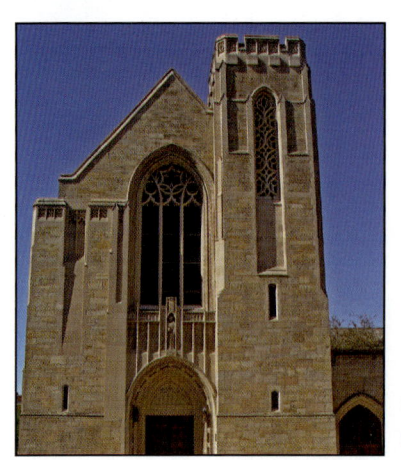

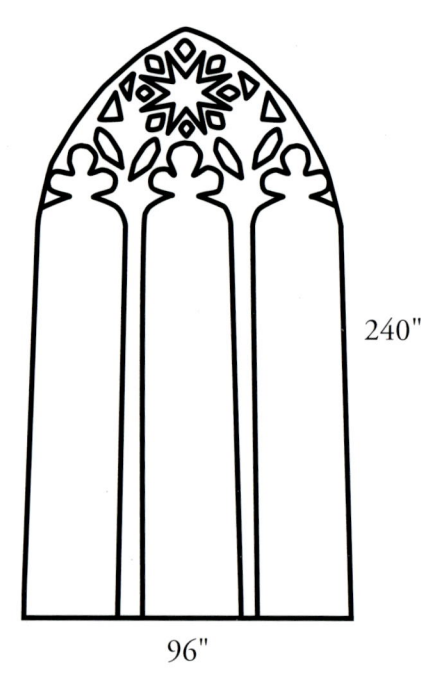

240"

96"

### Christ Church Episcopal
### Grosse Point Farms, Mich.

SALVATOR MUNDI

# Judson

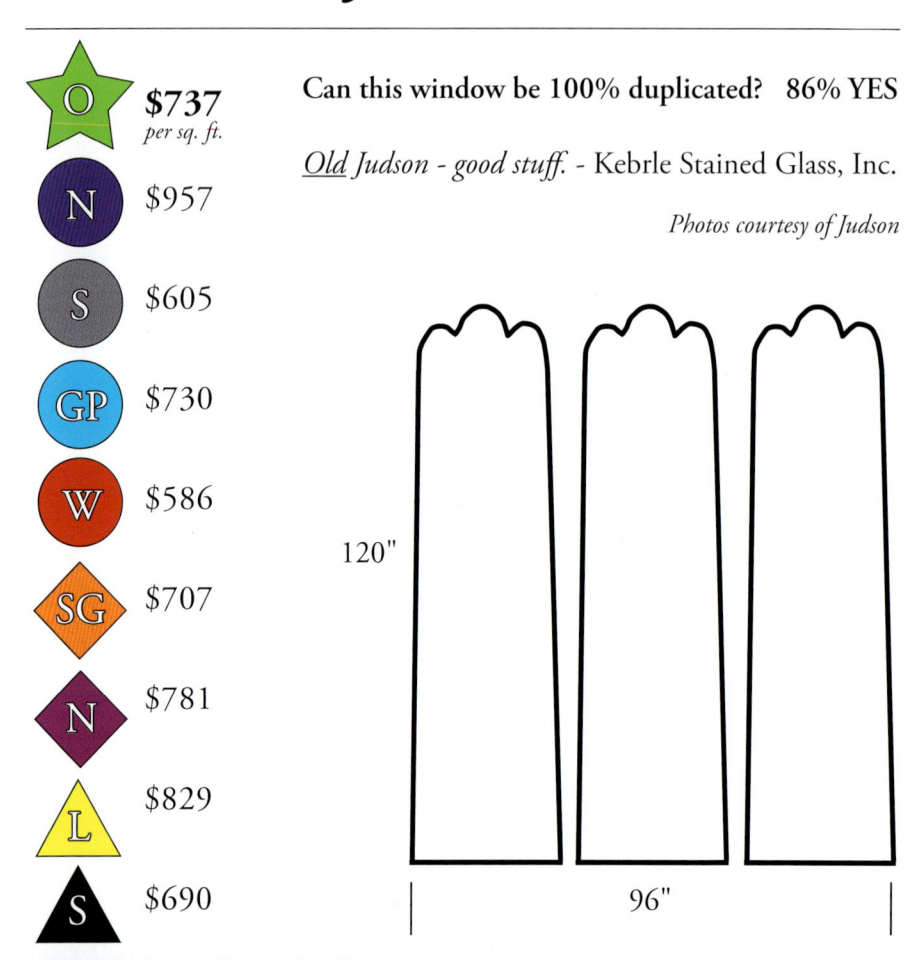

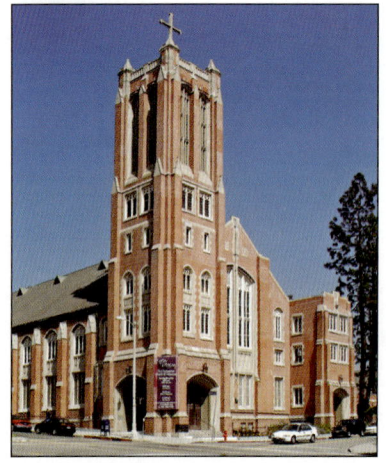

| | |
|---|---|
| O | **$737** per sq. ft. |
| N | $957 |
| S | $605 |
| GP | $730 |
| W | $586 |
| SG | $707 |
| N | $781 |
| L | $829 |
| S | $690 |

Can this window be 100% duplicated?    86% YES

<u>Old</u> *Judson - good stuff.* - Kebrle Stained Glass, Inc.

*Photos courtesy of Judson*

120"

96"

FIRST PRESBYTERIAN CHURCH
HOLLYWOOD, CALIF.

The Prodigal Son

# Judson

| | | |
|---|---|---|
| ⭐ O | **$511** per sq. ft. | Can this window be 100% duplicated? 100% YES |
| ● N | $621 | |
| ● S | $485 | |
| ● GP | $499 | |
| ● W | $403 | |
| ◆ SG | $504 | |
| ◆ N | $522 | |
| ▲ L | $541 | |
| ▲ S | $496 | |

*Photos courtesy of Judson*

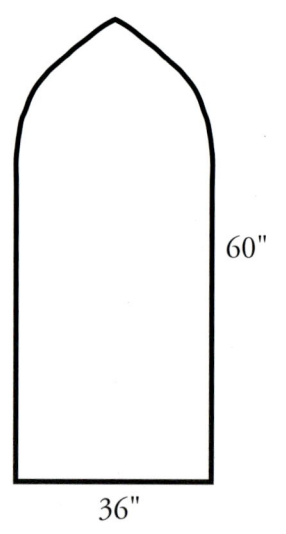

60"
36"

## St. Aidan's, Westwood
## Los Angeles, Calif.

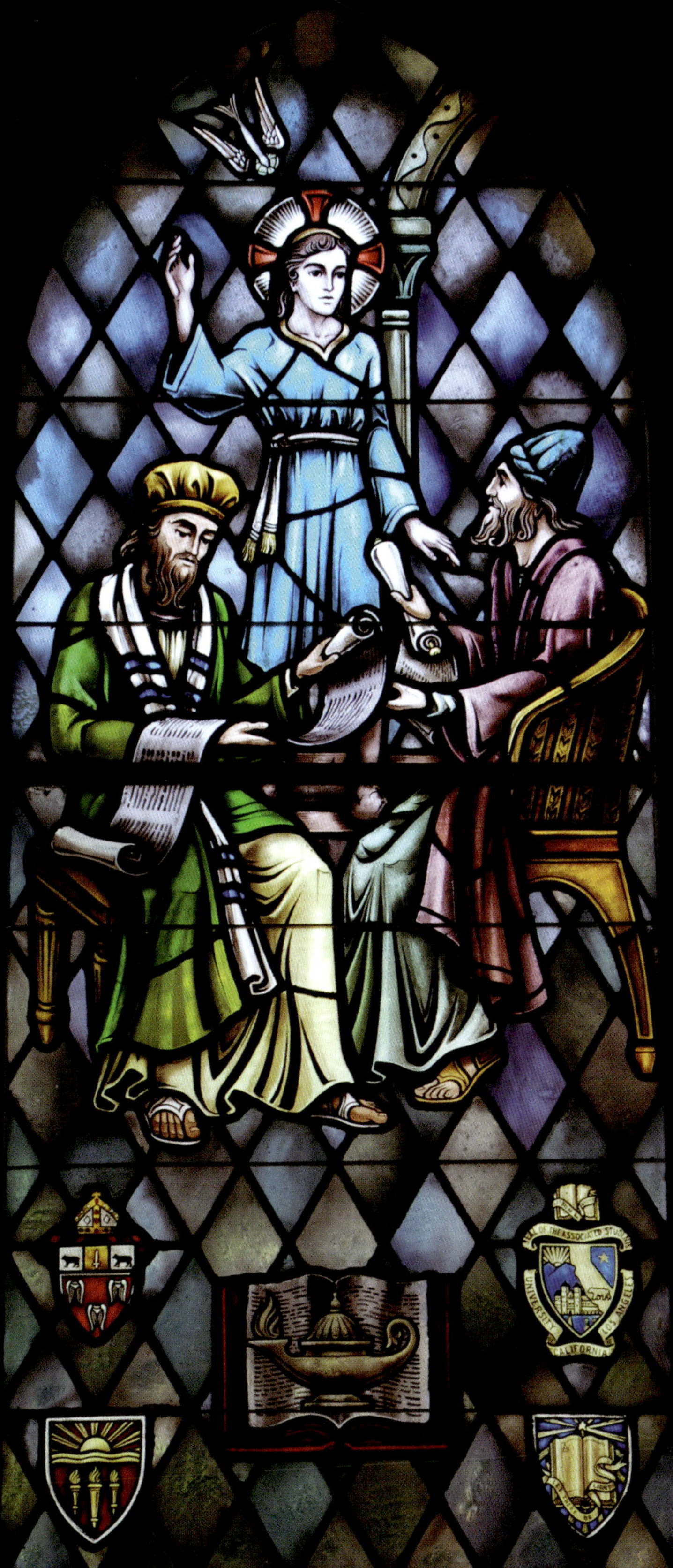

UNIVERSITY
LOS ANGELES
CALIFORNIA

# La Farge

| | |
|---|---|
| O | **$1292** *per sq. ft.* |
| N | $2070 |
| S | $1119 |
| GP | $948 |
| W | $988 |
| SG | $1308 |
| N | $1273 |
| L | $1256 |
| S | $1357 |

**Can this window be 100% duplicated?   35% YES**

Visit of Mary to Elizabeth, 1885. The historic window is dedicated to Cleveland industrialist Amasa Stone, who committed suicide after the twin tragedies of his son drowning and the collapse of a bridge he'd built, which killed a trainload of people. - *from the Conrad Schmitt catalog, page 48.*

*Beauty and talent.* - Kebrle Stained Glass, Inc.

*Unique glass and drapery glass.* - Raynal Studios

*The Confeti glass is amazing, design and hand painting is timeless – one of a kind.* - Enterprise Art Glass Works, Inc.

*This window is probably plated. It is virtually impossible to duplicate the color of every piece as shown. The result will be close but not 100%. Appraisal is for "close" result.* - Tooley Art Glass Studio

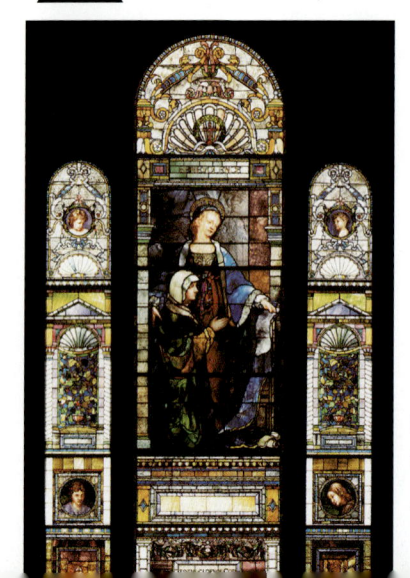

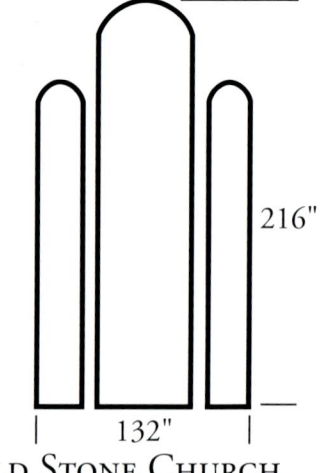

216"

132"

## Old Stone Church
## Cleveland, Ohio
*Photos courtesy of Conrad Schmitt Studios*

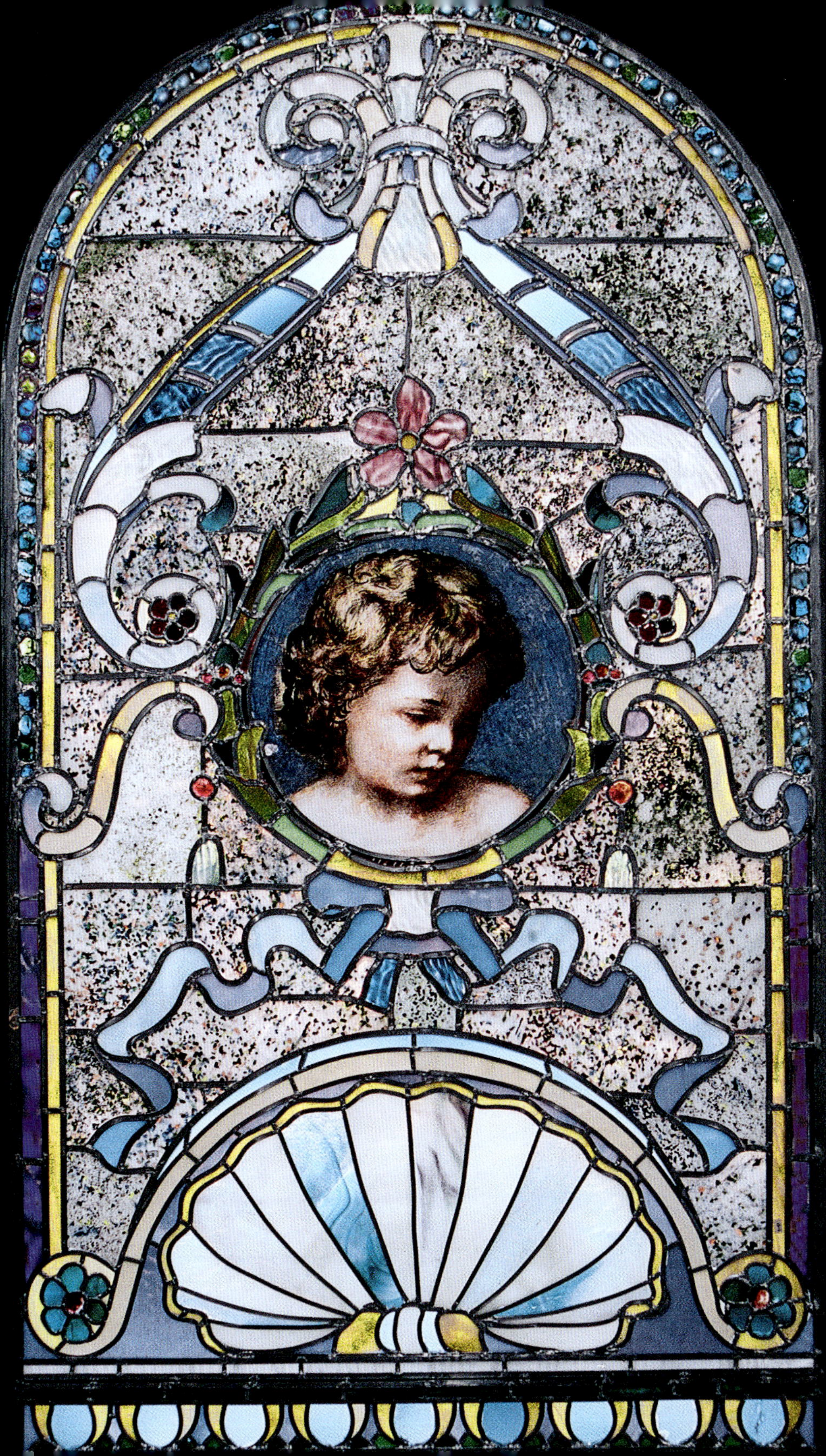

# La Farge

| | |
|---|---|
| O | **$1178** *per sq. ft.* |
| N | $1842 |
| S | $925 |
| GP | $920 |
| W | $888 |
| SG | $1092 |
| N | $1293 |
| L | $1275 |
| S | $1158 |

**Can this window be 100% duplicated?   43% YES**

St. Paul's Historical Landmark, where this window is located, used to be St. Paul's Episcopal Church. It was where the Trial of Peter Zenger (Freedom of Speech) took place. In 1980, the site was transferred from the Episcopal Dioceses of New York to the National Park Service.
*- from Rohlf Studios, Inc. and www.thingstodo.com.*

*Early opalescent glass.* - Raynal Studios

*La Farge and Tiffany windows are very difficult to replicate because of the plating and availability of matching glass.* - Rohlf's Studio, Inc.

*Some glass used is no longer available.*
- Tooley Art Glass Studio

*Nearly impossible to replicate the glass.*
- SLFirpo Design/Craft

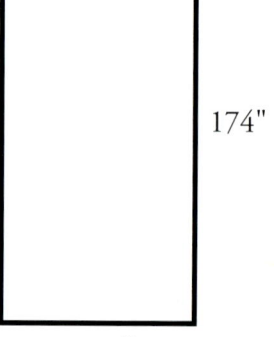

174"

50.5"

ST. PAUL'S NATIONAL HISTORIC LANDMARK, MT. VERNON, N.Y.
*Photos courtesy of Rohlf Studios, Inc.*

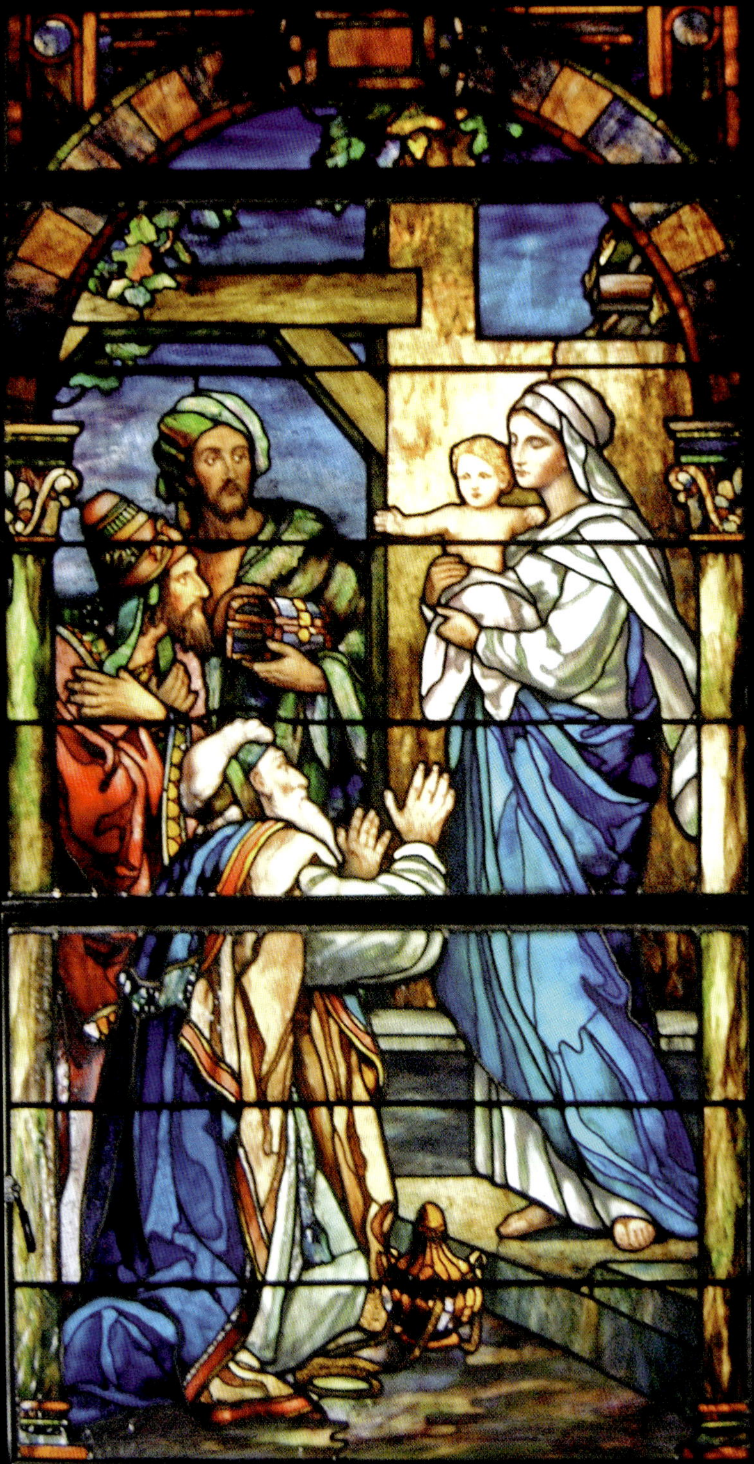

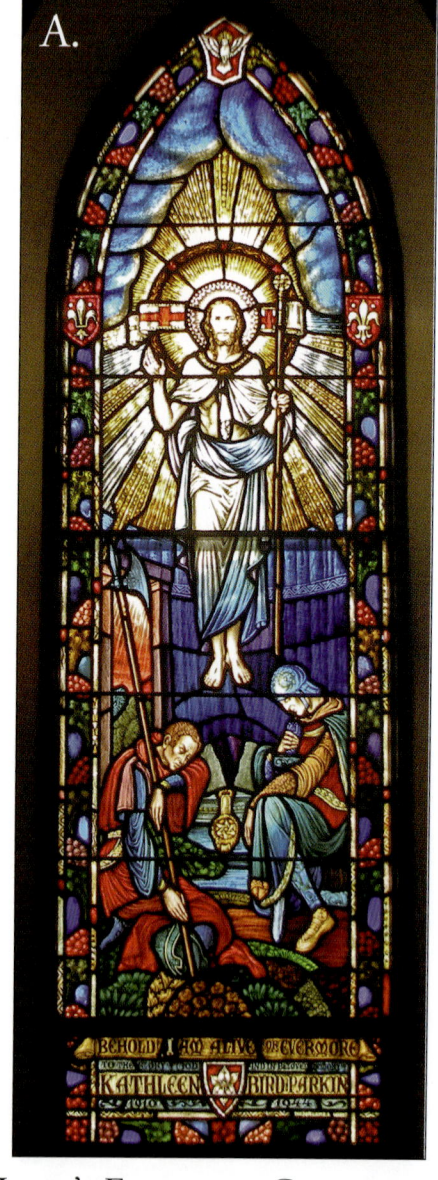

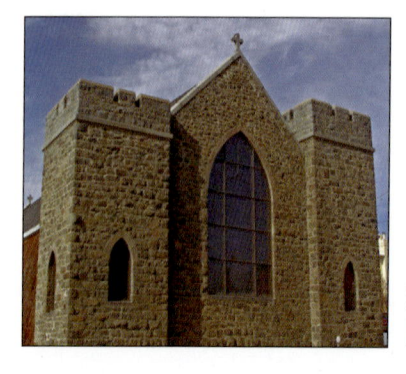

# Lamb

|   | A. $668 per sq. ft. | B. $681 per sq. ft. |
|---|---|---|
| O | | |
| N | $888 | $967 |
| S | $590 | $560 |
| GP | $623 | $614 |
| W | $523 | $540 |
| SG | $588 | $596 |
| N | $770 | $792 |
| L | $648 | $665 |
| S | $690 | $702 |

Can this window be 100% duplicated?
A. & B.  95% YES

A.

St. John's Episcopal Church
Butte, Mont.

125

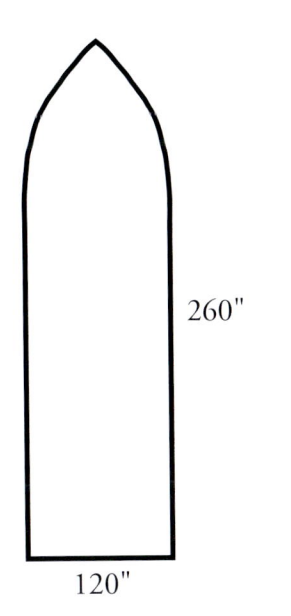

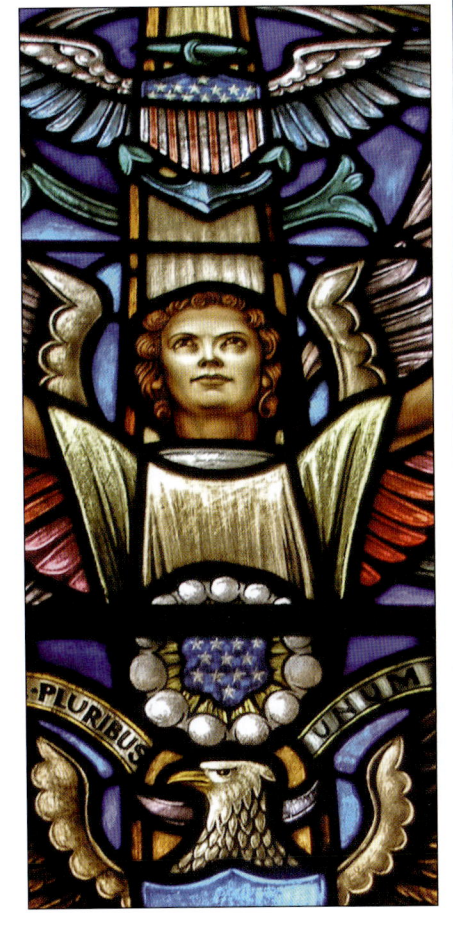

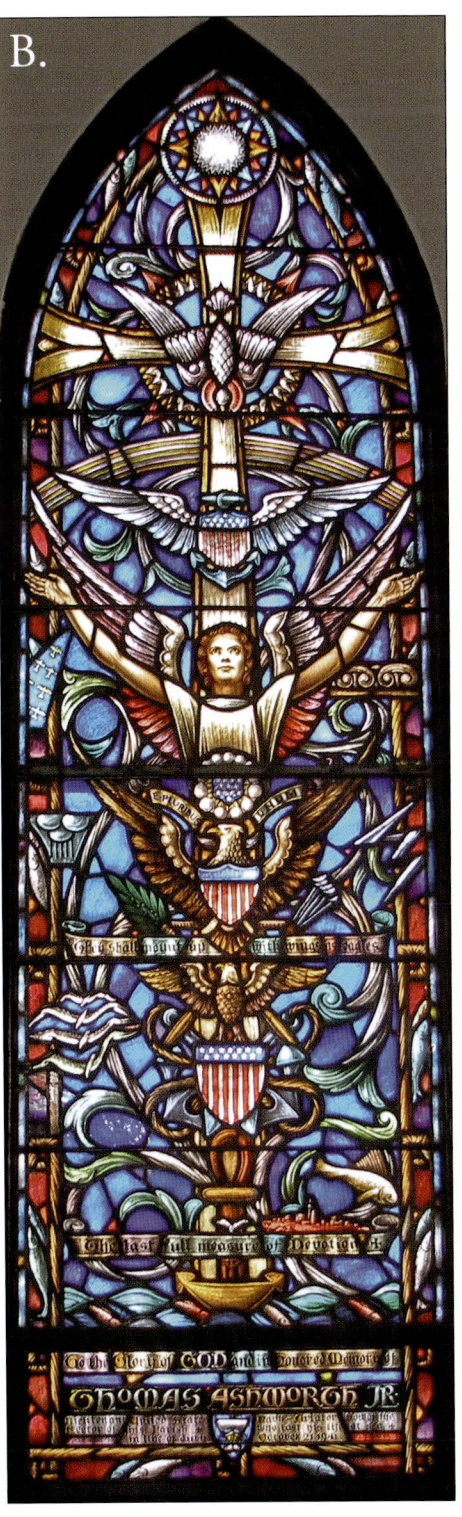

260"

120"

B.

# Lamb

| | | |
|---|---|---|
| O | **$557** per sq. ft. | |
| N | $689 | |
| S | $511 | |
| GP | $497 | |
| W | $533 | |
| SG | $518 | |
| N | $606 | |
| L | $500 | |
| S | $615 | |

Can this window be 100% duplicated? 100% YES

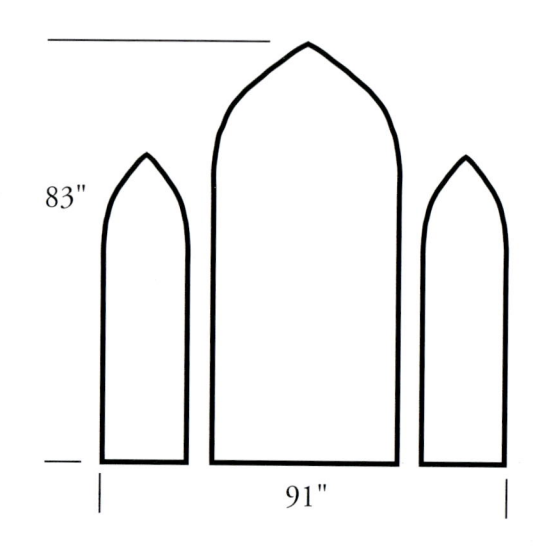

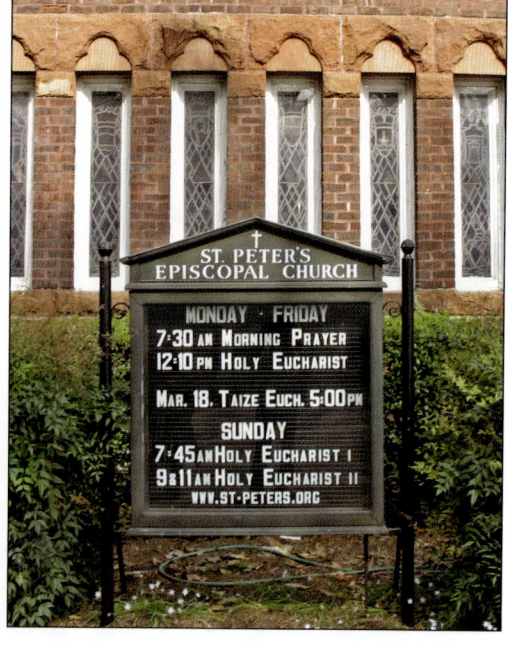

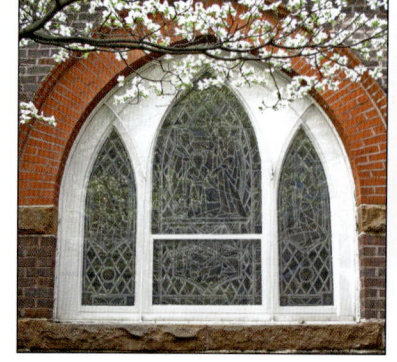

83"

91"

St. Peter's Episcopal Church
Charlotte, N.C.

I am the Light of the World

# Munich Studio, Chicago

| | |
|---|---|
| O | **$714**<br>*per sq. ft.* |
| N | $1058 |
| S | $553 |
| GP | $589 |
| W | $648 |
| SG | $582 |
| N | $885 |
| L | $679 |
| S | $761 |

Can this window be 100% duplicated?   91% YES

*Not as intricate as the German style. Yet, very involved with wide variety of glass.* - Enterprise Art Glass Works, Inc.

Diameter of 104"

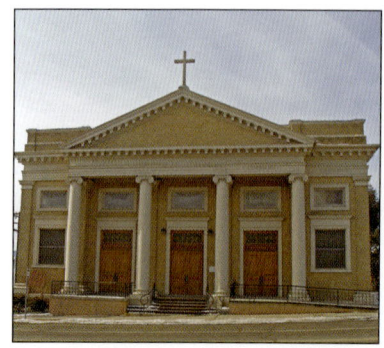

St. Joseph Catholic Parish
Butte, Mont.

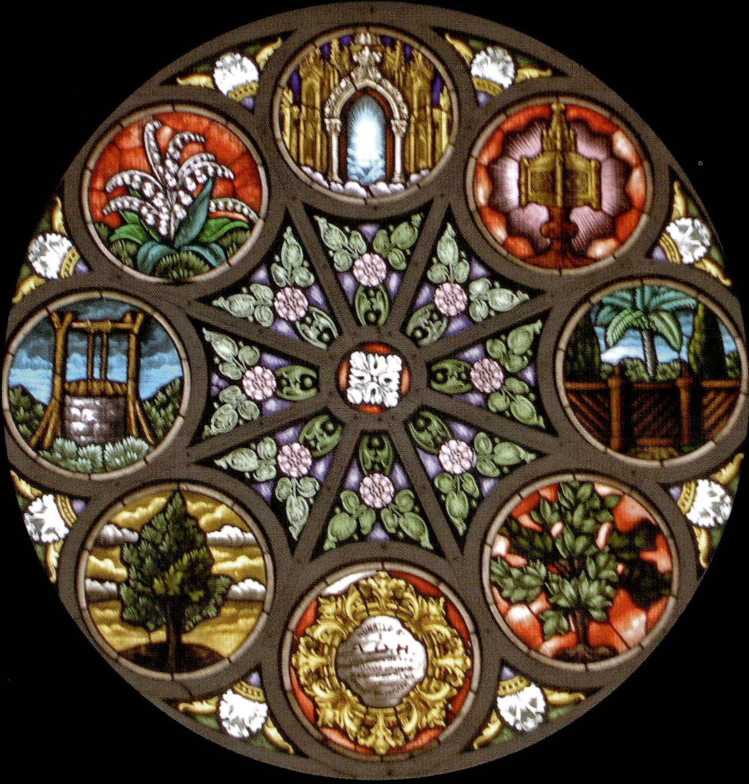

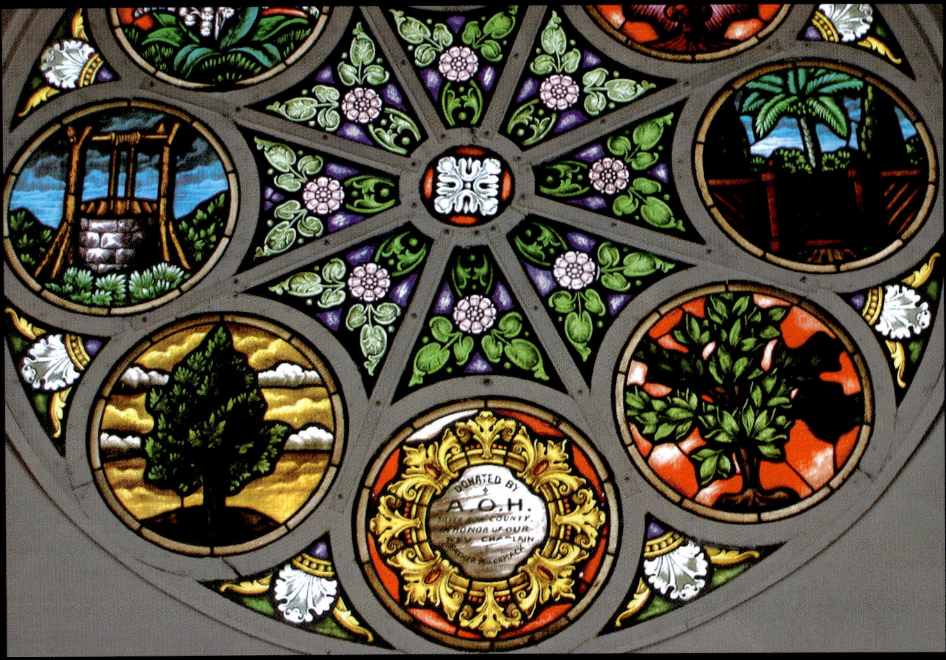
DONATED BY
A.O.H.
COUNTY
HONOR OF OUR
REV.
CHAPLAIN

# Munich Studio, Chicago

| | |
|---|---|
| O | $1006 per sq. ft. |
| N | $1583 |
| S | $768 |
| GP | $792 |
| W | $923 |
| SG | $886 |
| N | $1149 |
| L | $933 |
| S | $1082 |

Can this window be 100% duplicated?   77% YES

The Annunciation. "And coming to her, he said, "Hail, favored one!" The Lord is with you." But she was greatly troubled at what was said and pondered what sort of greeting his might be. Then the angel said to her, "Do not be afraid, Mary, for you have found favor with God. Behold, you will conceive in your womb and bear a son, and you shall name him Jesus." *Luke 1:28-31*

*Looks imported from F.X. Zettler.* - Kebrle Stained Glass, Inc.

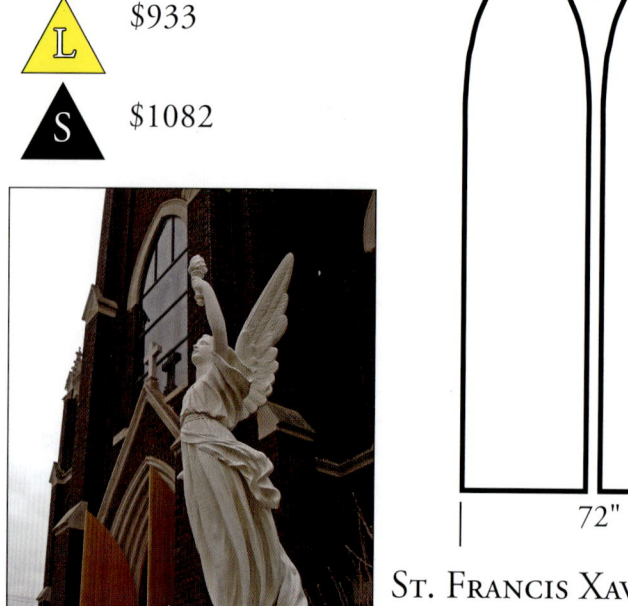

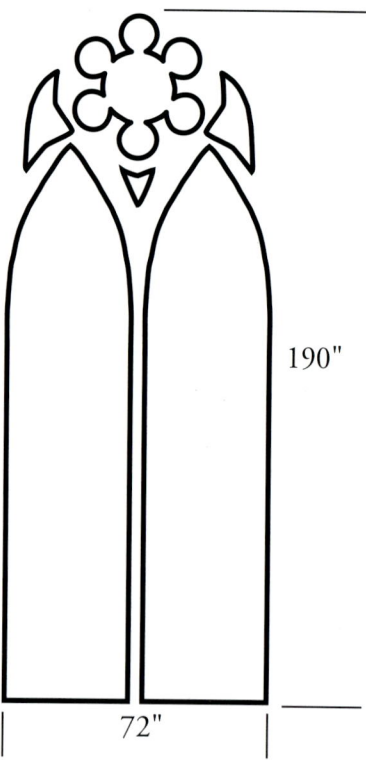

190"

72"

St. Francis Xavier
Enid, Okla.

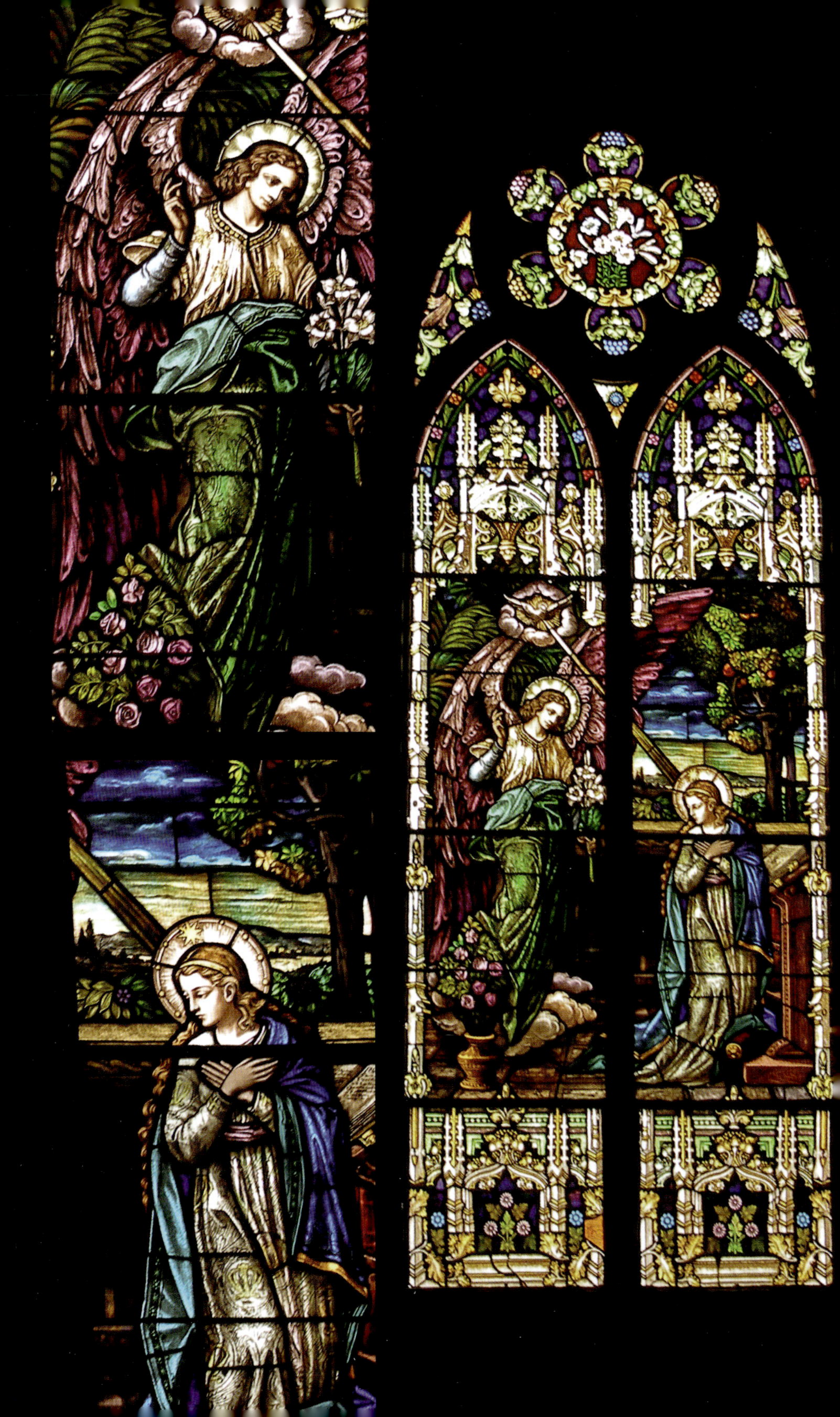

# Payne

| | |
|---|---|
| O | **$881** per sq. ft. |
| N | $1253 |
| S | $780 |
| GP | $798 |
| W | $615 |
| SG | $862 |
| N | $906 |
| L | $856 |
| S | $925 |

Can this window be 100% duplicated?   90% YES

234"

152"

Church of the Incarnation
Episcopal, Dallas, Texas

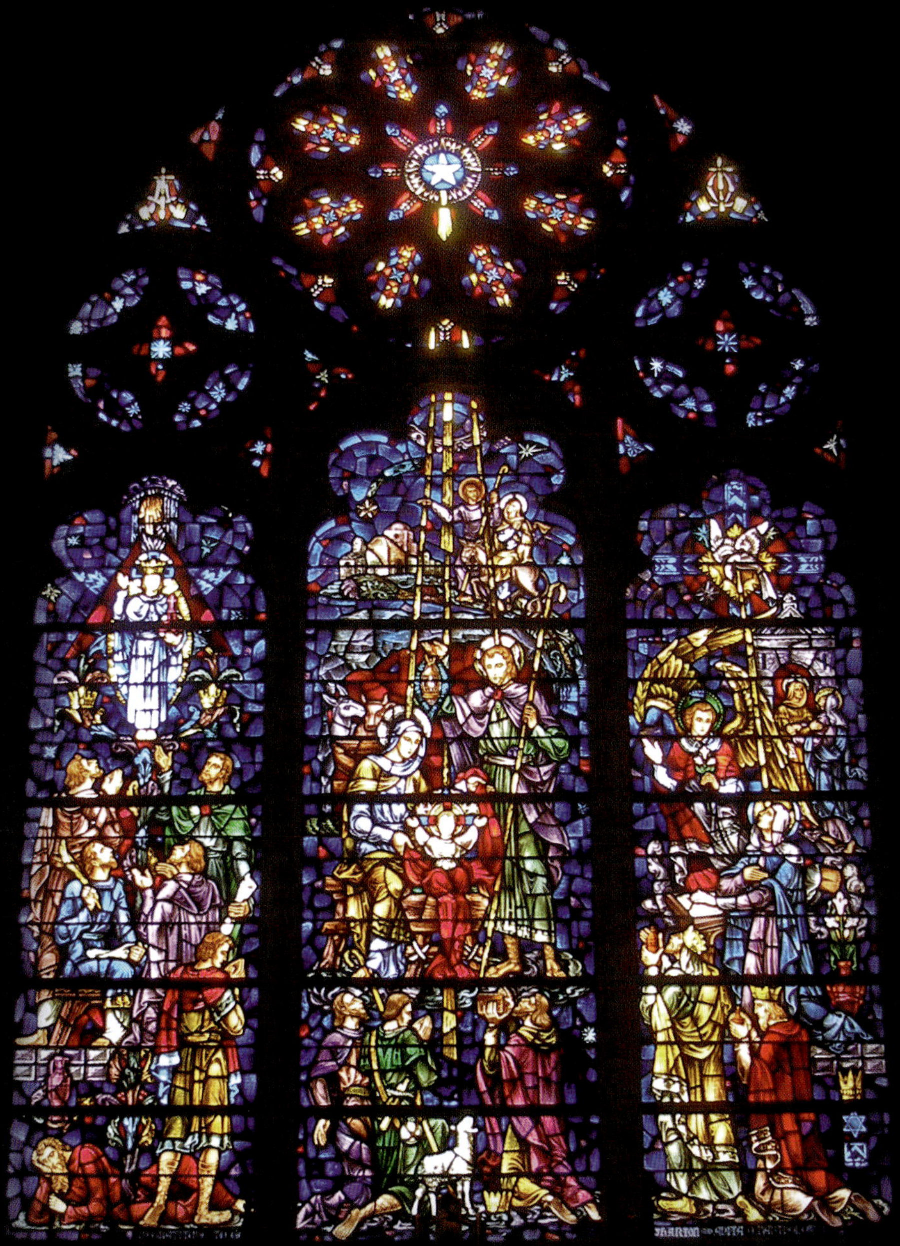

# Payne

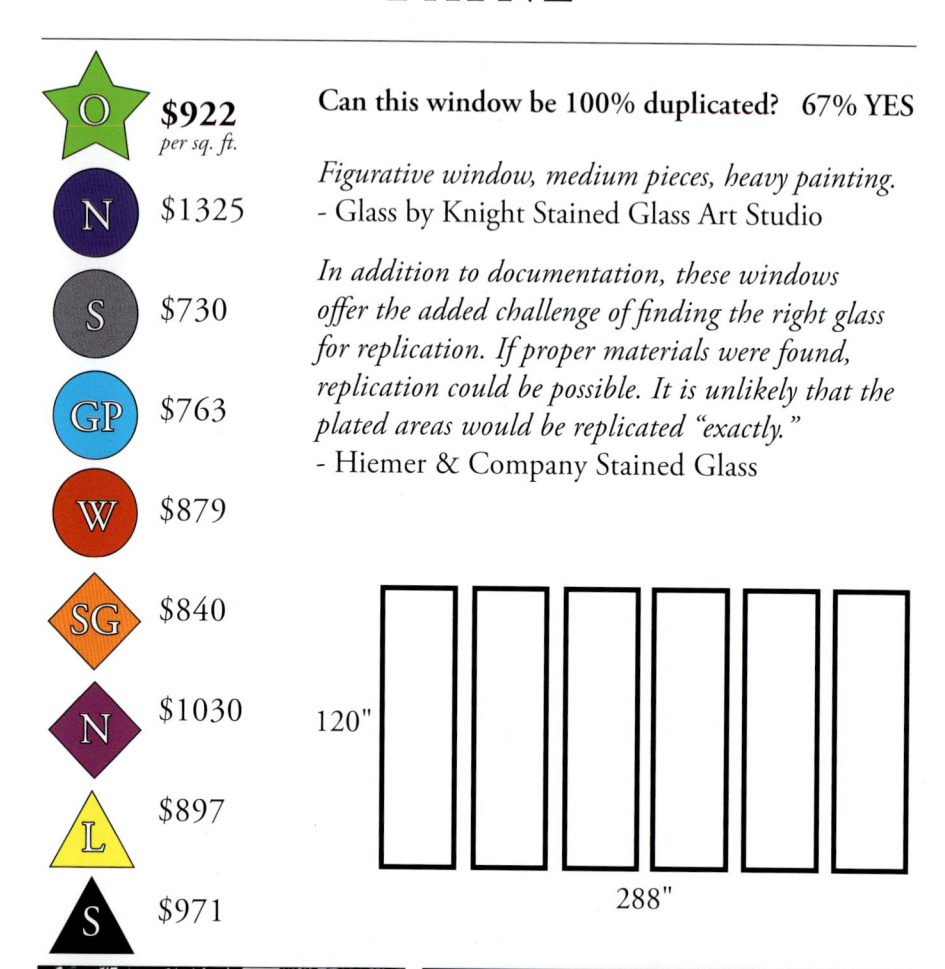

| | |
|---|---|
| O | **$922** per sq. ft. |
| N | $1325 |
| S | $730 |
| GP | $763 |
| W | $879 |
| SG | $840 |
| N | $1030 |
| L | $897 |
| S | $971 |

Can this window be 100% duplicated?   67% YES

*Figurative window, medium pieces, heavy painting.*
- Glass by Knight Stained Glass Art Studio

*In addition to documentation, these windows offer the added challenge of finding the right glass for replication. If proper materials were found, replication could be possible. It is unlikely that the plated areas would be replicated "exactly."*
- Hiemer & Company Stained Glass

120"

288"

First United Methodist,
St. Petersburg, Fla.

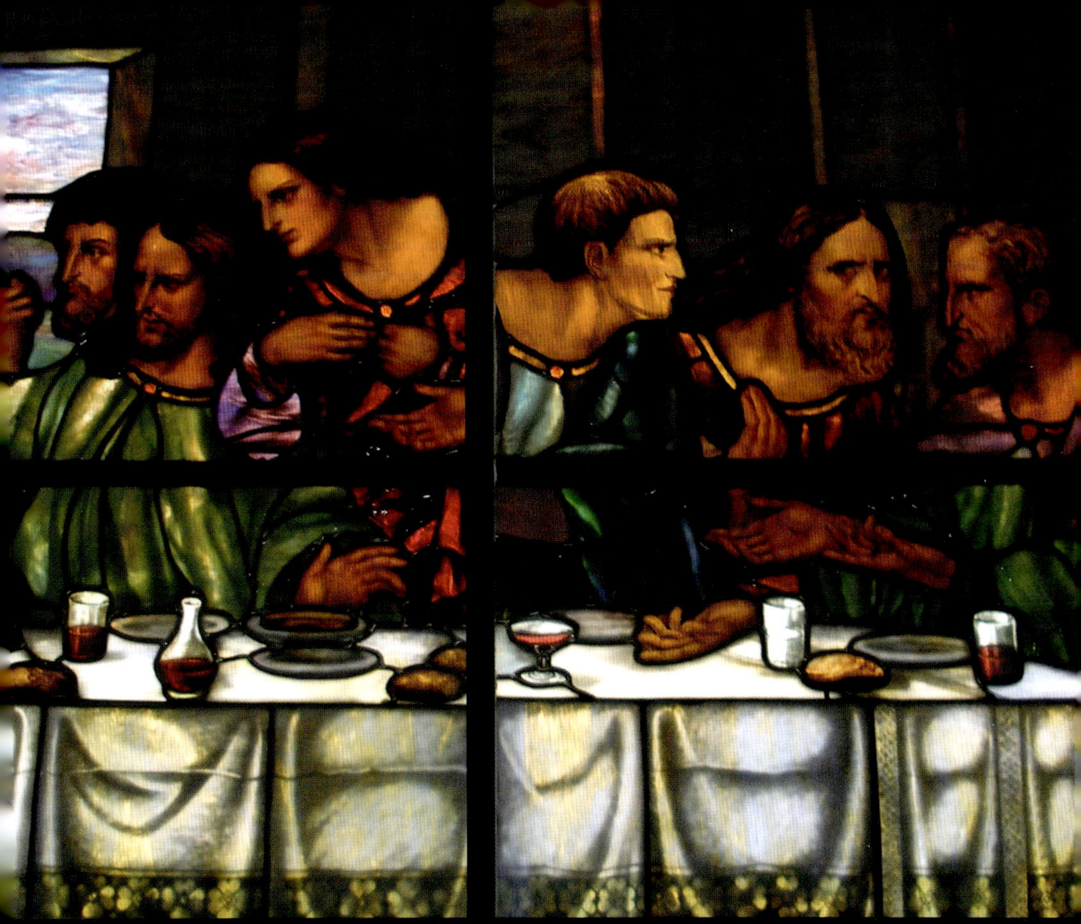

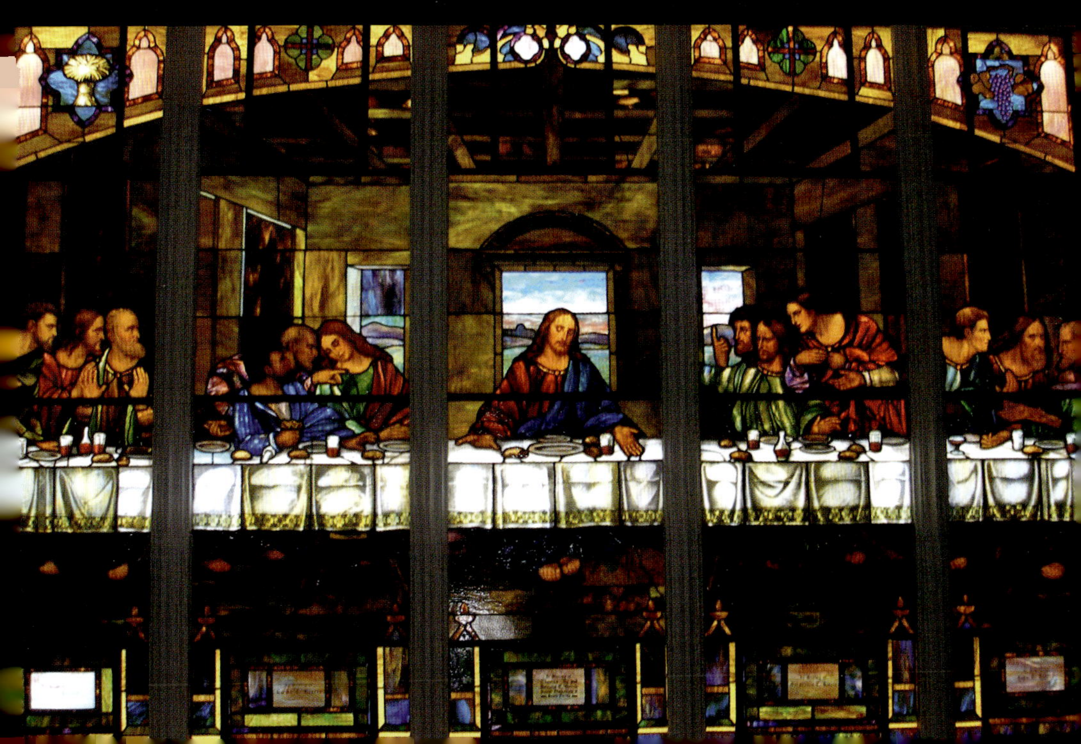

# Payne

| | |
|---|---|
| O | **$938** per sq. ft. |
| N | $1513 |
| S | $694 |
| GP | $772 |
| W | $711 |
| SG | $886 |
| N | $1005 |
| L | $983 |
| S | $932 |

Can this window be 100% duplicated?   86% YES

The Last Supper is depicted with all heads turned toward Christ except the head of Judas. A nimbus (the "halo") surrounds all heads except Judas. The shaft of wheat and cluster of grapes symbolize the basis of the Eucharist in the Last Supper...In the center is Christ the Great High Priest with the shield of three nails symbolic of His suffering and the crown symbolic of His rule through suffering. *- from St. John Cathedral, Guide to a walking, meditative self tour of the life of Jesus through some of our windows, page 6.*

*Generally, in all windows, the number of painted heads, silver stain, etc. are major considerations for cost to replicate as well as detail.* - Anonymous

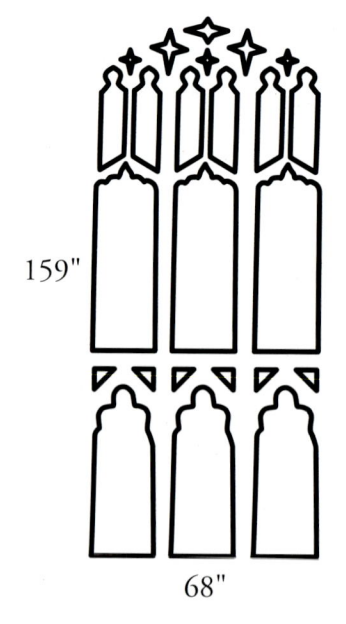

159"

68"

## St. John's Episcopal Cathedral
### Jacksonville, Fla.

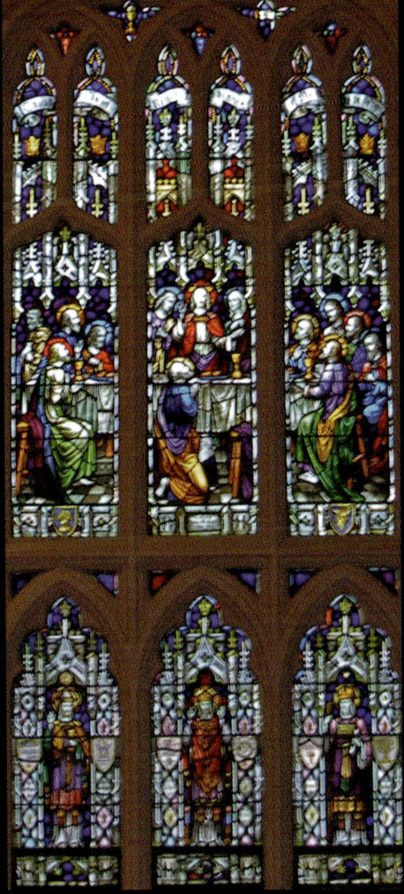

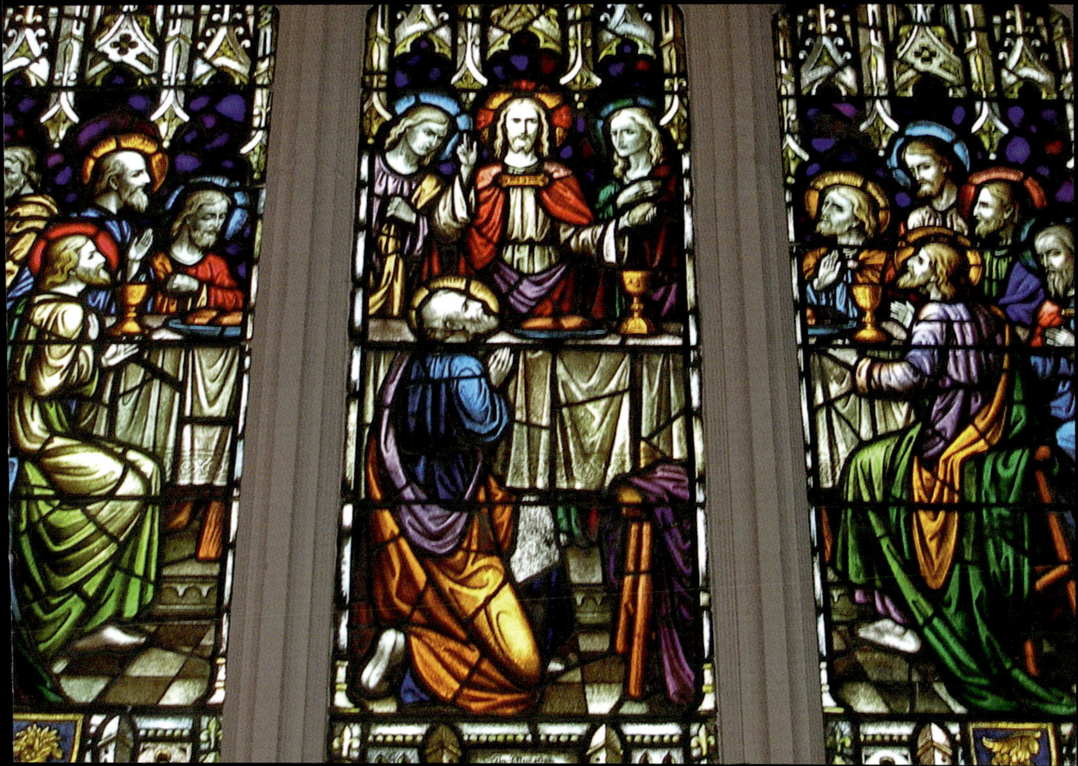

# Phipps, Ball, & Burnham
## 1920

O  **$749**
*per sq. ft.*

Can this window be 100% duplicated? 100% YES

Jesus welcomes and embraces the children who have come to him willingly and unafraid. The open-faced flowers, particularly the daisies, are symbols of youth and innocence. "Let the children come unto me for to such belongs the Kingdom of God."

"It is a testament to the fervor of St. Paul's congregation over the years that has established this cathedral-esque gallery of fine stained glass art. This artistic glory, sitting side-by-side with the T-shirt shops and bars on Key West's busy Duval Street, is a potent reminder to tourists and locals alike, to stop for a moment and absorb the sacred, revel in the creative spirit, and give thinks for the gift of worship."

From "Self-guided Tour, The Stained Glass Windows, St. Paul's Episcopal Church, Key West, Fla.

*Early English style. Love the colors! - Enterprise Art Glass Works*

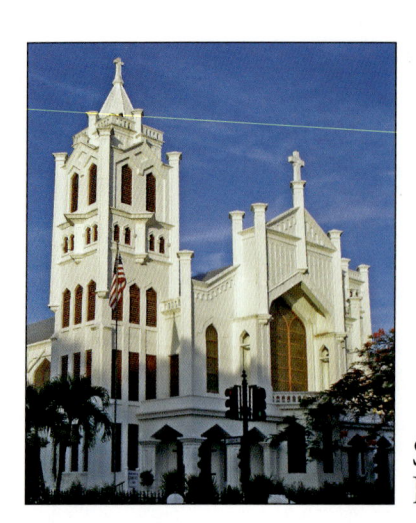

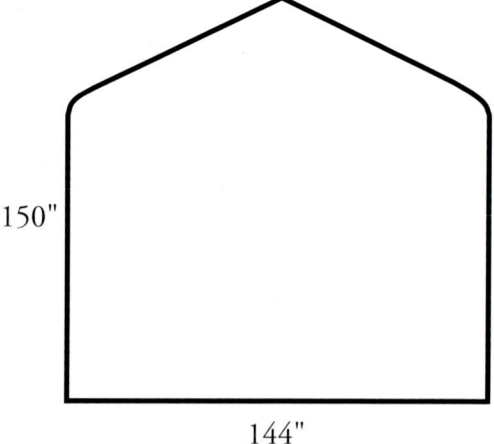

150"

144"

St. Paul's Episcopal Church, Key West, Fla.

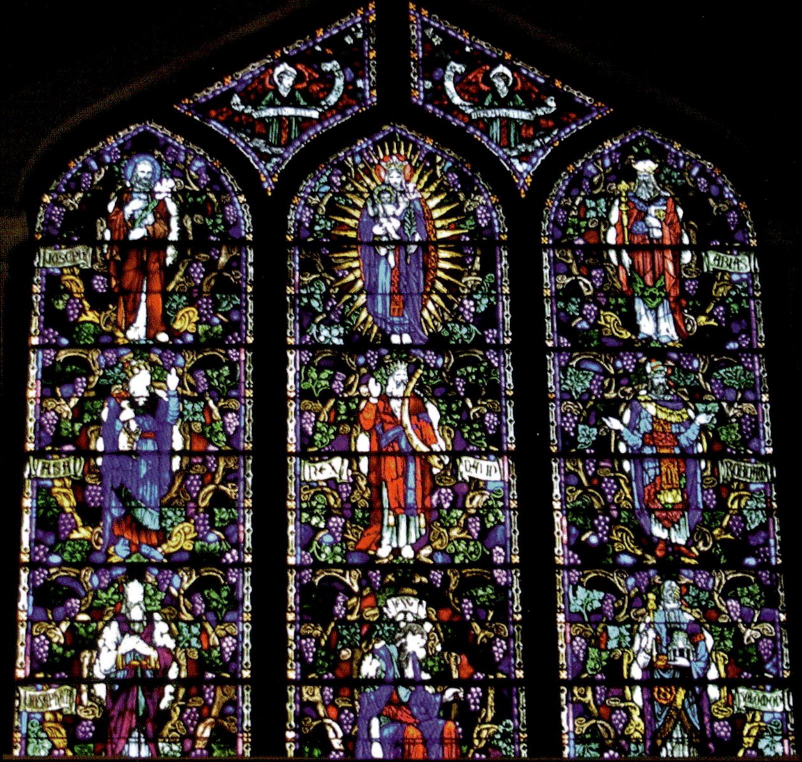

# Rambusch

| | |
|---|---|
| O | **$288** per sq. ft. |
| N | $277 |
| S | $295 |
| GP | $291 |
| W | $290 |
| SG | $300 |
| N | $275 |
| L | $293 |
| S | $287 |

Can this window be 100% duplicated?   96% YES

In 1901, Jacksonville experienced a massive fire that swept thru the downtown and one of the casualties was St. John's Church. The congregation decided to re-build and the new church, now a cathedral, has become the home of some of finest stained glass windows in Florida. Studios including Tiffany, Payne, and D'Ascenzo have contributed traditional windows that adorn the nave. In 1970, a chapel was added for which Rambusch designed a series of panels in a more modern style.

*This is a fairly simple geographic design in that the individual pieces are straightforward cuts, although the design is dense in pieces per square foot. The panels are divided symmetrically which would allow for easy repair and replacement.* - Cottage Glass

*Antique glass, large lead.* - Creative Glassworks

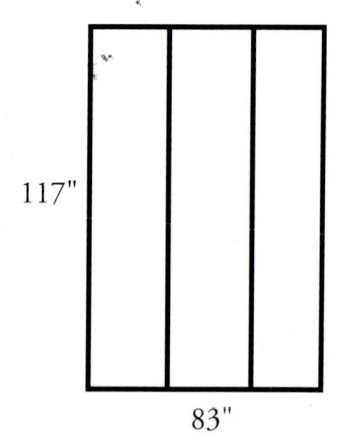

117"

83"

Cummings Memorial Chapel
St. John's Episcopal
Cathedral, Jacksonville, Fla.

AS I HAVE LOVED YOU

# Rohlf

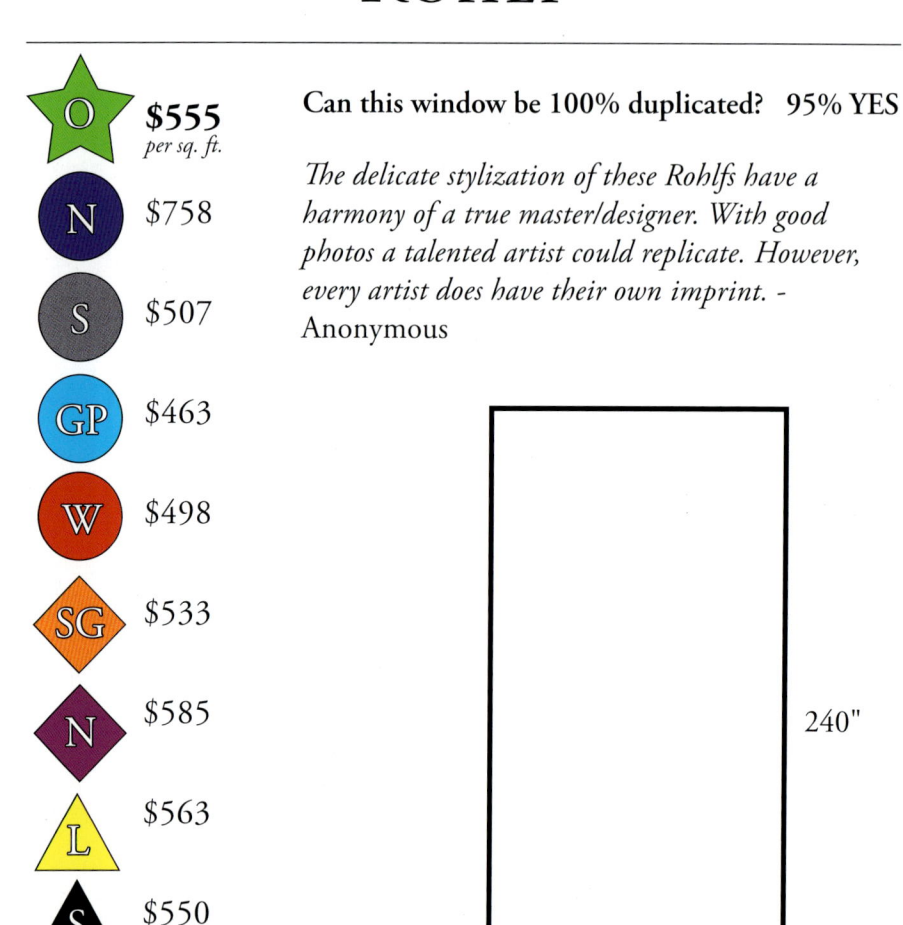

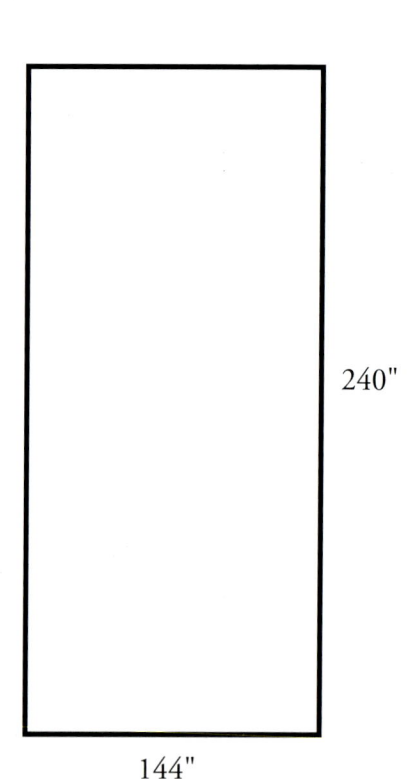

| | |
|---|---|
| O | **$555** per sq. ft. |
| N | $758 |
| S | $507 |
| GP | $463 |
| W | $498 |
| SG | $533 |
| N | $585 |
| L | $563 |
| S | $550 |

**Can this window be 100% duplicated?  95% YES**

*The delicate stylization of these Rohlfs have a harmony of a true master/designer. With good photos a talented artist could replicate. However, every artist does have their own imprint. - Anonymous*

240"

144"

**Broadmoor United Methodist, Shreveport, La.**
*Rendering photos courtesy of Rohlf's Studio, Inc.*

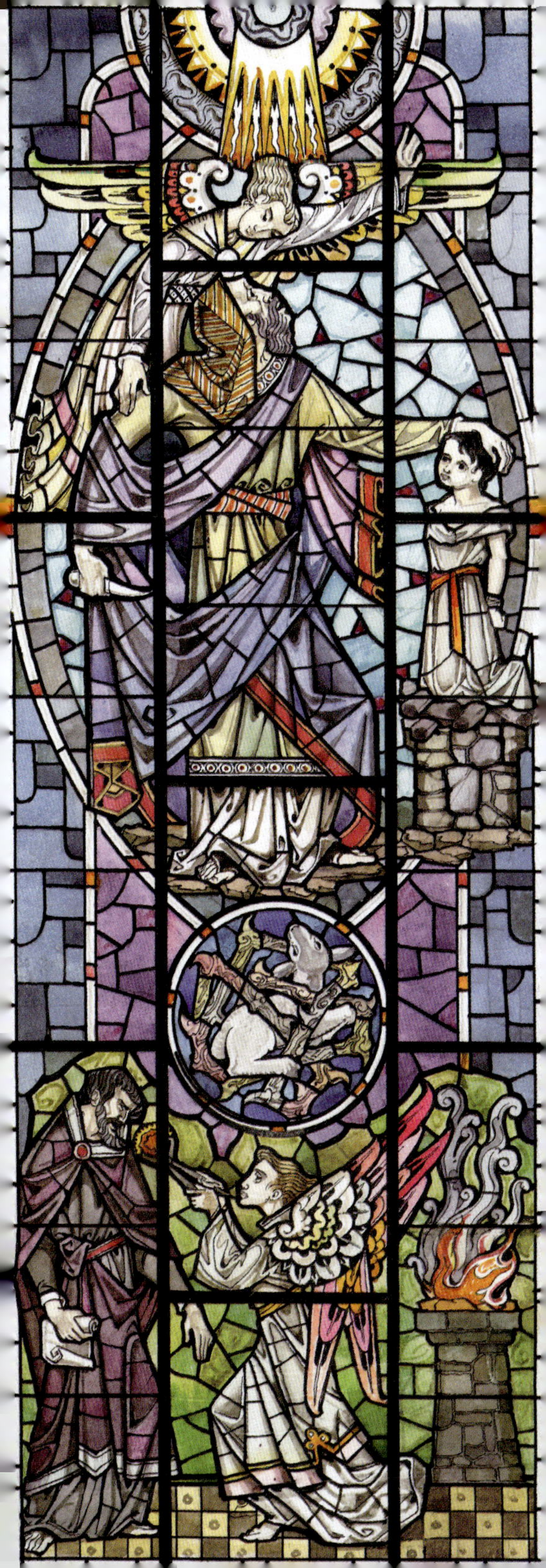

# Rohlf

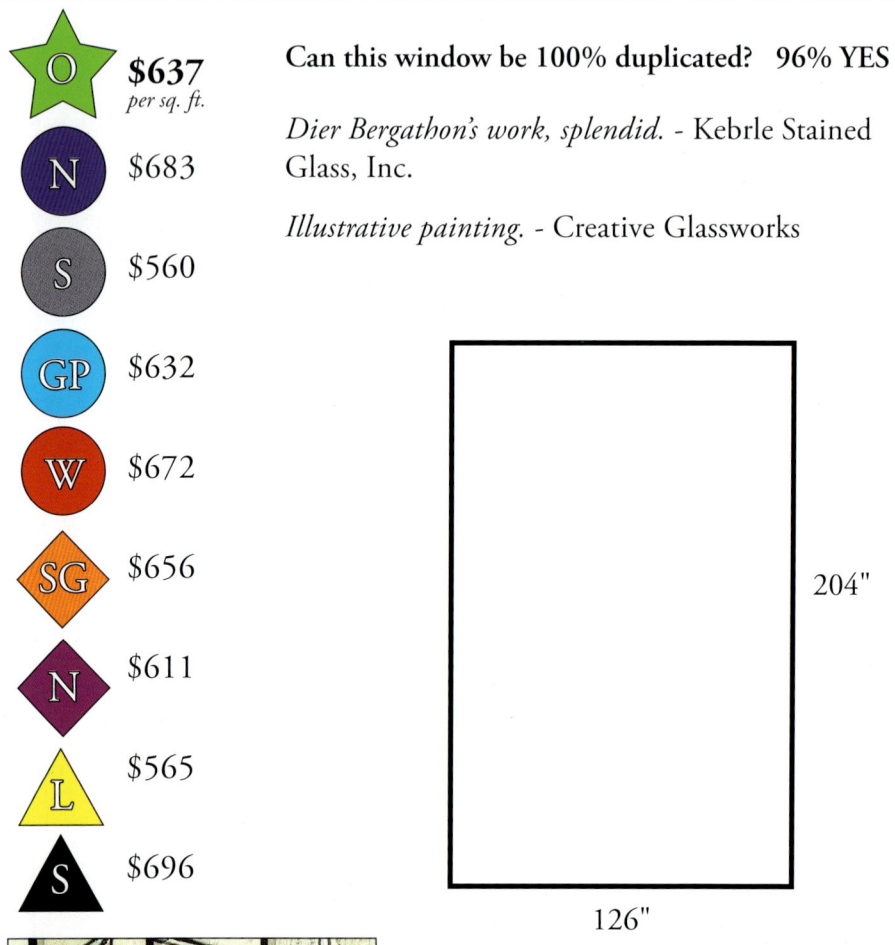

| | |
|---|---|
| O | **$637** per sq. ft. |
| N | $683 |
| S | $560 |
| GP | $632 |
| W | $672 |
| SG | $656 |
| N | $611 |
| L | $565 |
| S | $696 |

Can this window be 100% duplicated?   96% YES

*Dier Bergathon's work, splendid.* - Kebrle Stained Glass, Inc.

*Illustrative painting.* - Creative Glassworks

204"

126"

**Blessed Sacrament Church, Valley Stream, N.Y.**
*Rendering photos courtesy of Rohlf's Studio, Inc.*

HAIL MARY

FULL OF GRACE

INSCRIPTION
INSCRIPTION

# Tiffany

| | | |
|---|---|---|
| O | **$1676** *per sq. ft.* | |
| N | $2948 | |
| S | $1306 | |
| GP | $963 | |
| W | $1211 | |
| SG | $1573 | |
| N | $1780 | |
| L | $1870 | |
| S | $1552 | |

**Can this window be 100% duplicated?   27% YES**

*Drapery glass unavailable.* - Raynal Studios

*Some of this glass was specifically made to create certain areas and effects.* - Whitworth Stained Glass

*The glass speaks for itself. One of a kind. Everyone tries but no one can 100% replicate this window.* - Enterprise Art Glass Works, Inc.

*It is difficult to value a Tiffany as they have moved from the realm of stained glass to valuable antiquity whose value could be greatly increased at auction. The market may have rendered these virtually invaluable.* - Hiemer & Company Stained Glass

*Yes, everything can be replicated at a price, even a Tiffany. Although, as close to the original as the replication may be, it would still be a mere replication.* - Ascalon Studios, Inc.

*The resale value of a Tiffany is so high (and the glass type so scarce) that I don't think he can be replicated in the minds of the clients!*
- Anonymous

103"

47"

## National Presbyterian Church, Washington, D.C.

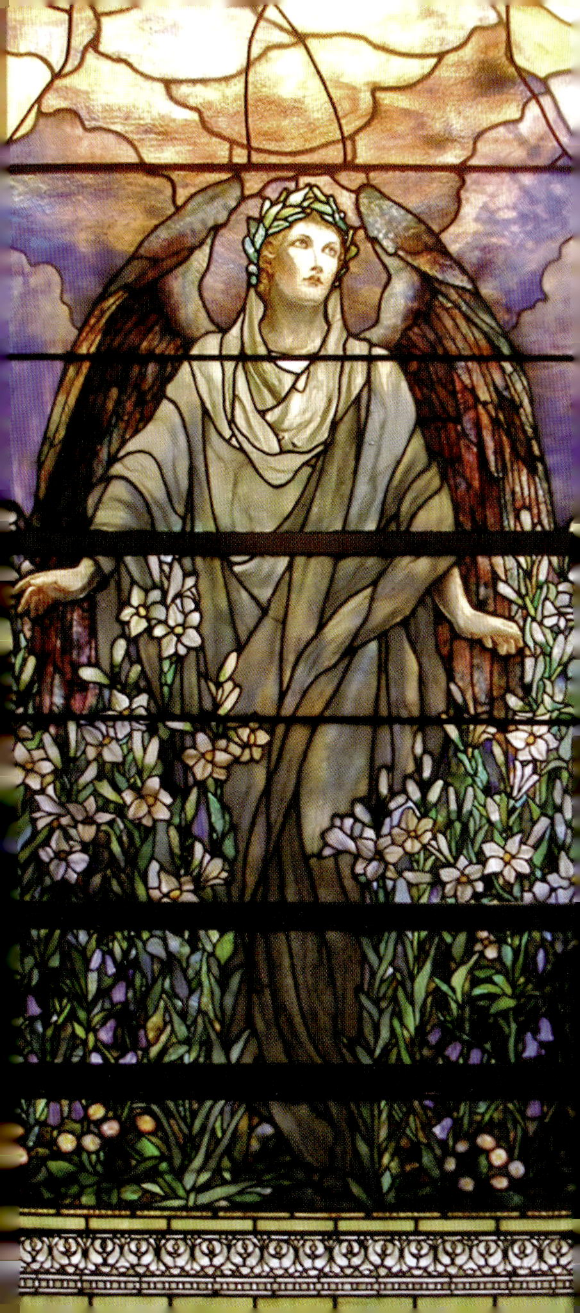

# Tiffany Family

| | |
|---|---|
| O | **$1214** *per sq. ft.* |
| N | $2270 |
| S | $863 |
| GP | $727 |
| W | $474 |
| SG | $1257 |
| N | $1171 |
| L | $1433 |
| S | $1084 |

Can this window be 100% duplicated?   24% YES

*Unusual amount of paint for Tiffany; Drapery glass unavailable.* - Raynal Studios

*(Editor's Note: This window has not been authenticated as a Tiffany).*

*Nearly impossible to replicate the glass.*
- SLFirpo Design/Craft

*In addition to documentation, these windows offer the added challenge of finding the right glass for replication. If proper materials were found, replication could be possible. It is unlikely that the plated areas would be replicated "exactly."*
- Hiemer & Company Stained Glass

*High quality painting with plated glass, intricate (custom glass).* - Creative Glassworks

*Obtaining an exact duplicate means locating the several layers of glass that blended to give the varied colors. Won't be exact.* - Tooley Art Glass Studio

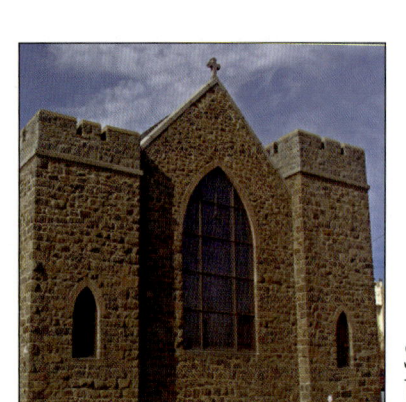

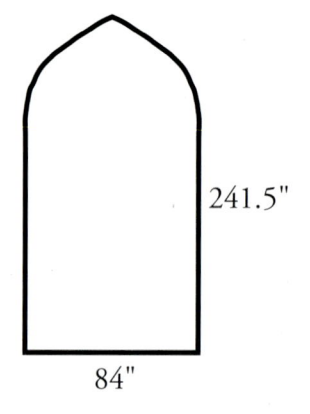

241.5"

84"

St. John's Episcopal, Butte, Mont.

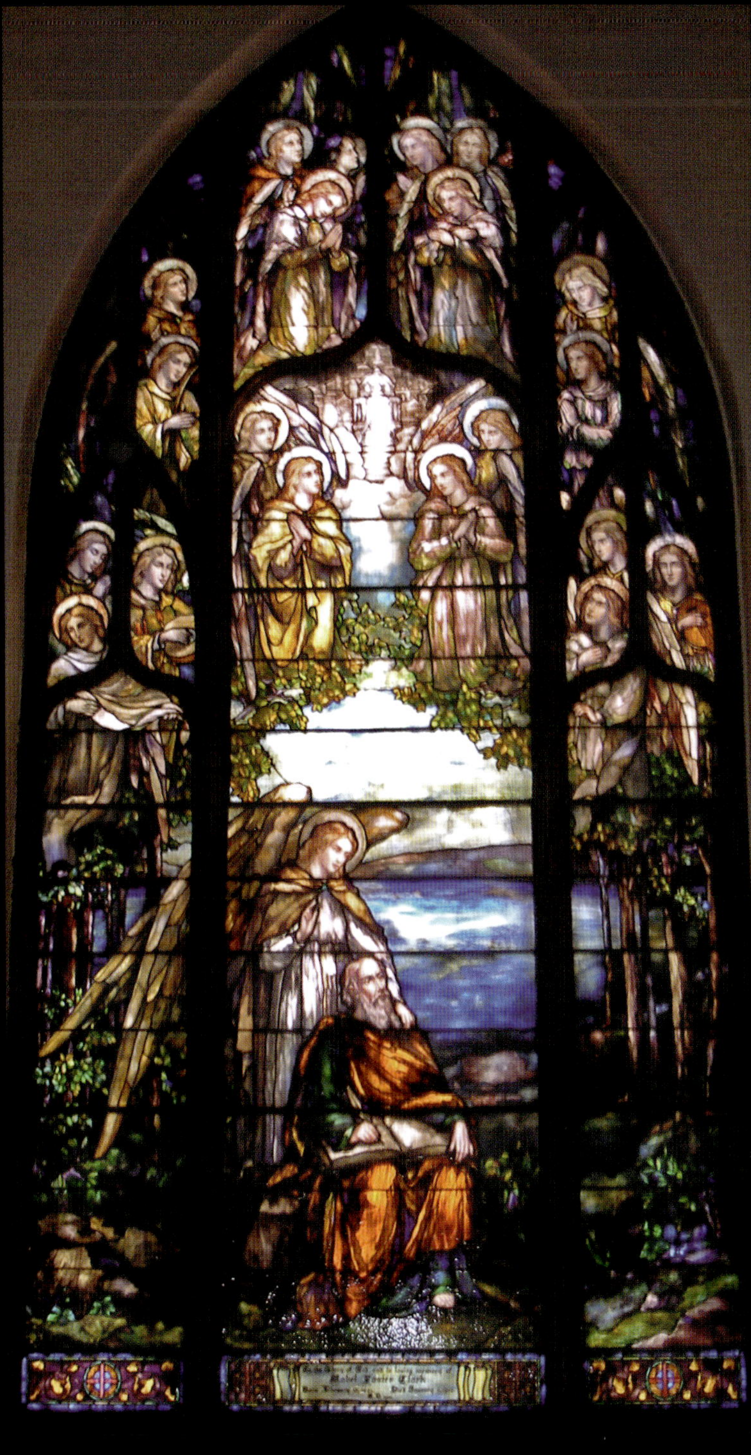

# WILLET

| | |
|---|---|
| O | **$710** per sq. ft. |
| N | $842 |
| S | $710 |
| GP | $691 |
| W | $548 |
| SG | $704 |
| N | $717 |
| L | $695 |
| S | $714 |

**Can this window be 100% duplicated?   90% YES**

Personally signed by Henry J. Willet, the Christmas Window (1962) illustrates the Incarnation. The artist's hand swirls through the story of our Savior's birth. In the center is the serene child in the manger where Mary and Joseph gaze lovingly. Heavenly hosts frame the star that notarizes the divine birth. Kings at right and shepherds at left proceed to see the child while a scowling Herod's threats become real in the slaughter of innocents at the feet of the kings. - *from Myers Park Presbyterian Church (stained glass pamphlet), page 21.*

*Just visited this church and saw the incredible detail and work in this and the other windows there.*
- Whitworth Stained Glass

*Fully painted.* - Creative Glassworks

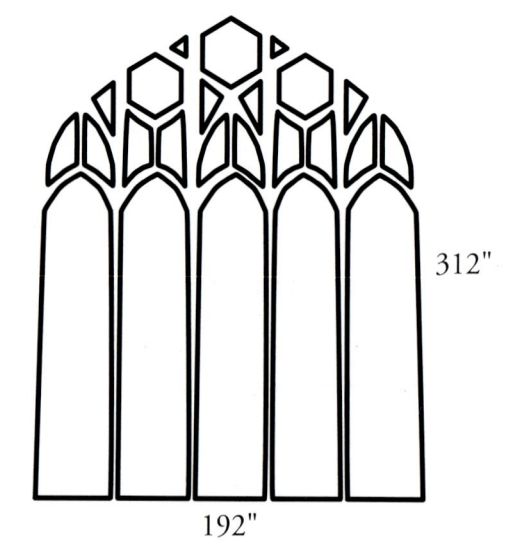

312"

192"

MYERS PARK PRESBYTERIAN, CHARLOTTE, N.C.

ON
GOOD
WILL
TOWARD
MEN
WONDERFUL
COUNSELOR
MIGHTY
FATHER
PEACE
OUT OF EGYPT

GOOD
WILL
TOWARD
MEN
HIS
NAME
SHALL
BE
CALLED
WONDERFUL
COUNSELOR
THE
MIGHTY
GOD
THE
EVER
LASTING
FATHER
THE
RINCE
OF
PEACE

# WILLET

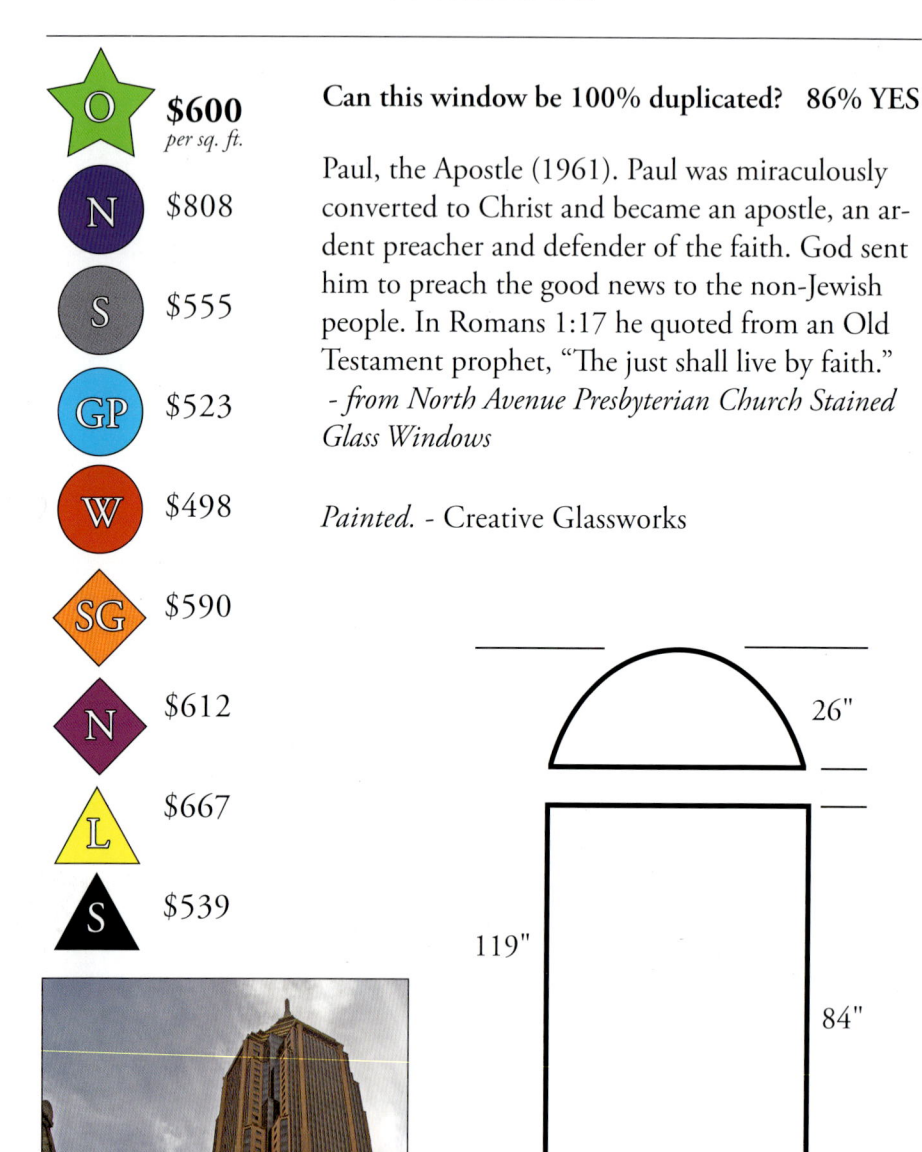

| | |
|---|---|
| O | **$600** per sq. ft. |
| N | $808 |
| S | $555 |
| GP | $523 |
| W | $498 |
| SG | $590 |
| N | $612 |
| L | $667 |
| S | $539 |

**Can this window be 100% duplicated?   86% YES**

Paul, the Apostle (1961). Paul was miraculously converted to Christ and became an apostle, an ardent preacher and defender of the faith. God sent him to preach the good news to the non-Jewish people. In Romans 1:17 he quoted from an Old Testament prophet, "The just shall live by faith."
*- from North Avenue Presbyterian Church Stained Glass Windows*

*Painted.* - Creative Glassworks

26"
119"
84"
55"

## NORTH AVENUE PRESBYTERIAN, ATLANTA, GA.

THE JUST SHALL LIVE BY FAITH

IN LOVING MEMORY
MARY METCALFE TULLER

# WILLET

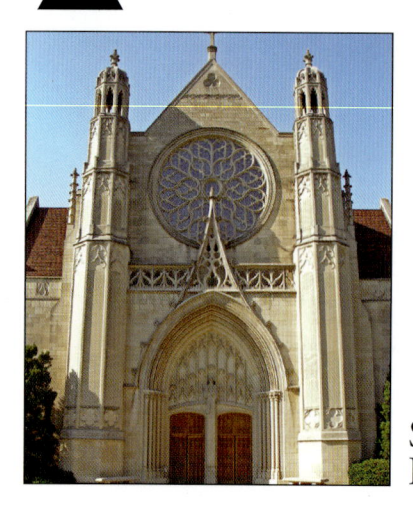

- O $632 per sq. ft.
- N $869
- S $590
- GP $544
- W $503
- SG $630
- N $634
- L $671
- S $586

Can this window be 100% duplicated?   86% YES

*Good Willet.* - Kebrle Stained Glass, Inc.

*Fully painted, moderate complexity.*
- Creative Glassworks

*There is low representation of this Romanesque style which was popular in the Northeastern U.S. from approximately 1930 through the early 1950s. Hiemer Studio created lots of them during that period.* - Hiemer & Company Stained Glass

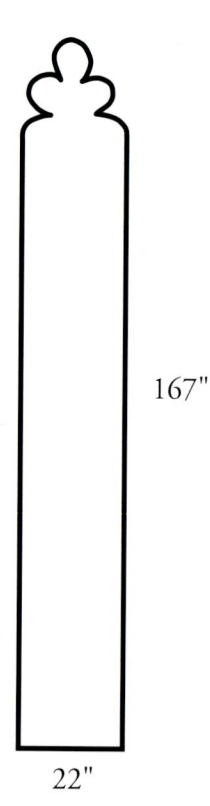

167"

22"

SECOND PRESBYTERIAN, INDIANAPOLIS, IND.

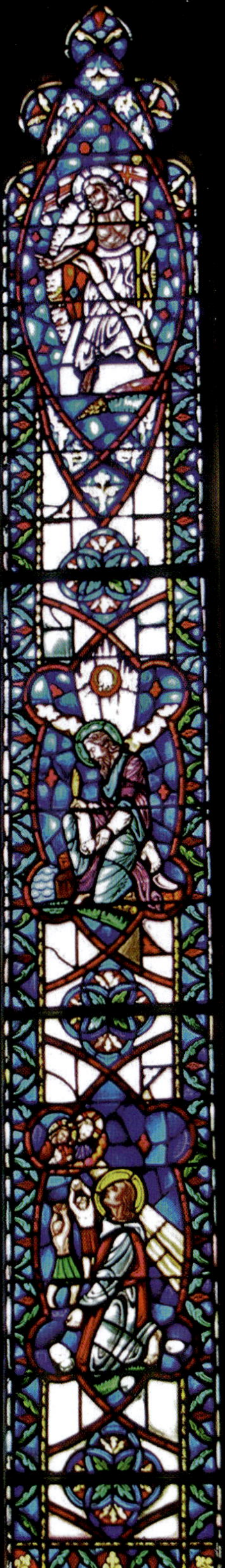
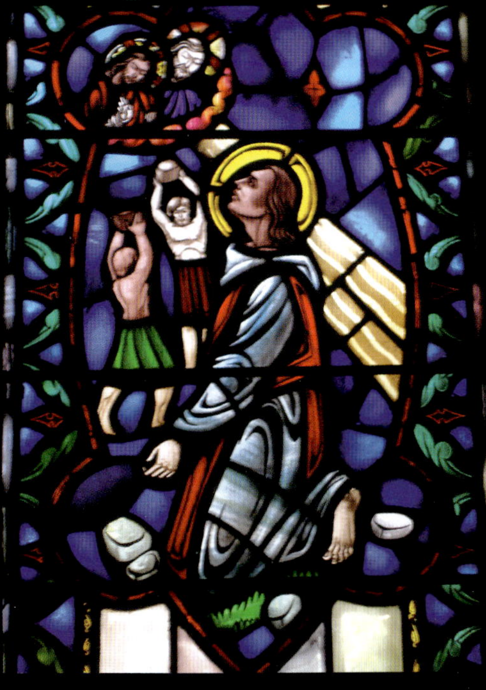

# Zettler

| | |
|---|---|
| O | **$1117** per sq. ft. |
| N | $1692 |
| S | $875 |
| GP | $977 |
| W | $777 |
| SG | $1212 |
| N | $1004 |
| L | $1201 |
| S | $1056 |

Can this window be 100% duplicated?   76% YES

*Ornate, painted.* - Creative Glassworks

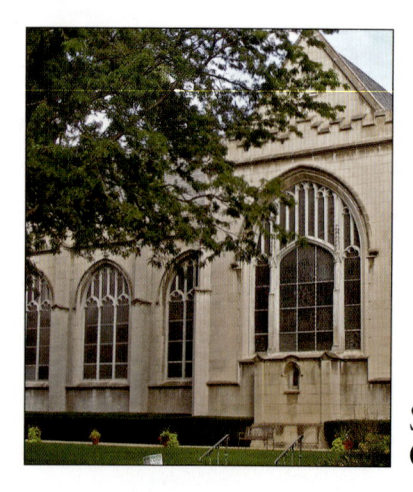

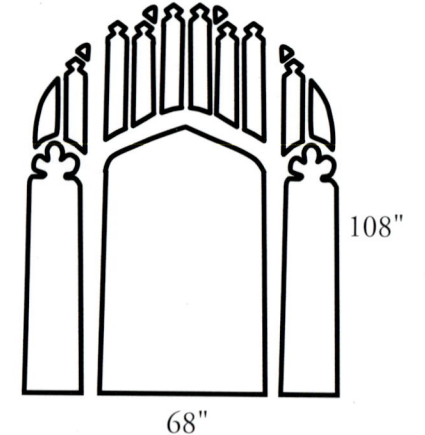

108"
68"

## St. Edmond Catholic
## Oak Park, Ill.

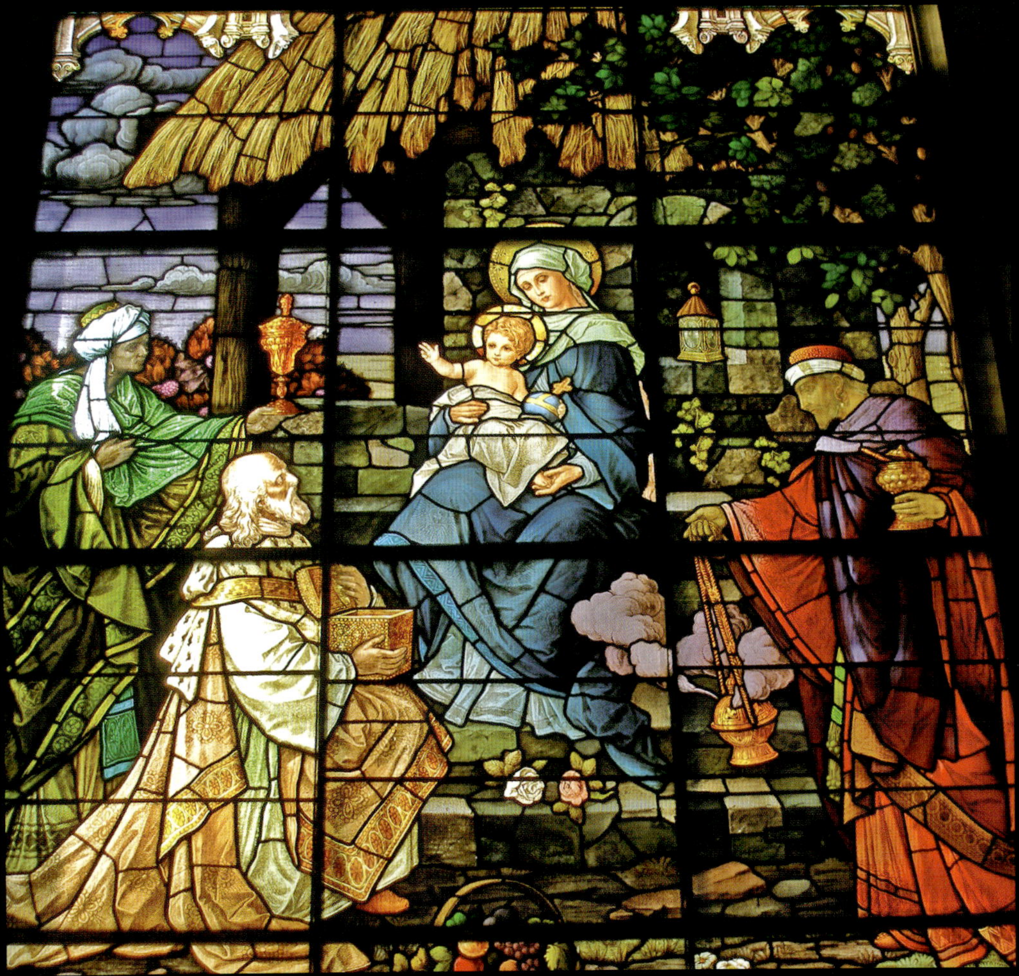

# Zettler

| | |
|---|---|
| O | **$1016** *per sq. ft.* |
| N | $1376 |
| S | $838 |
| GP | $977 |
| W | $732 |
| SG | $1030 |
| N | $998 |
| L | $1004 |
| S | $1018 |

Can this window be 100% duplicated?   75% YES

1913. The Cathedral upholds the traditions of the great Churches of the Middle Ages telling the consecutive stories of the Old and New Testaments in its stained glass windows. The making of these windows was awarded to the world-renowned firm of F. X. Zettler of Munich, Bavaria. - *from the "Cathedral of St. Helena, Helena Montana," page 8.*

*Great Zettler.* - Kebrle Stained Glass, Inc.

*Ornate, painted.* - Creative Glassworks

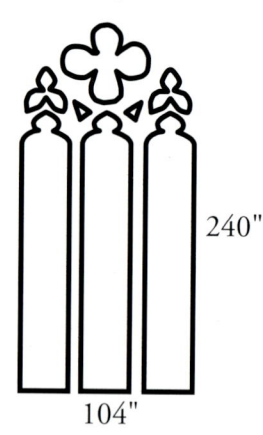

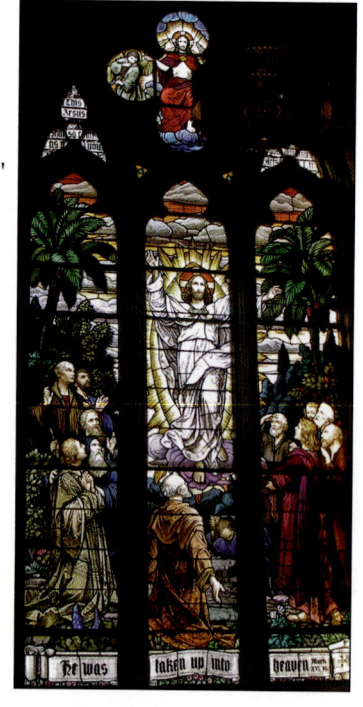

240"
104"

Cathedral of St. Helena, Helena, Mont.

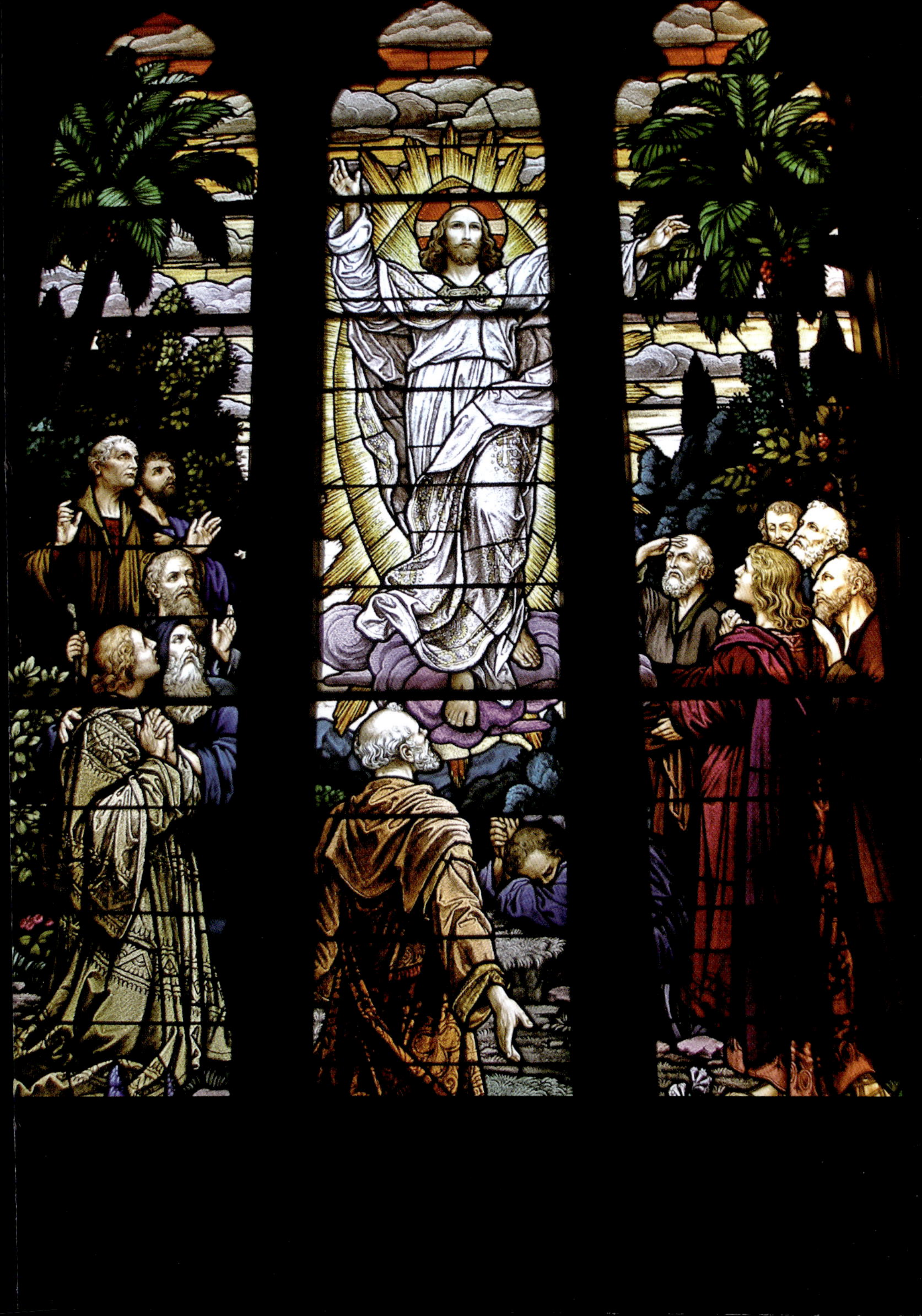

*Photo courtesy of Rohlf's Studios, Inc.*

# Section 3

A stained glass revival is again sweeping America. Artistic voids of these last few decades are being filled with light, brilliance and beauty. As America is returning to the scriptures in record numbers, stained glass continues to be used to help tell the story. Likewise, as America returns to old fashioned craftsmanship, so too are stained glass studios gathering the world's great artists and craftsmen to design and fabricate modern masterpieces.

# The Modern Stained Glass Studios

# Conrad Schmitt

- ⭐ O    **$344** *per sq. ft.*
- 🔵 N    $350
- ⚫ S    $415
- 🔵 GP    $302
- 🔴 W    $337
- 🔶 SG    $343
- 🔷 N    $344
- 🔺 L    $299
- 🔺 S    $366

**Can this window be 100% duplicated? 96% YES**

*Spiritual Awakening* incorporates a range of glass types, some of which have been shaded with air-brushed enamel paint prior to firing. The abstract design engages the viewer's imagination, allowing for individual interpretation of the figure. Its dynamic, flowing lines stir the living movement of one's own faith and uplift the human spirit.

*This design is entirely composed of glass with no painting and can be replicated with relative ease. The window is divided into symmetrical panels which would allow for easy repair and replacement.*
- Cottage Glass

*Relatively simple painted and antique hand blown glass.* - Creative Glassworks

136"

186"

### St. Elizabeth Ann Seton Catholic Church, New Berlin, Wis.

*Photo courtesy of Conrad Schmitt Studios*

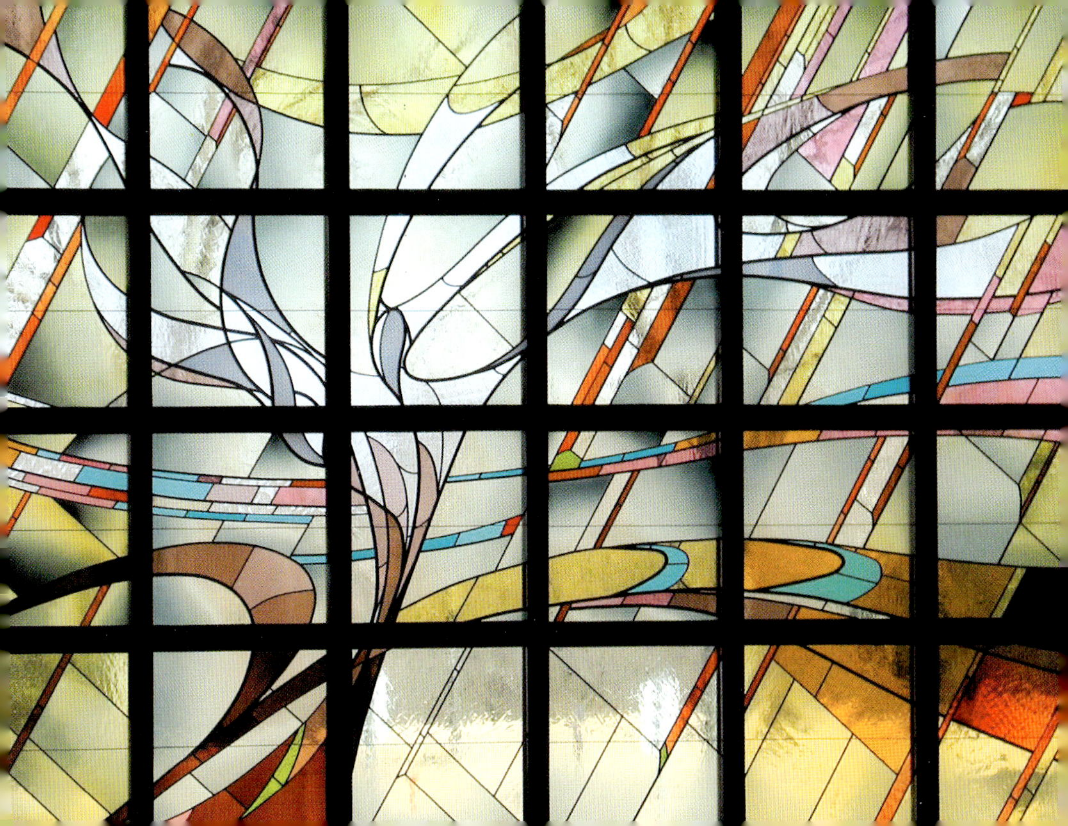

# Conrad Schmitt

| | |
|---|---|
| O | **$600** per sq. ft. |
| N | $729 |
| S | $710 |
| GP | $470 |
| W | $530 |
| SG | $682 |
| N | $494 |
| L | $640 |
| S | $543 |

Can this window be 100% duplicated?   85% YES

A new, multi-layer (plated) window of Jesus and the Children has been created to coordinate with existing Tiffany windows.

*Appears to contain drapery glass, partially painted, moderately ornate.* - Creative Glassworks

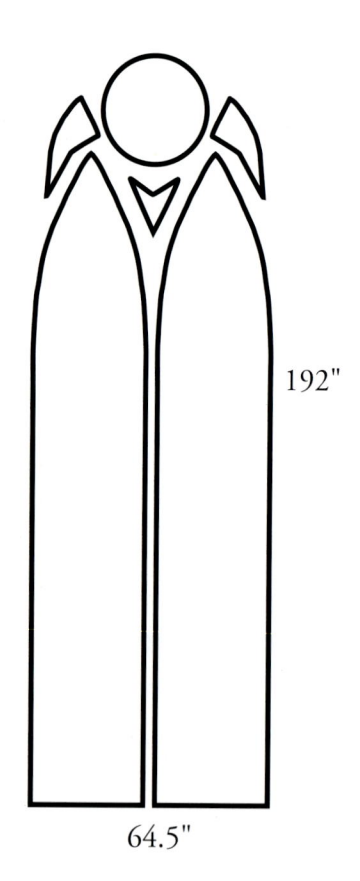

192"

64.5"

## First Congregational, Kenosha, Wis.
*Photo courtesy of Conrad Schmitt Studios*

From the
lips of infants
and children You
have ordained praise.
Psalm 8:2

Let the
little children
come unto Me.
Luke 18:16

# Franz Mayer, Munich

| | |
|---|---|
| O | **$912** per sq. ft. |
| N | $1285 |
| S | $725 |
| GP | $877 |
| W | $602 |
| SG | $865 |
| N | $964 |
| L | $954 |
| S | $879 |

Can this window be 100% duplicated?  81% YES

*Highly ornate and painted.* - Creative Glassworks

*Replication of any window required clear and absolute documentation of the original including, but not restricted to, detailed photos, color notes and/or samples. Without adequate documentation, replication is not possible.*
- Hiemer & Company Stained Glass

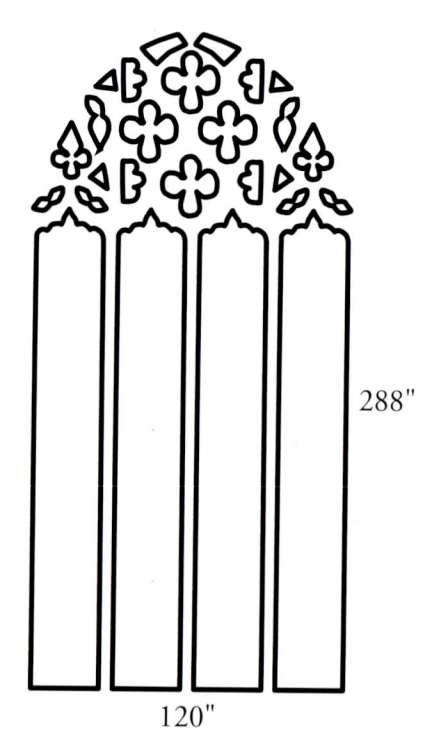

288"

120"

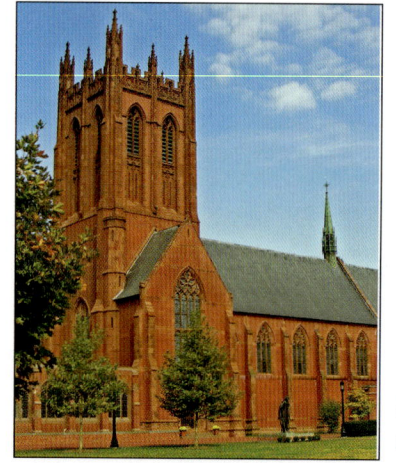

St. Paul School, Concord, N.H.

NOW GET UP AND GO INTO THE CITY AND YOU WILL BE TOLD WHAT YOU MUST DO

THE SECRETS OF THE KINGDOM OF GOD HAS BEEN GIVEN TO YOU

# Judson

| | |
|---|---|
| O | **$383** per sq. ft. |
| N | $419 |
| S | $359 |
| GP | $369 |
| W | $387 |
| SG | $358 |
| N | $416 |
| L | $383 |
| S | $389 |

Can this window be 100% duplicated?   95% YES

*With the exception of the faces of the figures and the hands, it appears the other design lines are stenciled/traced lines. It is not clear to me whether the red portions of some of the flames have been painted.* - Cottage Glass

*Very simple, some painting.* - Creative Glassworks

*This stylized art has an inconsistency that a professional studio would not expect. The two heads and the hands of Jesus just don't belong with the overall stylization. Excellent photos would be important and with them the art could be easily duplicated.* - Anonymous

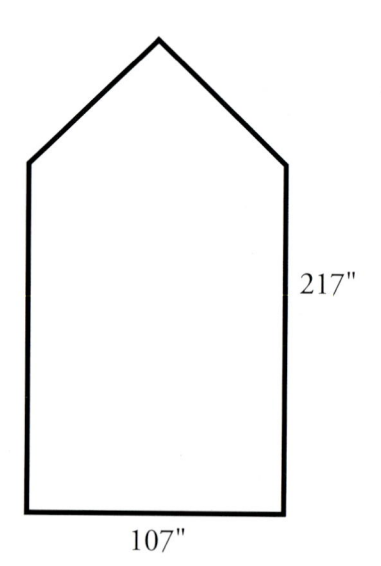

217"

107"

## All Saints Episcopal, Los Angeles, Calif.
*Photos courtesy of Judson*

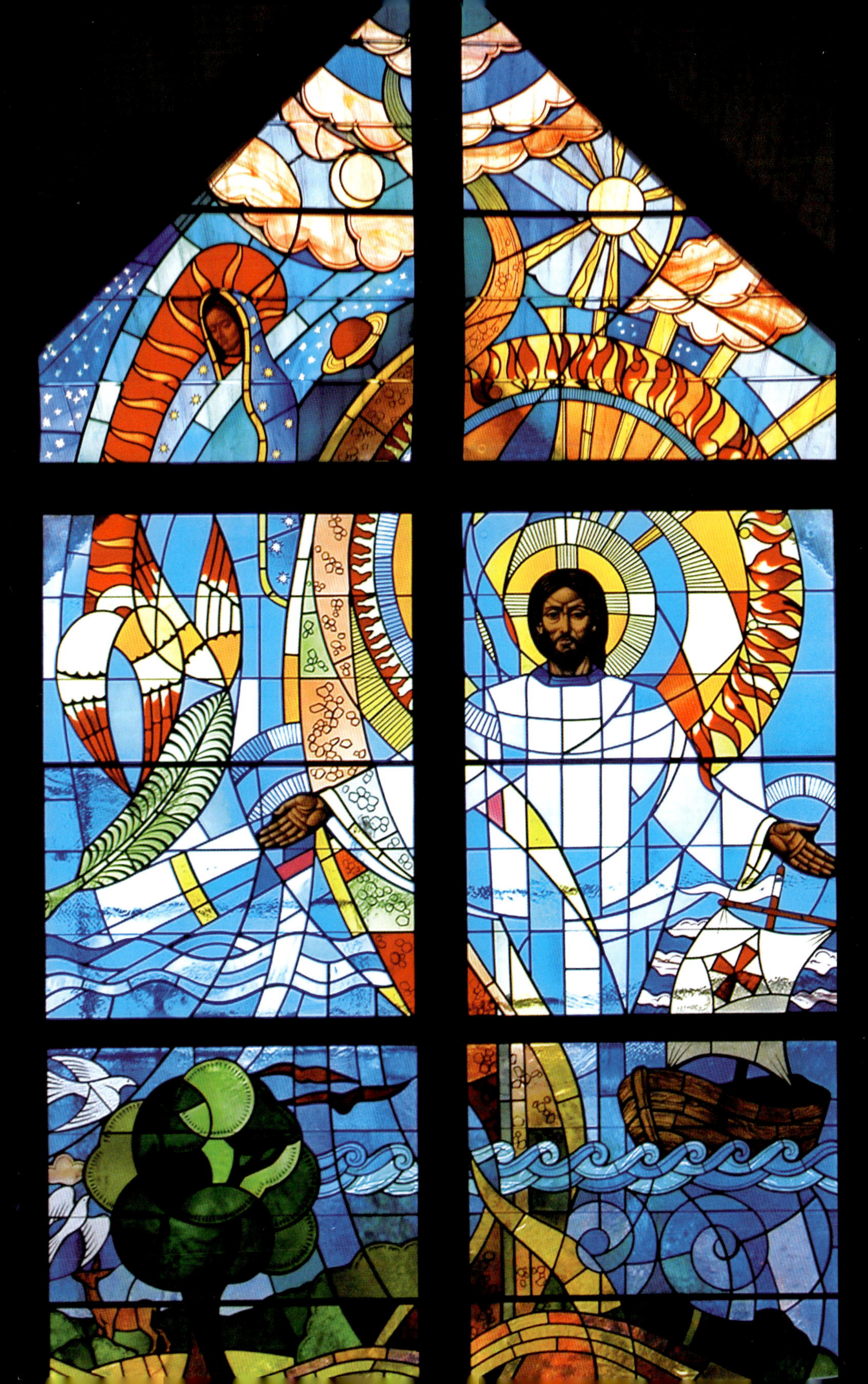

# LeCompte

| | |
|---|---|
| O | **$506** *per sq. ft.* |
| N | $633 |
| S | $463 |
| GP | $460 |
| W | $459 |
| SG | $522 |
| N | $485 |
| L | $535 |
| S | $481 |

Can this window be 100% duplicated?   91% YES

Rowan LeCompte designed windows with literary and musical themes for the chancel, and they were executed and installed by Dieter Goldkuhle in 1992 and 1997. Given a blank canvas and instructions to inspire, LeCompte chose to celebrate music, both in terms of the composer who produced it and the poets who provided the words to sing. Figures in the "Spring" window are W. A. Mozart, Walt Whitman and E. E. Cummings. - *from A Journey of Hope, The House of Hope Presbyterian Church, 1849-1999, pages 118-119*

*French style, simple yet colorful. Beautiful composition.* - Enterprise Art Glass Works, Inc.

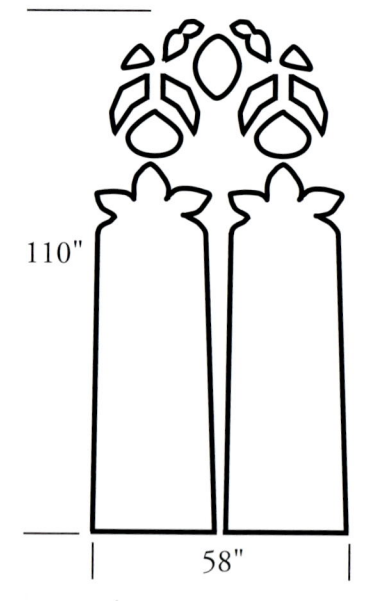

110"

58"

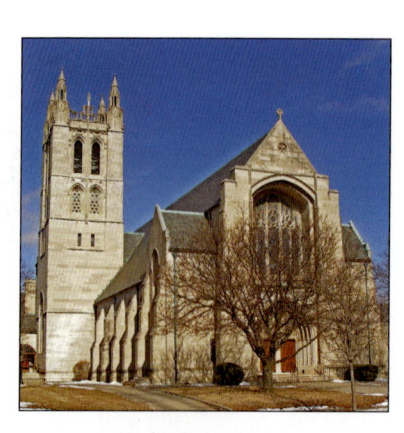

House of Hope Presbyterian
St. Paul, Minn.

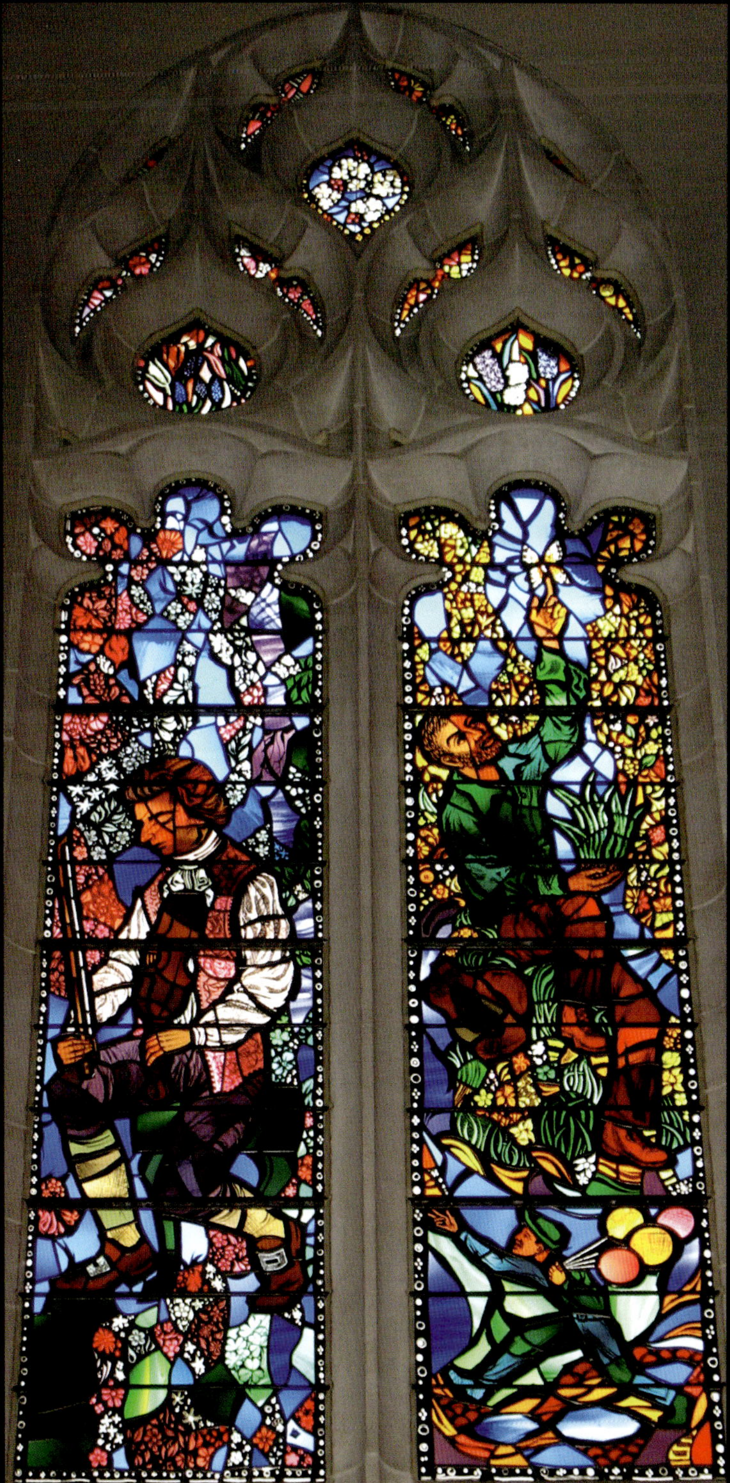

# Rohlf

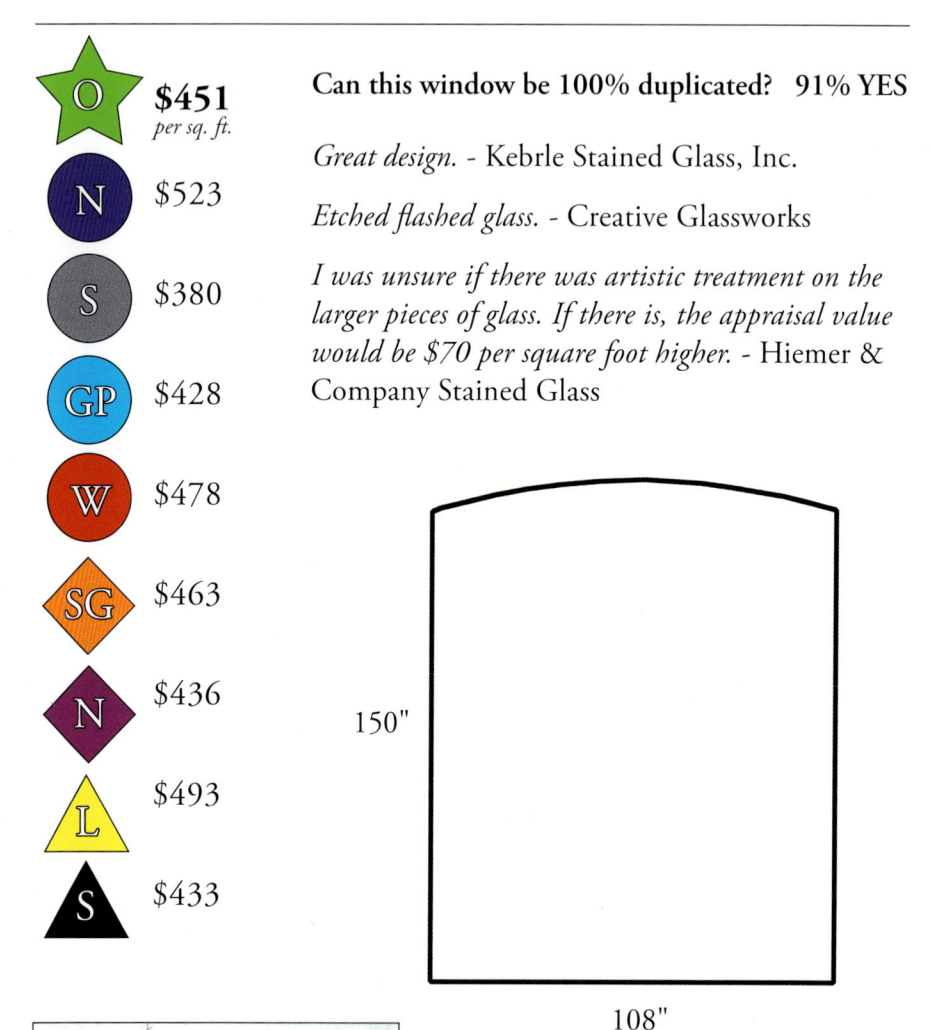

| | |
|---|---|
| O | **$451** per sq. ft. |
| N | $523 |
| S | $380 |
| GP | $428 |
| W | $478 |
| SG | $463 |
| N | $436 |
| L | $493 |
| S | $433 |

Can this window be 100% duplicated?   91% YES

*Great design.* - Kebrle Stained Glass, Inc.

*Etched flashed glass.* - Creative Glassworks

*I was unsure if there was artistic treatment on the larger pieces of glass. If there is, the appraisal value would be $70 per square foot higher.* - Hiemer & Company Stained Glass

150"

108"

PRESIDENT'S WINDOW,
IONA COLLEGE,
NEW ROCHELLE, N.Y.
*Photos courtesy of Rohlf's Studios, Inc.*

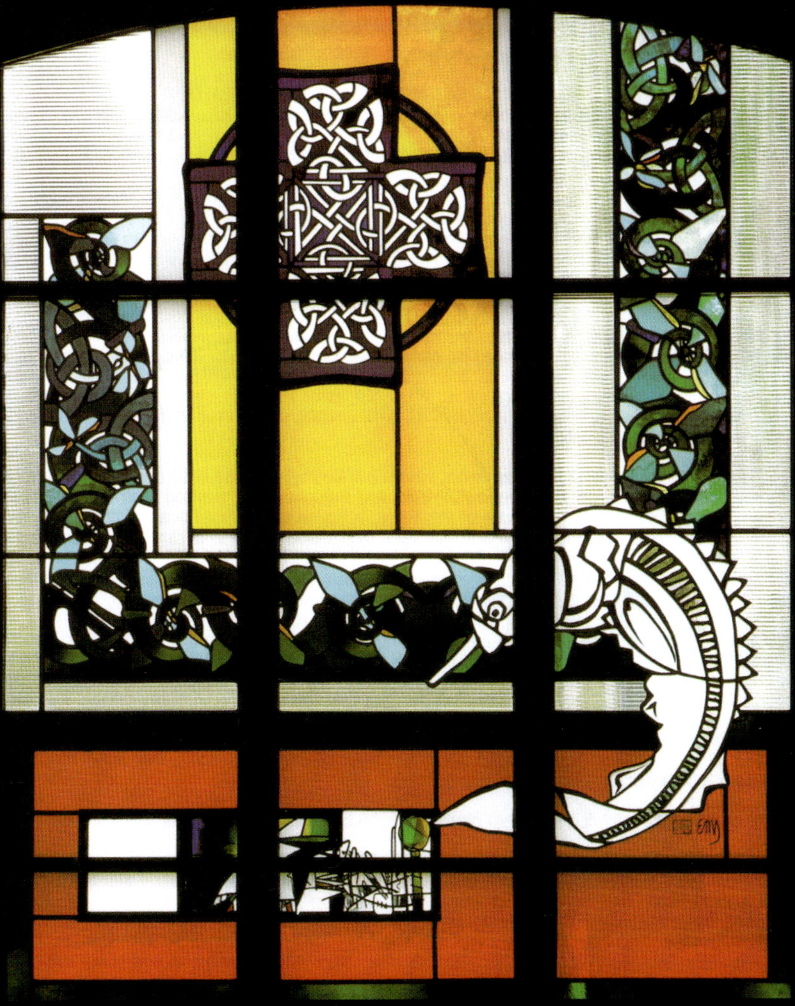

# Rohlf

| | |
|---|---|
| O | **$506** per sq. ft. |
| N | $651 |
| S | $440 |
| GP | $474 |
| W | $435 |
| SG | $522 |
| N | $485 |
| L | $575 |
| S | $449 |

Can this window be 100% duplicated?   96% YES

*Great Bergathon.* - Kebrle Stained Glass Inc.

*Beautiful coloration, many pieces. Studio still exists so windows can be remade.* - Enterprise Art Glass Works, Inc.

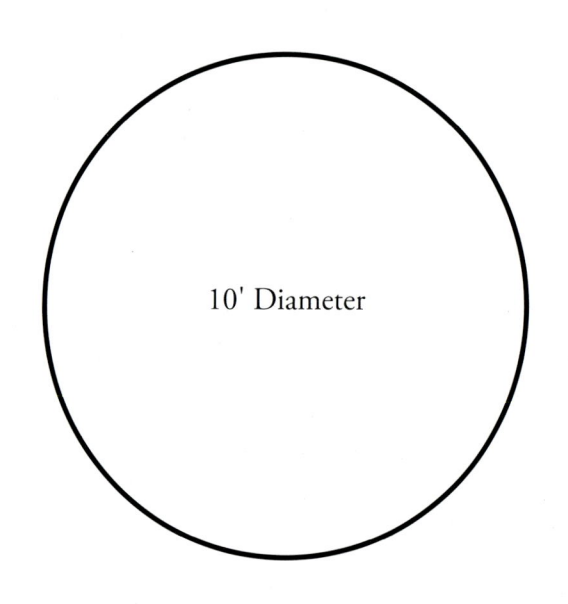

10' Diameter

FIRST PRESBYTERIAN CHURCH, RIDGEWOOD, N.J.
*Photos courtesy of Rohlf's Studios, Inc.*

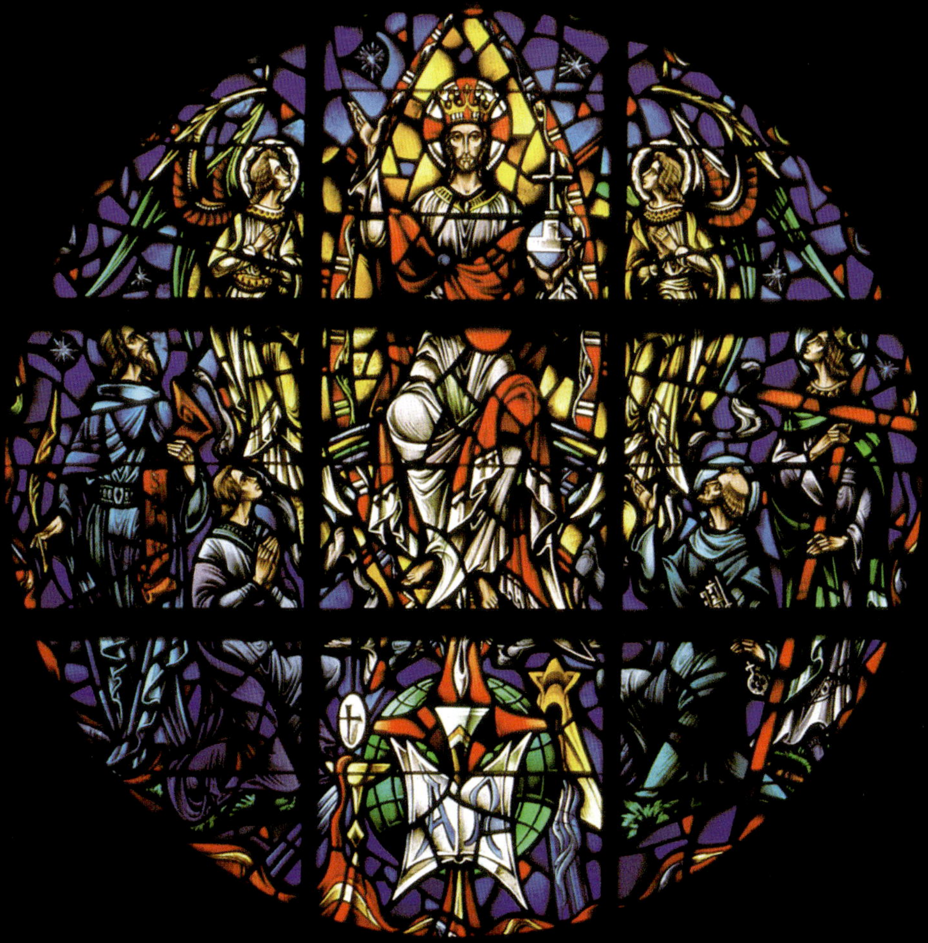

# Willet

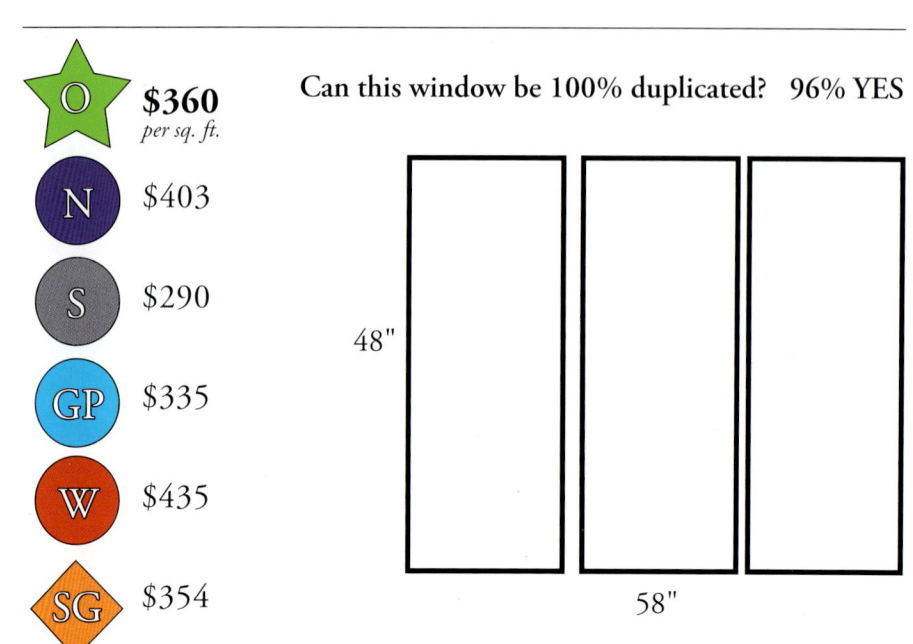

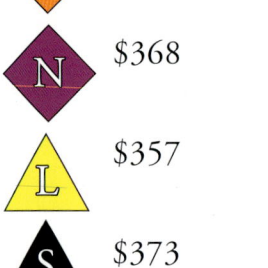

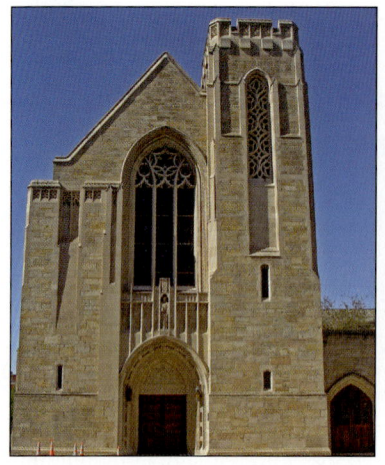

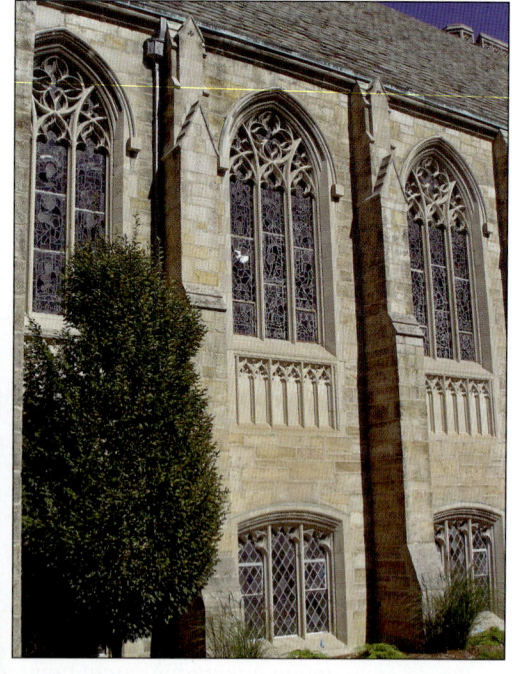

| | | |
|---|---|---|
| O | **$360** per sq. ft. | Can this window be 100% duplicated? 96% YES |
| N | $403 | |
| S | $290 | |
| GP | $335 | |
| W | $435 | |
| SG | $354 | |
| N | $368 | |
| L | $357 | |
| S | $373 | |

48"

58"

Christ Church Episcopal
Grosse Point Farms, Mich.

"In memory of Betty Bird by her friends and family."

*Photo courtesy of Judson*

## FACETED GLASS
(Also known as *dale de verre*)

French artists began experimenting with a thick colored glass style in the 1920s that had first been used in a decorative way by Byzantine artists. Faceted glass is thick, modern cast glass set into epoxy resin which results in a mosaic-like approach of pure color effects. Epoxy resin is very strong and works with 1" thick glass effectively, both having very similar coefficients of expansion and contraction.

A prominent early designer of faceted projects was Father Anthony Lauck of the Notre Dame Art Department, who described the concept by saying, "Some materials have a more marked character about them than others. Among these is dale de verre. Not only is it deeply translucent, but it transmits light in clear brilliant colors. The thickness gives more depth and intensity to its color. The unusual means of shaping it by chiseling adds to its character. Hammer cutting fractures the glass in uneven sizes with notched and somewhat jagged edges. Faceting the edges breaks up the surfaces with shell-like ripples and facets, which bring out the crystalline, angular structure of the glass. Each broken facet transmits its own hue, catches a different angle of the sun's rays or the sky's brightness and brings a varied pattern of sparkling light into the window. It is precisely this unique and individual charm of slab glass that appeals to artists, connoisseurs and patrons alike."

# Faceted Glass

# Faceted Glass

| | |
|---|---|
| O | **$283** per sq. ft. |
| N | $381 |
| S | $247 |
| GP | $264 |
| W | $250 |
| SG | $268 |
| N | $307 |
| L | $285 |
| S | $280 |

Can this window be 100% duplicated?   89% YES

*Personal opinion: faceted glass works best when not designed as leaded design. This one is very labor intensive.* - Anonymous

*Can only be replaced, not repaired.*
- Creative Glassworks

*This window could be replicated with excellent photos. I suspect that the camera film has not done an excellent job of recording the subtle colors. It is a simple, but complicated composition of colors. The cross is barely visible within the rose. Perhaps I've put the cost per square foot too low for the time the studio would need to make good studies of this color arrangement.* - Anonymous

180" × 540"

First Baptist Church
Wichita Falls, Texas

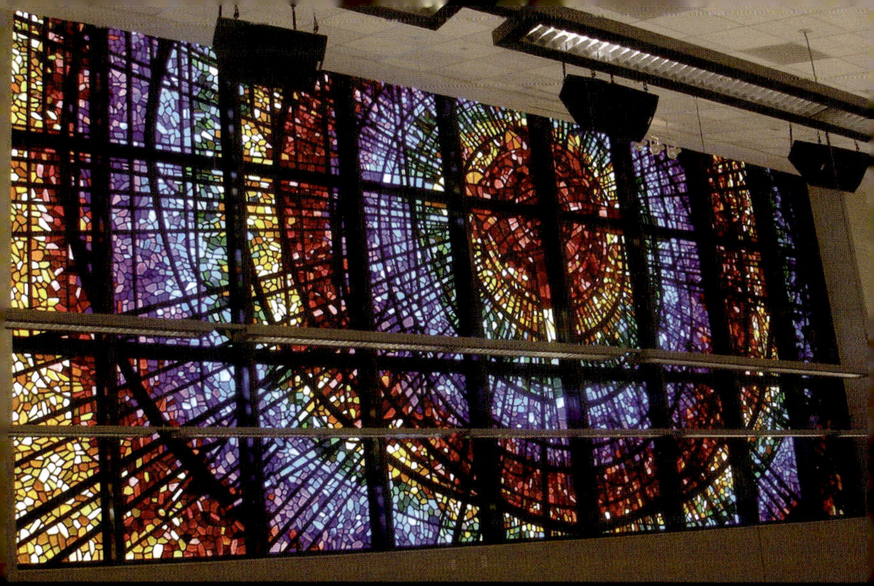

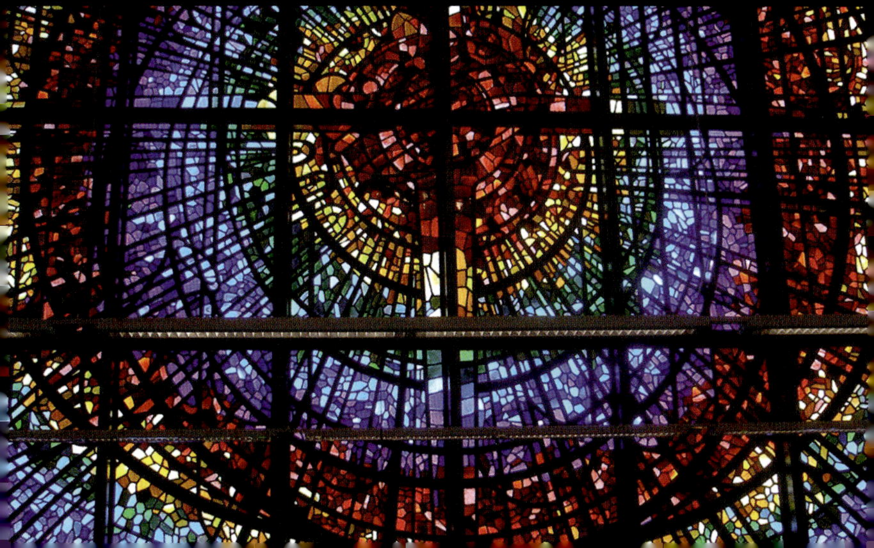

# Faceted Glass

- O — **$247** per sq. ft.
- N — $303
- S — $237
- GP — $241
- W — $203
- SG — $237
- N — $263
- L — $253
- S — $248

**Can this window be 100% duplicated?   95% YES**

The "Window of Compassion" pictures many traditional symbols of the Resurrection. At the bottom of the design, two angels kneel in adoration as Christ fulfills the promise of His ministry on earth. Designed and fabricated by Smith Studios, Fort Worth, Texas, 1987.

*This window is the type of faceted glass that is easy to duplicate because the dale glass colors are so limited and the cuts are easy (not many inside curves). When a designing artist strictly limits the color range (this is for both faceted glass and leaded glass) the crafting of the window is simple. My comment is not negative to the artist or studio. I'm well aware that the church budget may dictate what can be done artistically. - Anonymous*

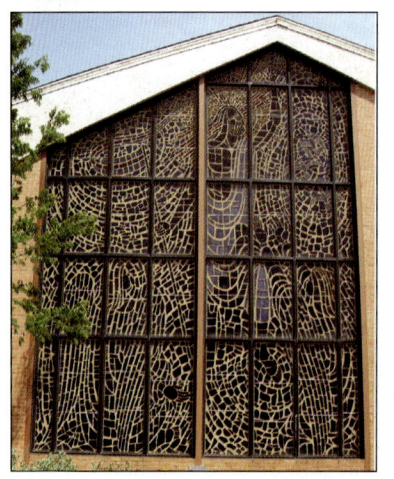

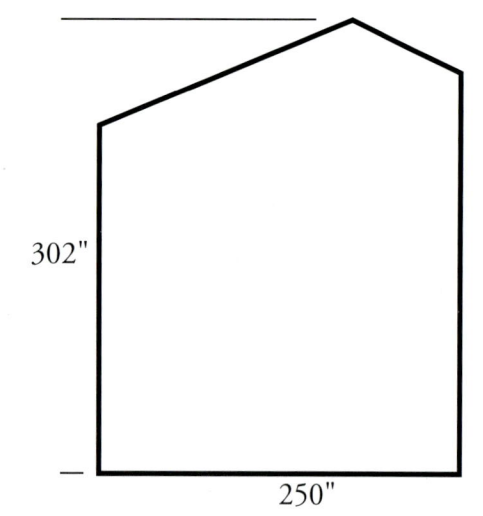

302"

250"

**Arborlawn United Methodist Church**
**Fort Worth, Texas**

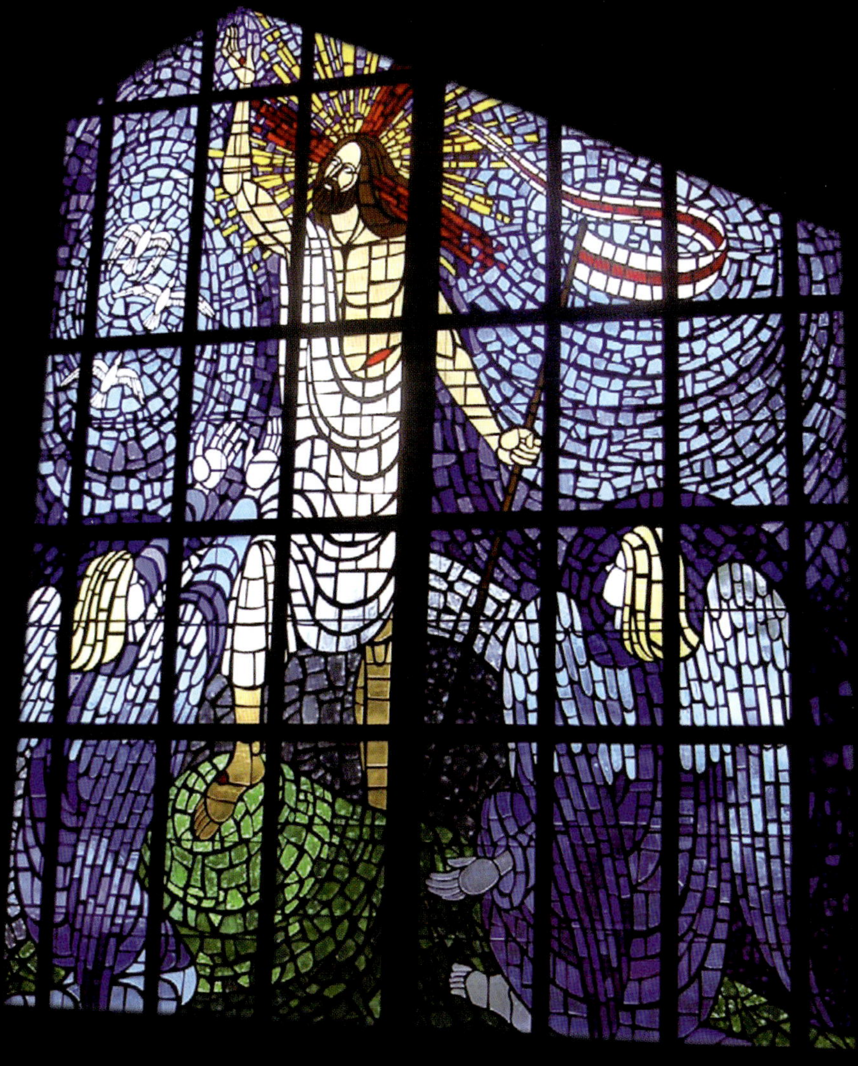

# Willet

| | |
|---|---|
| O | **$388** per sq. ft. |
| N | $331 |
| S | $260 |
| GP | $322 |
| W | $273 |
| SG | $315 |
| N | $274 |
| L | $308 |
| S | $296 |

Can this window be 100% duplicated?   94% YES

*Better with some negative space.* - Anonymous

*It could be unlikely that the variety of rubies in this window is still available.* - Hiemer & Company Stained Glass

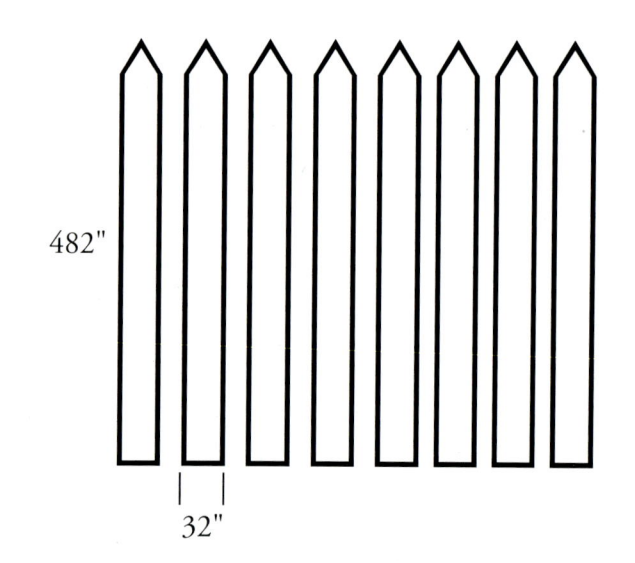

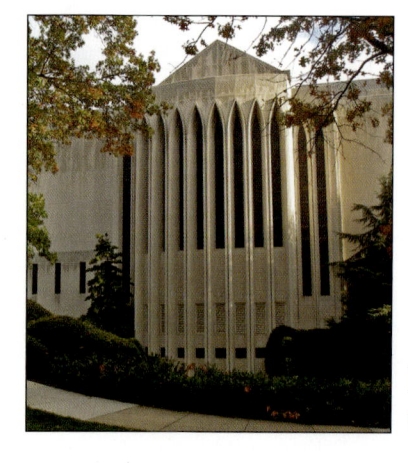

482"

32"

NATIONAL PRESBYTERIAN CHURCH, WASHINGTON, D.C.

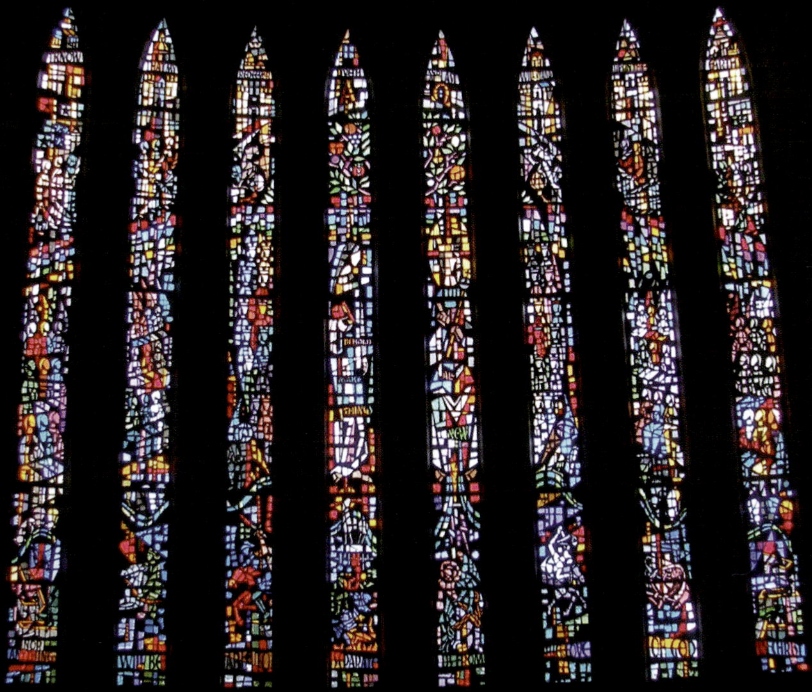

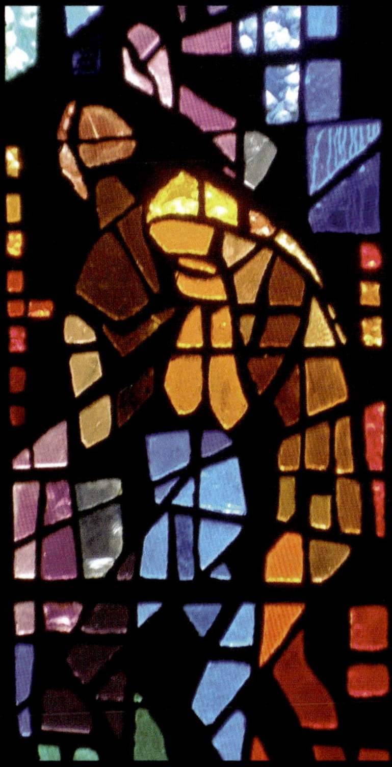

# Conrad Schmitt

| | |
|---|---|
| O | **$296** per sq. ft. |
| N | $338 |
| S | $238 |
| GP | $339 |
| W | $250 |
| SG | $309 |
| N | $275 |
| L | $300 |
| S | $303 |

Can this window be 100% duplicated?    94% YES

*From the 50s.* - Kebrle Stained Glass, Inc.

*Photos courtesy of Conrad Schmitt Studios*

St. Mary's Greek Ruthenian
New York City, N.Y.

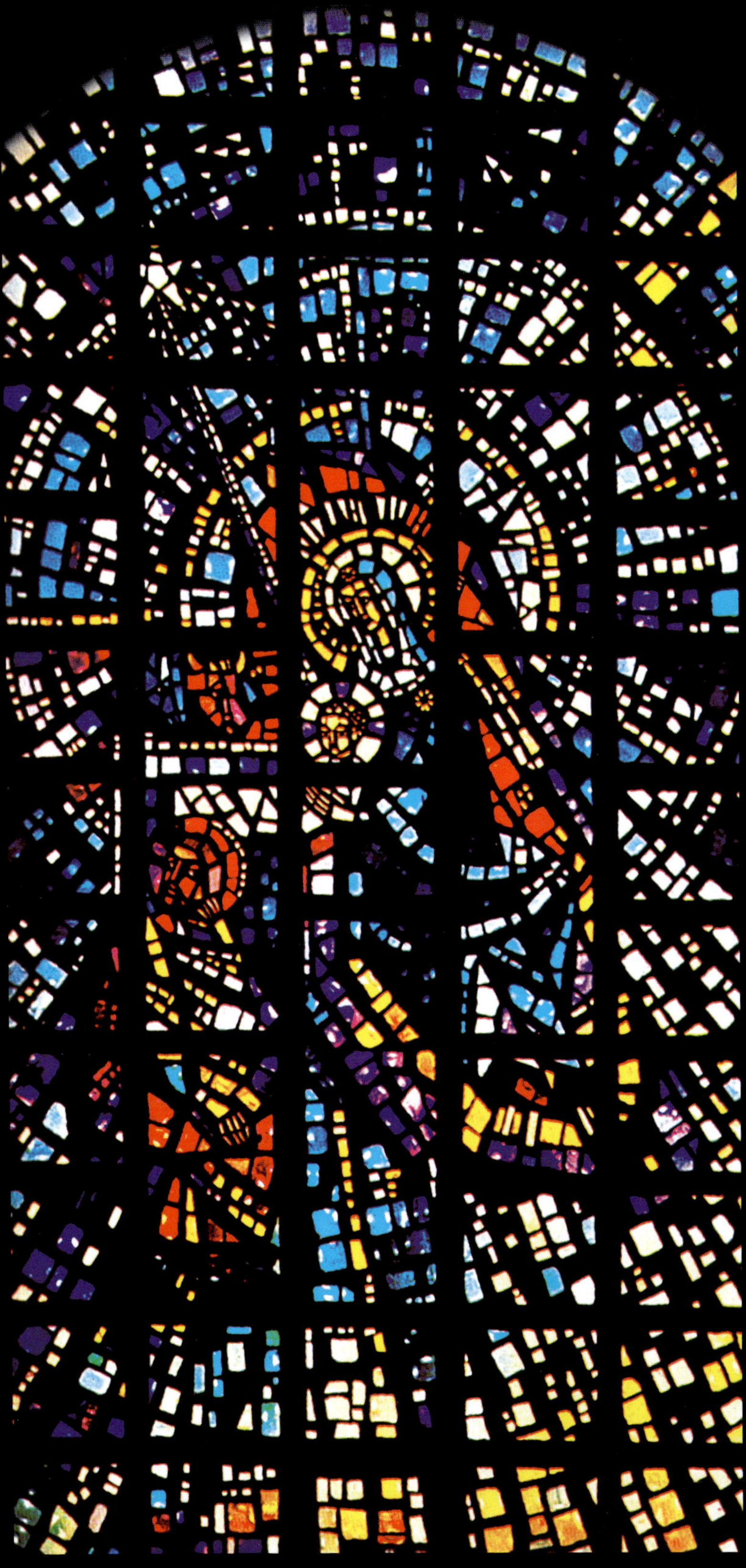

# CONRAD SCHMITT

| | |
|---|---|
| O | **$285** *per sq. ft.* |
| N | $333 |
| S | $235 |
| GP | $311 |
| W | $255 |
| SG | $295 |
| N | $271 |
| L | $283 |
| S | $297 |

**Can this window be 100% duplicated?   95% YES**

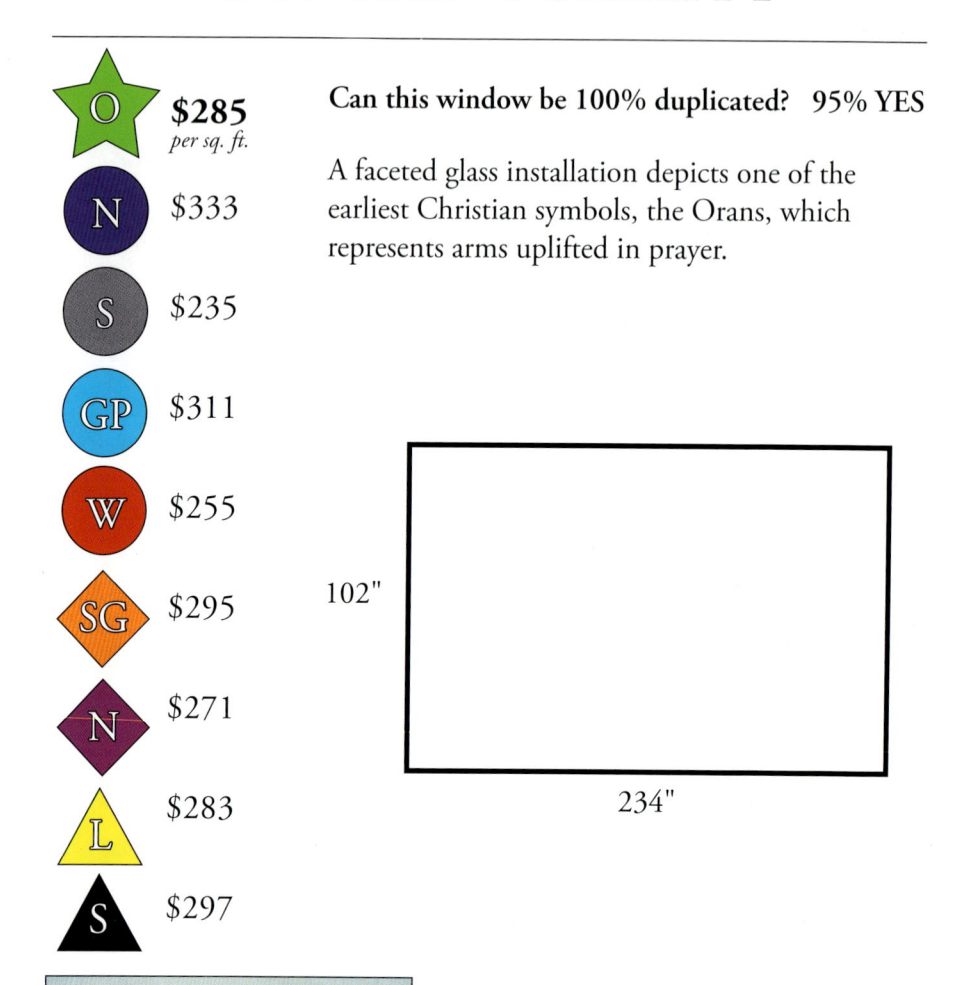

A faceted glass installation depicts one of the earliest Christian symbols, the Orans, which represents arms uplifted in prayer.

102"

234"

St. Michael the Archangel Cemetery, Palatine, Ill.
*Photos courtesy of Conrad Schmitt Studios*

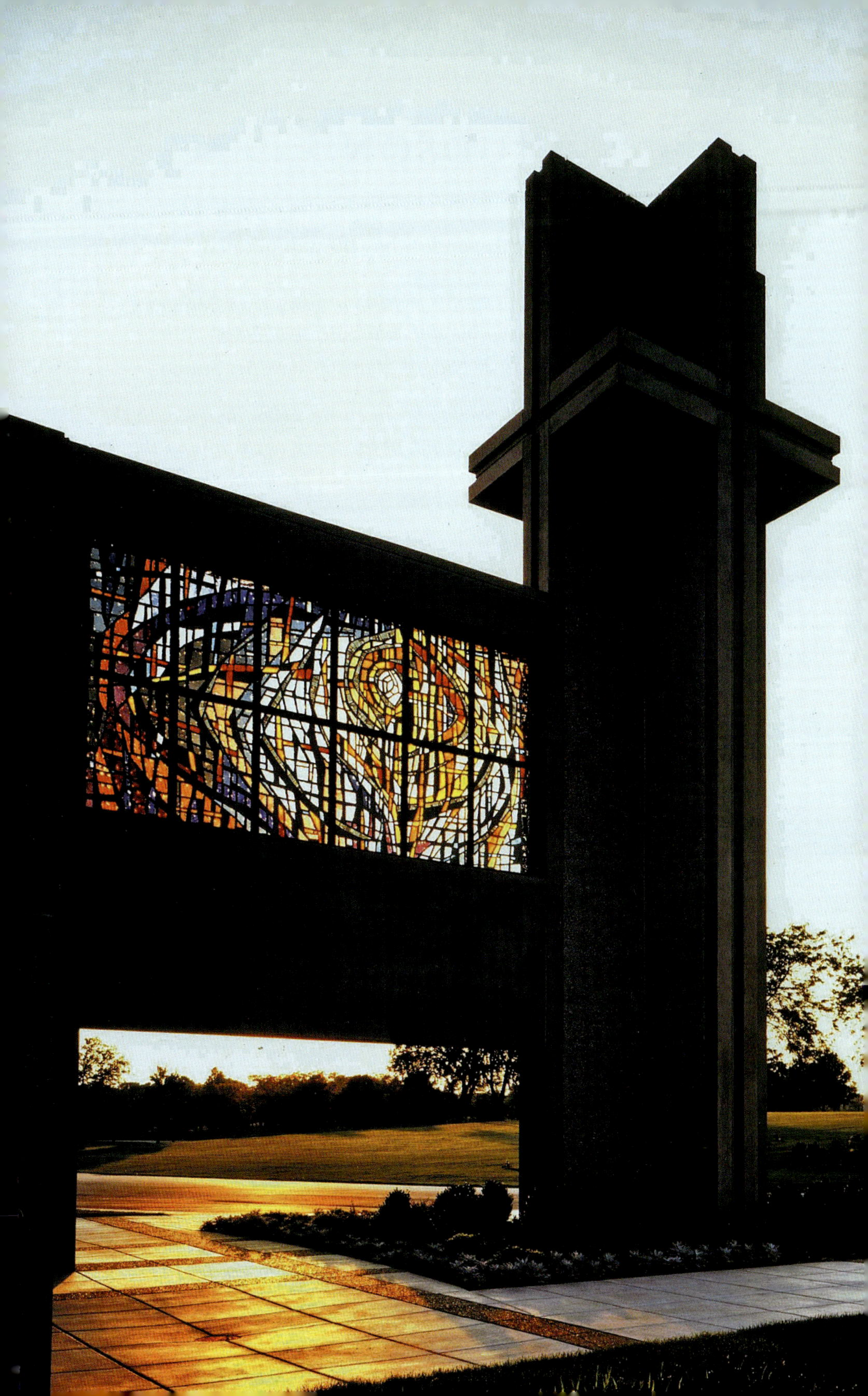

# Judson

| | | |
|---|---|---|
| O | **$252** per sq. ft. | Can this window be 100% duplicated?   95% YES |
| N | $275 | Glass available at Blenko, epoxy resin line clean and clear, no difficulty cuts, good layout.<br>- Glass by Knight Stained Glass Art Studio |
| S | $255 | |
| GP | $264 | This appears to be an entirely glass design with the possible exception of the black circle around the dove's face. If the colors can be matched, then yes, this can be 100% replicated. However, it is a dense design and would involve a fair bit of labor.<br>- Cottage Glass |
| W | $190 | |
| SG | $240 | Segments are very large, apparently requires heavy equipment. - Creative Glassworks |
| N | $269 | |
| L | $238 | 99.5" |
| S | $255 | 30.25" |

Rancho Bernardo Community Presbyterian Church
San Diego, Calif.
*Photos courtesy of Judson Studios*

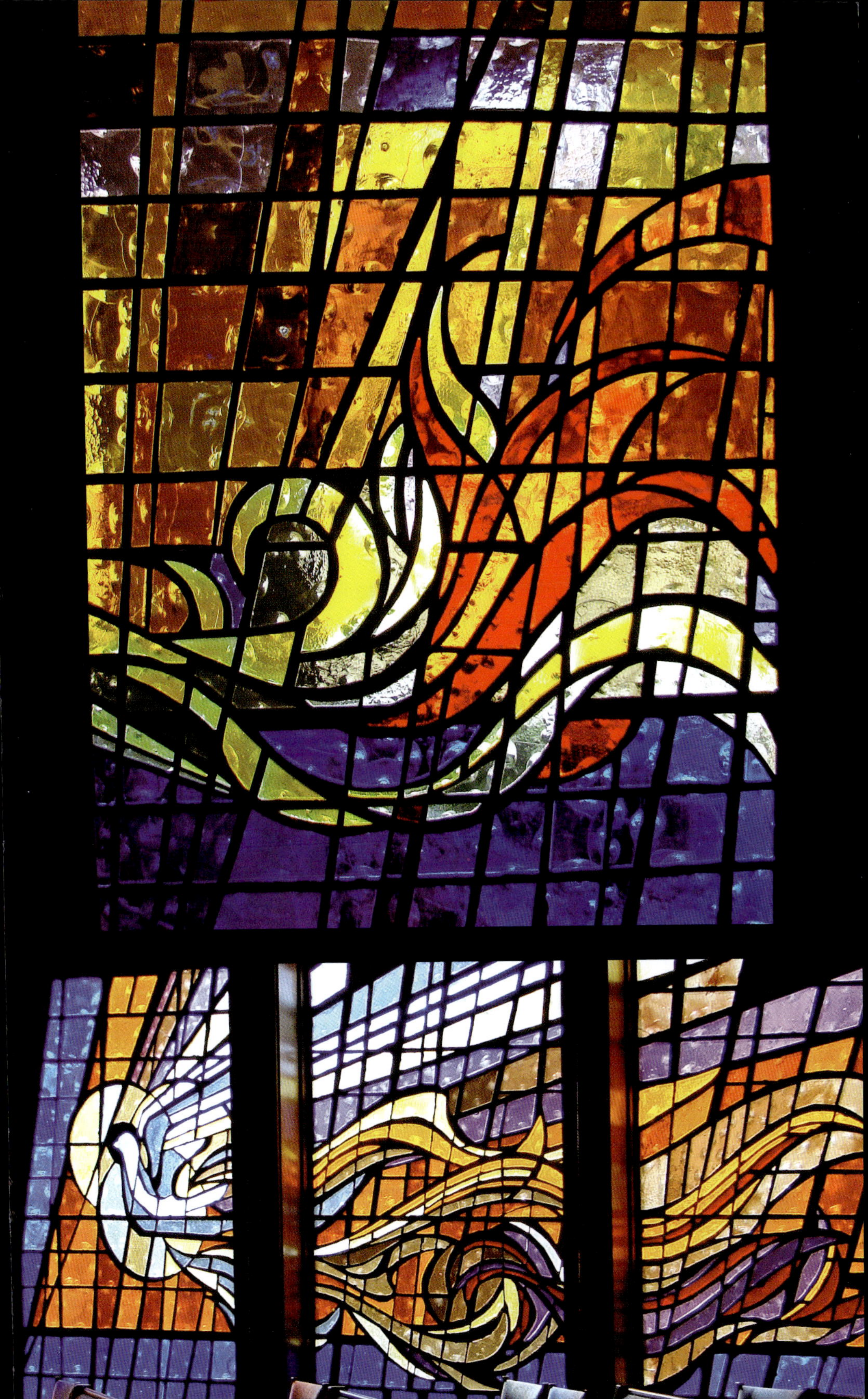

# Loire

| | |
|---|---|
| O | **$277** per sq. ft. |
| N | $290 |
| S | $236 |
| GP | $297 |
| W | $287 |
| SG | $302 |
| N | $236 |
| L | $253 |
| S | $301 |

Can this window be 100% duplicated?   94% YES

*The master of dalleglass!* - Anonymous

*Wonderful color and design, it's falling apart in places.* - Kebrle Stained Glass, Inc.

*Loire windows are usually multi-colored (many blues, for example). The glass was anvil cut in the ones I'm familiar with. Anvil cut means lots of glass waste and slick edges that don't bind well to epoxy. Loire is the "master" in faceted glass for designing color — a great like our American Tiffany. Tiffany did some, a sort of faceted glass long before it was used as a medium for church windows. Tiffany doesn't "hold a candle" to Loire, but a Tiffany would have a higher resale value. One of the details that always makes a faceted glass window hard to exactly duplicate is the facets. Good photos would show the line, design plan and colors — but the facets that give life to the window would be hard to replace if the original window was destroyed by fire.* - Anonymous

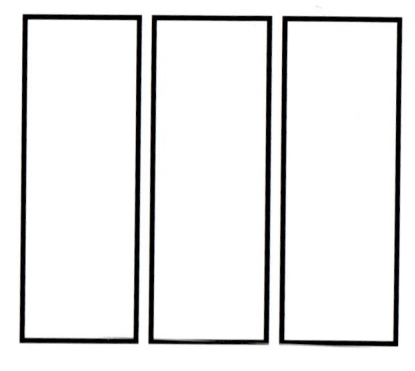

Moody Memorial First United Methodist Church, Galveston, Texas

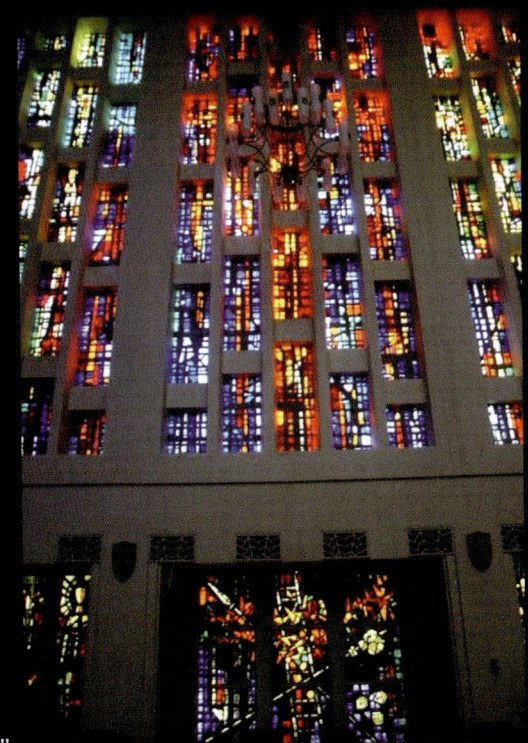

180" x 340"

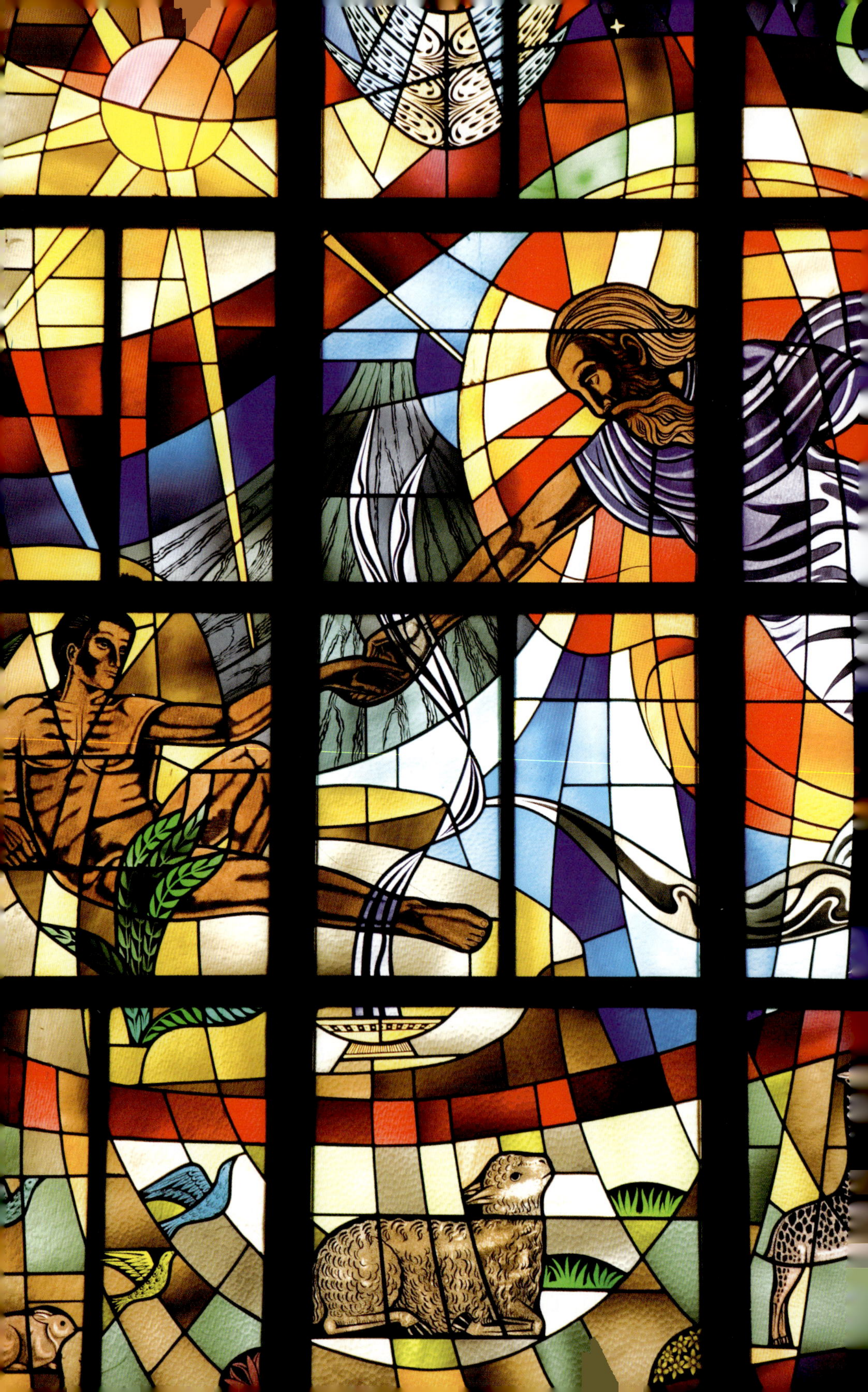

## *Afterword*

# STAINED GLASS IN THE NEW MILLENNIUM

The trend in the first decade of the new millennium is to build large, inexpensive church buildings and to have few, if any, windows, let alone stained glass windows. Audio-visuals and artificial lights are the current rage. Anything that allows permanent light into the darkness is almost taboo!

This is most likely a fad that will soon end. There is simply something inherently wrong with shutting God's light out of worship. There are too many basic needs being unfulfilled. To paraphrase Matthew 5:15-16, *let the church not hide itself under a bushel, but rather let the light shine.* For nine hundred years stained glass has been a theological beacon of inspiration to the world. Sermons end, music stops, and audio-visual programs come and go, but light continues to shine day after day after day. Even more important, the story told by stained glass never ends.

There is the argument that stained glass is too expensive. That it is! But an equal truth is its power to be funded with ease. Families who have lost loved ones are often happy to fund a stained glass memorial window. It is a vision tens of thousands will witness over the lifetime of the window—especially those windows that are lit from the inside, so the world can experience the visual story from the highways of life. What a way to tell God's loving message!

Some leaders may fear the upkeep stained glass requires. Stained glass is, however, much like the motor of an automobile. Drive a car hard and never change the oil and filter, and the major overhaul will not be far ahead. On the other hand, if stained glass receives preventive maintenance and remains protected from the elements, its story telling power will last 150 years before it needs re-leading. It is then ready for another 150 years, as

*Left: Window by Reinarts Stained Glass Studios featured on the cover of "Stained Glass Quarterly of the Stained Glass Association of America"*

long as it receives systematic preventive care. Human beings who have half that lifespan are considered lucky!

There are those who fear the great loss the church would suffer if disaster strikes the stained glass. True, it does happen and the potential of that very fact is the reason for this volume. Obviously, this book recommends those steps to reduce the church's potential for great disaster. Preventive maintenance and proper protective coverings go a long way to help avoid damage involving weather, accidents, vandalism or robbery. Further, stained glass appraisals, photographic records and fine arts insurance coverage decrease the impact of catastrophic loss. Stained glass can rise to inspire again!

Nine hundred years ago, stained glass was created as a way of communicating the Bible to the illiterate masses. Today, most Americans can read, but many are biblically illiterate.

Young people and old men still go to sleep during sermons, yet many confess to have stared with wonder at the magnificence and storytelling ability of the altar's stained glass window. Hopefully, the church and temple will never abandon its greatest communication tool as the next one thousand years of its existence is unfurled.

*Above: Bellevue Baptist Church, Cordova (Memphis), Tenn.*
*Right: First Baptist Church, Germantown, Tenn.*

GO YE INTO ALL THE WORLD AND PREACH THE GOSPEL TO EVERY CREATURE

*Temple Israel, Columbus, OH*

# About the Artists[i]

# Note to Readers

*This list of studios is partial, at best. Many of the great regional artists and studios are not mentioned here. Knowledge of the studio is critical, however, in understanding the replacement value of stained glass. The best volume available to learn the studio background of your stained glass is the* **Biographical Index of Historic American Stained Glass Makers**, *(compiled by Robert O. Jones in conjunction with The SGAA Stained Glass School) published by the Stained Glass Association of America (ISBN: 0-9619640-2-2). The Biographical Index was crucial to this About the Artists section of the Stained Glass Appraisal Guide.*

# Maitland Armstrong

*David Maitland Armstrong* (1836-1918) the founder of Maitland Armstrong & Company was educated at Trinity College, Hartford, CT. Helen Maitland Armstrong (1869-1948) was a designer, painter and studio owner.

Selected Work: *Church of the Ascension; First Presbyterian Church; St. Michael's Catholic Church; Church of the Holy Communion; St. Marks in the Bowery, Appellate Court Building, New York City. All Souls Church, Asheville, NC; Gould Memorial Church, Roxbury, NY; St. Margaret's Church Hibernia, FL; Faith Chapel, Jekyll Island, GA; Sailors Snug Harbor Church, Staten Island; Christ's Church, Marlborough, NY; and Our Lady of Perpetual Hope, Bernardsville, NJ.*[ii]

**All Saints Episcopal Church, Pasadena, Calif.**

# Burnham

*William Herbert Burnham* (1887-1974) was a Boston designer and studio owner. Burnham was educated at the Massachusetts School of Art, and began work with Harry Goodhue from 1904-1908, and then designed for Horace J. Phipps from 1908-1916. In 1920, Burnham became partners with the Phipps, Ball and Burnham Company. He left the firm in 1922 and traveled Europe studying glass, then returned to begin his own studio as designer and craftsman, retiring in 1968. Burnham embraced the Gothic Revival style and did much work for architect Ralph Adams Cram. Burnham is regarded as one of the top American designers of the 20th century. He was honored by the Craftsmanship Medal by the AIA and was made a Fellow and served as President of the Stained Glass Association in 1939-1941.

His son, Wilbur H. Burnham, Jr. joined his father's studio in 1939 after study at the Yale School of Fine Arts. The studio was turned over to his son, Wilbur C. and a partner in the early 1980s.

Selected Works: *Washington Cathedral, Washington, DC; Cathedral of St. John the Divine, NYC; Princeton University Chapel; Church of St. Vincent DePaul; First Cumberland Presbyterian Church, Chattanooga; St. Paul's Episcopal Cathedral, Key West, FL; Mellon Memorial Chapel, Pittsburgh; Worcester Polytechnic Institute; Church of St. Vincent de Paul, Los Angeles; St. Mary's Cathedral, Peoria, IL; and Norfolk Navy Chapel, Norfolk VA.*[iii]

***House of Hope Presbyterian Church, St. Paul, Minn.***

# Connick

*Charles J. Connick* (1875-1945), Boston, MA. Connick was the most prominent advocate of 20th Century American Gothic Revival Windows. He apprenticed with the Rudy Brothers from 1894-1897, then served as manager of Rudy Brothers after J. Horace moved to York in 1903. He then did design work for Spence, Moakler and Bell of Boston, in 1909. The study of windows took him to Europe in 1910. His first actual job was for Ralph Adams Cram, in Arthur Cutter's shop.

Charles J. Connick opened his stained glass studio in Boston in 1913. From this time until it closed in 1986, the Connick Studio designed impressive windows for churches, cathedrals, libraries and chapels. In 1937, Connick authored "Adventures in Light and Color," and served as president of SGAA, from 1931 through 1938. After the death of Charles Connick, the firm continued as Connick & Associates, under the direction of Orin Skinner.

Using pure, intense color and strong linear design, this guild of artists led the revival of the medieval style of stained glass craftsmanship. Their work reflected a strong interest in symbolism in design and color, and stressed the importance of the relationship between the window's design and its surrounding architecture. Windows created by the Connick Studio can be found in approximately 5,000 churches, schools and hospitals around the world.

***Christ and Holy Trinity Church, Westport, Conn.***

Shortly after closing, the studio gave its tremendous collection of records, working drawings and related materials to the Boston Public Library. Selected materials are now available to scholars, historians and researchers from churches and museums throughout the world. The extensive archive contains glass panels and paintings; cartoons for more than 6,000 commissions; watercolor sketches of stained glass windows; light boxes illuminating glass panels; correspondence, insurance appraisals and financial records; clippings about American stained glass craftsmen and the Connick Associates; photographs, glass plate negatives, color slides and blueprints; brass stencils and copper printing plates; and an extensive reference library.[iv]

Selected Works: *Skinner Heinz Chapel, Pittsburgh; St. James Episcopal Cathedral, Hyde Park Union Church and Fourth Presbyterian, Chicago; Emmanuel Episcopal Church, West Roxbury, MA; Chapin Memorial Chapel, Niles, MI; Boston University Theological School; Children's Hospital, Cincinnati; Massachusetts General Hospital Chapel, Boston; National Education Association Building, Washington, DC; Seabury Western Theological Seminary Chapel, Evanston, IL; Buckham Memorial Library, Mt. Holyoke College, Fairbault, MN; St. Vincent Ferrer Church, NYC; Pierce Hall, Kenyon College, Gambler, OH; St. Charles College Chapel, Cantonsville, MD; Sulpician Seminary, Catholic University, Washington, DC.*[v]

# D'Ascenzo

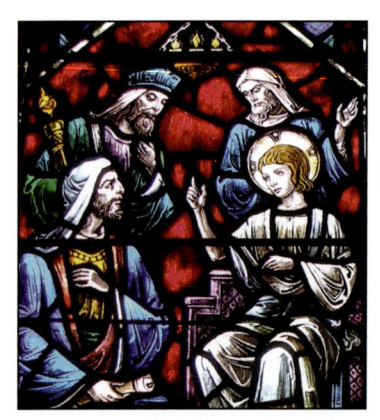

**First Presbyterian Church, Birmingham, Ala.**

*Nicola D'Ascenzo* (1868-1954). Studio Owner; Designer. Philadelphia, PA. Born in Torricella, Italy, he immigrated to the U.S. in 1879. He then studied at the Pennsylvania Academy of Fine Arts, the Pennsylvania Museum, the School of Industrial Art, the New York School of Design, and the *Scoula Libera*, Rome. He was also a musician and played the fiddle. He then served as President of the SGAA, in 1929-1930. Due to illness, he retired in 1948. The Studio during this era was run as a team effort, with profit sharing for its employees. Early work of the Studio was basically Renaissance Style; but by the 1920s this emphasis had evolved to Gothic Revival Style windows. The Studio was run by David Bramick after the death of D'Ascenzo.

Founded in 1896 by Italian and now elderly Nicola D'Ascenzo, the Studios sought to perpetuate in America a long-lost Old World art. The first true 13th Century 'medallion' type window made in the United States is generally credited to Nicola D'Ascenzo (1906). Associated with the studios and following in the footsteps of his illustrious father is his son, Nicola Goodwin D'Ascenzo, who made a name for himself initially as a designer and maker of fine mosaics. It was he who rediscovered the formula for making gold mosaics, held secret by the Venetians for hundreds of years, and which many an artist had spent a lifetime trying to accomplish. The artists of D'Ascenzo Studios rank among the three or four in the world today who are atop the lists in the art of making stained glass windows. They are the designers and makers of many of the outstanding church windows, both in America and in Europe.

The glass used in the memorial windows in the First Presbyterian Church of Birmingham is of the very highest quality. It uses the best French, Belgian and English antique 'pot metal' and ruby-flashed glass obtainable. The techniques employed in making them were substantially the same as those used during medieval times. And, like the centuries-old windows of the cathedrals of Europe, their rich, translucent, jewel-like glass glows with colors that are ever changing, from sunrise, to zenith, to sunset.[vi]

Selected works: *Washington Memorial Chapel, Valley Forge, PA; Folger Shakespeare Library, and National Cathedral, Washington, DC; Riverside Church, NYC; chapels at Yale, Princeton, Georgetown, Garret Park, and Canterbury School, Milford, CT; St. John's Church, Bala Cynwyd, PA; Church of the Nativity, Scranton, PA; Girls' Catholic High School, and Horn and Hardary Restaurant, Philadelphia; Our Lady of Perpetual Help, Brooklyn; Camden, New Jersey, Public Library mosaic; St. George P.E. Church, Sea Bright, NJ; St. James P.E. Church, Bristol, PA.*

# Emil Frei

*Emil Frei, Sr.*, was born in Bavaria in 1869 and studied at the Munich Academy of Art. Upon completion of his studies, he immigrated to New York. In 1898, he was invited to come to St. Louis to undertake the design and execution of stained glass for a large new church then under construction. This project, the stained glass windows for the St. Francis Xavier (College) Church at 239 North Grand, did not, however, come to fruition until a generation later, when it was undertaken by Frei's son and successor, Emil Frei, Jr.

Emil Frei, Jr. was the other pillar of the firm between 1930 and his death in 1967. Born in 1896, he studied art at Washington University before joining his father's firm in 1917. Throughout the 1920s and 1930s he exerted a significant artistic influence within

*Nichols Hills United Methodist Church, Oklahoma City, Okla.*

Emil Frei, Inc., as he worked to recreate the vivid and colorful 13th century medallion style windows like those at the Cathedral of Chartres. It fell to him to design the windows at St. Francis Xavier (College) Church in St. Louis, a project that did much to build his reputation as one of the foremost designers of stained glass in the United States. After his father's death in 1942, Emil Frei, Jr. assumed the presidency of Emil Frei, Inc., retaining that office until 1963, when he became chairman of the board until his death in 1967.

Under the leadership of Emil Frei, Jr., Emil Frei, Inc. rose to even greater heights as a new generation of artists associated with the firm and brought new techniques and different artistic perspectives to the stained glass medium. Due in part to the disruption of World War II and the subsequent liquidation of Emil Frei, Inc.'s assets in Germany, the focus shifted from the German figure style windows to the modernistic and often abstract stained glass windows designed by the company's St. Louis based artists.[vii]

Selected Works: *St. Anthony's Church, St. Francis de Sales Church, Masonic Temple, Shaare Zedec Synagogue, St. Louis; KAM Isaiah Israel Temple, St. Xavier College Library, St Ignatius Church, St. Viator Church, Chicago; Eden Theological Seminary, Webster Grove, MO; Trinity Evangelical Lutheran, St. Petersburg, FL; St. Michael's Catholic Church, Pensacola, FL*.[viii]

# CLEMENT JOHN HEATON

*Clement John Heaton* (1861-1940). He was the founding inspiration for the firm of Heaton, Butler and Bayne of London. Young Clement was apprenticed to Burlison & Grylls, and spent lunch hours in study in the British Museum. At the death of his father, he assumed a position at the firm; but, frustrated by his lack of technical education, he left the firm to learn other techniques.

In 1912, Heaton came to the United States, at the urging of Ralph Adam Cram. He then did windows for the *Cleveland Museum of Art*, and for *Trinity Cathedral*, also in Cleveland for *Huguenot Memorial Church, Pelham Manor,* and for the *Church of the Blessed Sacrament*, NYC. These windows were all made in England.

**Christ Church Episcopal, Grosse Point Farms, Mich.**

Heaton set up a studio in the U.S. after the work at Blessed Sacrament; and then produced *St. Michael's, Litchfield, CT; Kent School Chapel, Kent; Grace Church, Colorado Springs, CO; Christ Church, Grosse Pointe Farms, MI; College of Preachers, Washington Cathedral; Old Colonial Church of St. Philip, Charleston;* and the *First Baptist Church, Montclair, NJ*.[ix]

# JUDSON

In 1897, The Judson Studios was established in Los Angeles by three Judson brothers (Walter H., J. Lionel, and Paul) and their father, William Lees Judson, a noted California artist. The three brothers came to Los Angeles in 1895 at the behest of their father who saw the need for a local stained glass shop. William Lees had apprenticed all three in Toronto, Canada.

The brothers began with the name "Colonial Art Glass Company" when they left Rafael Glass to go on their own in 1897. William Lees even did some of their art work at this time. After Paul left, the business became the W. H. Judson Art Glass Company, and finally incorporated in 1931 as The Judson Studios.

In the early days, work was balanced between religious and secular, between recreating the Gothic effect and working for Frank Lloyd Wright in glass and tile on the Ennis and Barnsdall Houses. Judson Studios became the primary West Coast employer of artist Frederick Wilson, from the 1920s.

By the early '50s the business was controlled by Horace T. Judson, son of Walter H. and his cousin William Rundstrom. In the '60s Horace became sole owner and by 1981 he had sold it to his younger son and daughter-in-law, Karen A. and Walter W. Judson.

**St. James Church, Los Angeles, Calif.**

Judson Studios is still family run, and is currently owned by Karen Judson, her husband Walter Judson having passed away suddenly in January of 2003, and directed by David Judson, fourth and fifth generation respectively. Today the current generation brings a 21st century aesthetic and technological sensibility to the facility and the craft, with over 100 years of tradition and experience.[x]

Selected Works: *Stanford Court Hotel dome, San Francisco; Hollywood Presbyterian Church, All Saints Church, Pasadena, CA; Church at Divinity School of the Pacific, Berkeley, CA; Air Force Academy Chapel, Colorado Springs.*[xi]

# LA FARGE

*John La Farge* (1835-1910). Designer; studio owner, New York City. La Farge was the one who conceived of the opalescent stained glass window, a new, decorative window form. He was granted the first patent for opalescent treatment of windows, in 1880; he then formed the La Farge Decorative Art Company with Mary Tillinghast, from 1883 to 1885. La Farge created the first 'cloisonné' window, '*The Old Philosopher*,' in 1883.

La Farge's work served as the primary inspiration for the stained glass work of Louis Comfort Tiffany. He closely supervised every aspect of the operation, including not only the design but the manufacture of the glass, the placement of lead lines, and the selection of

**Old Stone Church, Cleveland, Ohio**

individual pieces of glass. Until his death in 1909, he maintained the dictum "window decoration is the art of painting in air with a material carrying colored light."[xii]

Henry Adams described La Farge as *"the greatest innovator in the history of modern stained glass. His key breakthrough, of course, was the discovery of opalescent glass, which made possible a host of previously undreamed-of pictorial effects…La Farge manufactured glass of every type: glass that was textured by rollers; glass that was folded to resemble drapery; glass that was cast in molds to assume special shapes—for example, to resemble the petals of a flower; glass that was cut or chipped into facets like a jewel; and glass that had bits of colored glass sprinkled into it in decorative patterns."*[xiii]

These new varieties of glass suggested the incorporation of other materials; and La Farge exploited this idea exuberantly, utilizing broken bottles, slices of alabaster, bits of quartz, and even semi-precious stones.

Selected Works: *Chicago Board of Trade, and Second Presbyterian Church, Chicago; 'Battle' window, Harvard Memorial Hall; Trinity Church, Boston; Church of the Ascension, and Judson Memorial Church, New York City; Unity Church, North Easton, MA, and First Congregational Church, Methuen, MA; and First Unitarian Church, Philadelphia.*[xiv]

# Lamb

*J & R Lamb Studios*, New York (1857-present). J. and R. Lamb Studios was founded in 1857 in New York City by two British-born brothers, Joseph and Richard Lamb, who were enthusiastic about the Gothic Revival and related movements for religious reform.

Joseph was the chief designer and salesman, while Richard, a woodworker, managed the production side. Lamb Studios was apparently the first firm in the United States to specialize in religious artwork and played a significant role in promoting a higher standard of craftsmanship and design in American ecclesiastical art during the latter half of the nineteenth century.[xv]

The addition of stained glass was probably associated with the period when Joseph's son Charles Rollinson Lamb (1860-1942) left his college architectural studies and began designing for the Studios at age 16 in 1876. Under his influence and promotional talents, the firm soon expanded into stained glass and glass mosaic, including extensive secular commissions, and also began designing in a more eclectic mixture of revival and contemporary styles, including Celtic, Romanesque, Renaissance, Second Empire and Art Nouveau.[xvi]

Their workshops produced various ecclesiastical arts and published promotional catalogues of its work. The studios won medals at the Philadelphia Exposition in 1876, as well as at all later American expositions. They won gold medals at the Pan-American Exposition in Buffalo, and at the 1900 Paris Exposition.[xvii]

The J&R Lamb Studios has been serving the religious community for 150 years making it the oldest continuously operating stained glass studio in the United States. Over the years, Lamb has created approximately 15,000 original stained glass windows in every state in America and abroad, and more than 8,000 windows have been restored, some in the most important architectural works ever built in this country.[xviii]

Selected Works: *Stanford University Chapel, CA; Plymouth Church, Brooklyn; Church of the Advent, Kenmore, NY; Protestant and Catholic chapels, Camp Le Jeune, NC; Old Mariner's Church, Detroit; St. Michael's Church, Marble Collegiate Church, NYC; First Presbyterian Church, Orange, TX; St. Peter's Church, Charlotte Memorial Hospital, Charlotte, NC; Old Stone Church, Cleveland, OH; Church of the Ascension, Buffalo, NY; St. Philip's Church, Wrangell, AK; Flower Memorial Library, Watertown, NY; Sage Chapel, Cornell University, Ithaca, NY; Navy Family Chapel, Long Beach, CA; Puget Sound Navy Yard Chapel, Bremerton, WA; Parke Memorial Chapel, St. Andrews Cathedral, Honolulu; St. John's Episcopal Church, Tampa, FL.*[xix]

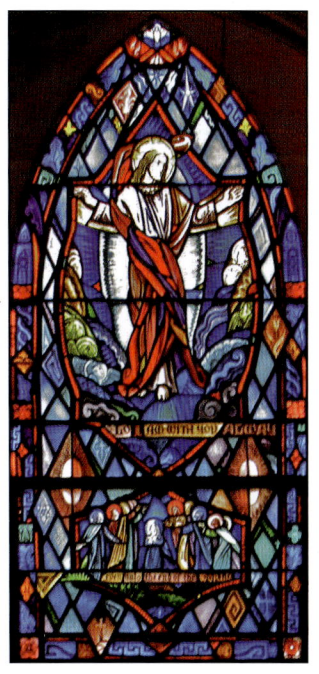

*St. Peter's Episcopal Church, Charlotte, N.C.*

# Rowan LeCompte

*Rowen LeCompte.* Born in Baltimore, Md., in 1925, LeCompte began making windows at age 14. His first commission at 16 was for the Episcopal Washington National Cathedral in 1941. Serving in Europe during World War II, LeCompte later attended the *New School of Social Research* and the *Institute of Contemporary Art.*

Selected Work: *Creation Rose Window and clerestory windows in National Cathedral; House of Hope Presbyterian Church, St. Paul, MN.*[xx]

*House of Hope Presbyterian Church, St. Paul, Minn.*

# Gabriel Loire

*Gabriel Loire.* Monsieur Loire was born in 1904 into a family of tanners in the small town of Pouance, in the northwest of France. He received his education at Combree College and at the Catholic University of Angers. There he met the stained glass masters of the cathedral and, at the age of 20, published his thesis on the art of stained glass.

In 1946, M. Loire founded his own studio, 'La Clarte' (or Clarity), in Leves. He has composed and installed or executed stained glass all over the world. Among his creations in this country are the *Presbyterian Church of Stamford, CT; Grace Cathedral in San Francisco;* churches in Allentown and Harrisburg, PA; Tacoma, WA; and Massillon, OH.

In the years before his death, on December 27, 1996, M. Loire designed the stained glass tower in Hakone, Japan; made windows for the *Thanksgiving Chapel in Dallas*; created windows for the *Prisoners' Conscience Chapel, in Salisbury Cathedral, England; the Catholic Church of St. George the Martyr, in Cape Town, South Africa,* and for the *Cathedral in Casablanca, Morocco;* and he worked in Windsor, England, on the windows in St. George's Chapel, dedicated to Lord Mountbatten.[xxi]

**St. Stephen Presbyterian, Fort Worth, Texas, 1969**

# Franz Mayer

In 1847, *Joseph Gabriel Mayer* (1808-1883) founded the '*Institute for Christian Art.*' He visualized a company that was "a combination of fine arts, architecture, sculpture and painting" to revitalize the medieval building trades. Around 1860, a stained glass department was created. In 1865, the first overseas branch was opened in London. Then, in 1882, the company was awarded the status, '*Royal Bavarian Art Establishment,*' by King Ludwig II. Following this, the studio moved into a rich and active period with over 500 employees and worldwide business connections. This was achieved during the management of Franz Borgias Mayer (1848-1926), who was the founder's son.

In 1888, a new branch was opened in New York City, a move that brought the company into full international status. Pope Leo XIII, in 1892 named the company a '*Pontifical Institute of Christian Art.*'

After the conclusion of World War I, Franz Borgias Mayer's sons, Anton (1886-1967), Karl (1880-1967), and Adaberrt (1894-1987) took over management. In 1925, the ecclesiastical sculpture department was dropped from the business and a mosaic department took its place.

The company was transformed into an artist's studio for stained glass and mosaic. From that point forward, many freelance artists and architects began to use the services of the studio. During the post-World War II years, mosaic was brought to new heights, in terms of its applications to architectural art, due to intensive artistic studies, and new technical and technological developments.

From the beginning, restoration and reconstruction of historic stained glass and mosaics were important. New experiences and procedures in these fields have, over the span of generations, assisted in the realization of these sorts of projects and programs. The complicated technique of thermo-insulated glass systems was studied in order to enable and expedite the preservation of medieval and stained glass from previous decades and centuries. This technique was used initially in 1952, for a large-scale restoration project for the Munich Cathedral (Germany).

*Saint Mary Cathedral, Austin, Texas*

In the early 1890s the 'Floatglass Painting' department was created. Today the company is managed by Gabriel Mayer (1938-) and his son Michael C. Mayer (1967-), who is of the fifth generation to find involvement at this level with the company.[xxii]

# Munich of Chicago

*The Munich Studio*, Chicago (1903-1957) was founded by Max Guler, a designer, Guler was trained as a china painter in Munich, and immigrated to Chicago in the United States. He founded Munich Studio and served as the primary designer for the firm. This studio designed richly detailed religious windows. Guler designed for Drehobl Brothers, in 1935.

Selected Work: *St. Agnes Church, St. Veronica Church, St. Leo's Church, St. Philip's Church, Our Lady of Sorrows Church, and St. Margaret Church, Chicago; St. Mary's, Easton, MA.*[xxiii]

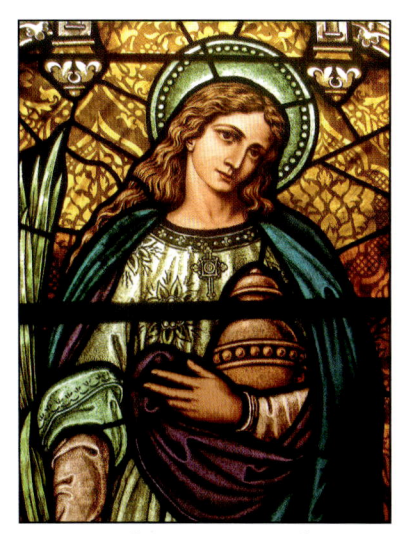

*Holy Rosary Parish, Bozeman, Mont.*

*St. John's Episcopal Cathedral, Jacksonville, Fla.*

# George Payne

George Hardy Payne originally founded the Payne Studios in 1896. The studio contributed to the early American arrival of stained glass. Working in both opalescent-type windows and painted stained glass, the Payne Studios rivaled both Tiffany and the Lamb Studios.

George Hardy Payne served his apprenticeship in England in 1862 under the direction of John Richard Clayton and Alfred Bell. His apprenticeship lasted seven years.

After working several years in the studios of Clayton and Bell, George Hardy Payne ventured to America along with his wife Elizabeth and established the Payne Studios.

Upon the death of George Hardy Payne, his son, George L. Payne, who had worked alongside his dad, continued to enlarge the operation of the studio.

The Payne Studio expanded to England and France having workshops design and fabricate their commissions for the U.S. The studio also included the services of Church lighting fixtures, bells, carillons and chimes, chancel furnishings and silverware and was located in Patterson, NJ.

In the early thirties, the studio ran into hard times and merged with the Spears Studio, which became the Payne Spears Studio. This lasted into the early forties when George Payne once again went on his own. One of America's foremost Designers and Painters, Per Bergethon, in the early fifties became an associate of the Payne Studio where he created hundreds of traditional and colonial style stained glass windows throughout America. Frederick Cole and Ronald Page also worked at this time in England for the Payne Studio.

George L. Payne died in 1980 and in 1981 his widow sold all assets to Rohlf's Studio in New York.

The Payne Studios were responsible for literally thousands of stained glass windows, along with some of the most renowned commissions and cathedrals in the U.S. and abroad.[xxiv]

Selected Work: *Church of the Ascension, Montgomery, AL; St. Stephen's Roman Catholic Church, Winooski, VT; St. Margaret's Episcopal Church, Boston, MA; Grace Methodist Church, Atlanta. Under the name of Payne-Spiers Studio: St. Mary's Hospital Chapel, Passaic, NJ, Presbyterian Hospital Chapel, Newark, NJ; French Hospital Chapel, Veteran's Hospital Chapel, Beth Israel Hospital Chapel, NYC; Chapel at Ft. Bragg, NC; St. John's Church, Flushing, NY; St. Marks Church, Baltimore; St. James Church, Hyde Park, NY.*[xxv]

*Trinity Lutheran Church, Houston, TX; Trinity Episcopal Church, Columbus, OH; St. Agnes Catholic Church, Dalton, OH; Church of the Ascension, Hickory, NC; St. Anna's Church, New Orleans, LA; Northminster Baptist Church, Richmond, VA; Zion Evangelist Church, Ridgefield, NJ; University of the South, Sewanee, GA; Trinity Episcopal Church, Tulsa, OK; Trinity Church, Fredericksburg, VA.*[xxvi]

# Rambusch

*F. C. V. Rambusch,* NYC. Rambusch emigrated from Denmark in 1889. He then worked for Gibson Art Glass, and then formed his own decorating company.

*Harold Rambusch.* Harold Rambusch was active from 1944 through 1985. He began stained glass production in 1930, with Gustav Bernhardt and William Haley as designers. He served additionally as President of SGAS in 1947.

*Rambusch Decorating Company,* NYC. 1898-present. Glass production since 1930. This firm was founded by F. C. V. Rambusch and William Hencken. Prior to 1930, their designs were fabricated by Puhl-Wagner-Heinersdorff studio in Berlin. Early designers included Gustav Bernhardt and William 'Bud' Haley.

Selected Work: *Chapel of the Holy Cross, and St. John Seminary, Brighten, MA; Notre Dame Seminary Chapel, New Orleans; Naval Air Station Chapels, Jacksonville, FL; St. Mary's Church, Omaha; St. Ambrose Church, Bridgeport, CT; Indiana World War Memorial Hall, Indianapolis; Lutheran Theological Seminary Chapel, Gettysburg, PA; Trinity Church, Hewlett, Long Island; German Catholic Orphanage, Buffalo; State Hospital, Massillon, OH; St. Anthony's Hospital, St. Petersburg, FL; Christ Episcopal Church, Pensacola, FL.*[xxvii]

**University Baptist Church, Fort Worth, Texas, 1974**

# Rohlf

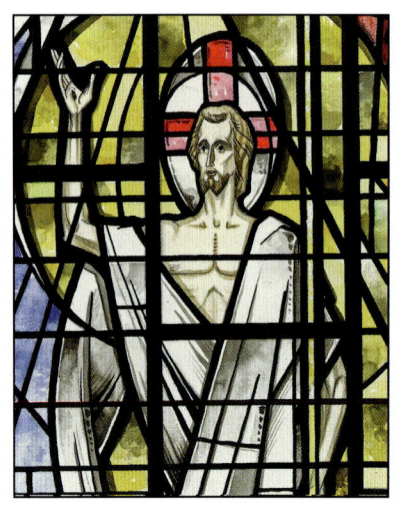

*Church of St. Frances of Rome, Bronx, N.Y.*

Rohlf's Studio was established in 1920. Hans Rohlf was the first generation by the name to run the company. The studio was located in the South Bronx. Hans died in 1958 at the age of 65. His son, Peter A. Rohlf (second generation) took the reins at age 17. In 1963, he moved the studio to the Cross Bronx Expressway in northern Bronx and expanded it from a five-person operation to fifteen persons.

In 1978, the studio was then moved again to its present location in Mount Vernon, NY. In 1985, Peter Hans Rohlf (third generation) joined the company full-time after graduating college. In 2001, Peter A. became Chairman and CEO and Peter Hans took the title of President. In 1988, Greg Rohlf joined the firm and spent fourteen years in the studio learning all aspects of the craft, including the management of the faceted glass operation and the exercise of the position of head selector. In 2000, Greg joined the sales staff and is currently Vice President. In January of 1981, following the death of George L. Payne, Rohlf's Studio acquired the Payne Studios of Patterson, NJ, one of America's oldest stained glass companies.

Rohlf's Studio has worked and collaborated with some of America's and Europe's greatest artists and painters, including Per Bergethon, Frederick Cole, Ron Page, Franz Schroeder and Frank Kaufel. Rohlf's Studio now employs approximately 35 craftspeople and four full-time artists and works with five additional freelance designers. Their commissions can be seen worldwide in places such as Africa, Israel, Iceland, Venezuela, Haiti and Mexico. In New York, Rohlf's Studio has performed restoration on stained glass edifices such as St. Patrick's Cathedral, the Riverside Church and Trinity Church on Wall Street. Rohlf's is presently the artisan for the Cathedral of St. John the Divine in New York City and Yale University in New Haven, CT.[xxviii]

# Conrad Schmitt

*Conrad Schmitt* (1867-1940). Designer, Studio Owner; Milwaukee, WI. Born in Wisconsin Conrad Schmitt entered business school in 1881 and was undertaking art commissions by 1889. By 1905, he and his group had organized as the Conrad Schmitt Studios. Conrad Schmitt Studios provided artwork for churches, estates, theatres, court houses, banks and other public buildings throughout the country; and stained glass work was began in 1920. This work included *St. John the Baptist Church*, Quebec, Canada; the *Apostolic Nunciature* (Vatican Embassy), in Washington, D.C.; the *Basilica of St. Josaphat* in Milwaukee; and the *Scared Heart Church* at the University of Notre Dame in South Bend, IN. An office in New York was opened in 1929.

When his father died, in 1940, Rupert Schmitt followed him as director of the studio; and he served as President of the Stained Glass Association, from 1950-1952. Employee Bernard O. Gruenke worked closely with Rupert after 1945 and then bought the Studio in 1953.

Gruenke produced what was probably the first faceted glass window in the U.S. '*Christ on a Rainbow*' in 1949. Bernard's original panels toured the country, demonstrating this novel window medium. Gruenke's son, Bernard M. Gruenke, joined CSS full time in the 1950s. Together with his father, he patented a glass etching technique known as "*Leptact*," in 1973.

A third Gruenke generation currently leads the Conrad Schmitt Studios. Heidi Gruenke Emery and Gunar Gruenke have directed and participated in hundreds of projects, from the *Wang Center for the Performing Arts* in Boston, to *St. Mary's Cathedral* in Colorado Springs.[xxix]

**St. Francis of Assisi Church, Donaldsonville, La.**

Selected Work: *St. Ambrose Cathedral, Des Moines, IA; Trinity Episcopal Church, Columbus, GA; St. Joseph's Catholic Church, Milwaukee; Marquette University.*[xxx] *St. Vincent de Paul Church, Chicago, IL; Annunciation Greek Orthodox Church, Wauwatosa, WI; All Faiths Chapel at Boys Town, Omaha, NE; St. Elizabeth Ann Seton Church, Keller, TX; St. Mary's Greek Ruthenain Church, New York, NY; St. Michael the Archangel Cemetery, Palatine, IL; Temple Emmanuel B'ne Jeshurun, Mequon, WI; and First Congregational Church, Kenosha, WI and St. Elizabeth Ann Seton Church, New Berlin, WI.*

# Louis Comfort Tiffany

As the scion of one of the country's most successful luxury goods merchants, Louis Comfort Tiffany (1848-1933) was exposed to the finer things in life. His father, Charles Lewis Tiffany, was a founder and principal owner of Tiffany & Company, the highly successful New York City jewelry and fancy goods store. Indeed, it was this family business, which gave Louis C. Tiffany both the "know how" and financial backing needed to form his own series of commercial enterprises.

After completing his formal schooling at the Eaglewood Military Academy in New Jersey, Louis Tiffany, enticed by the fine arts, continued to enrich his education through travel abroad and study with the highest-ranking artists of the period. Profoundly influenced by the American landscapist George Inness, Tiffany proved to be a competent painter and remarkable colorist in his own right. Although he was to remain a painter throughout his lifetime, while still in his twenties, Tiffany turned most of his attention and enormous creative energies to the design, manufacture and retail of decorative arts objects, a natural progression for a son of Tiffany & Company. Tiffany believed that the decorative arts were more important to a nation than were the 'fine' arts. "Artists who devote their talent to making things of use beautiful are educators of the people in the truest sense."

Tiffany began experimenting with glass, his own special area of interest. At first attempting to reproduce the properties found in medieval stained glass windows and ancient glass discovered in archaeological excavations, Tiffany raised the bar by striving for a combination of myriad colors and textures, as well as translucence in the flat opalescent and blown iridescent glass that he and his staff created. Eventually, Tiffany's enormous glass inventory of more than 5,000 different colors and textures enabled him to "paint with glass" and imbue his interior designs, windows and lamps with light and color effects heretofore unknown.

**North Avenue Presbyterian Church, Atlanta, Ga.**

Tiffany's work in glass brought him his greatest success as an artist and a businessman. In 1883 he established a succession of New York City-based firms primarily devoted to the manufacture and sale of glass objects. His firms initially made religious and figural windows for churches (his main source of income) and landscape and floral windows for the private and business sectors. Although Tiffany was the artist behind the glass, he hired the best creative talents of the era including the revered Hudson River school painter Frederic E. Church, the Albany muralist Will H. Low, and the Aesthetic Movement artist Elihu Vedder, to provide ideas, concepts, and designs for his window commissions.

During the early 1890s Tiffany, working with master glassmaker Arthur J. Nash and a team of chemists, designers and artisans based at his Corona (Queens), New York glass factory, produced the iridescent blown glass patented as *Favrile*. The resultant metallic iridescence became the hallmark of Tiffany glass.[xxxi]

Tiffany is considered the best known American stained glass designer and studio owner. His companies took several forms and names: 1879, Louis C. Tiffany and Associated artists; and in 1884-1892, the Tiffany Glass Company. It was changed briefly to Tiffany Glass and Decorating Company and finally simply as Tiffany Studios (1904-1933).[xxxii]

It is important to note that Louis Comfort Tiffany relied on the enormous financial and entrepreneurial resources of his father's firm, Tiffany & Company. Although Tiffany & Company and Tiffany Studios were two distinct and separate firms, Louis Tiffany was affiliated with both in an executive capacity. He was, therefore, able to advertise and sell Tiffany Studios' products at Tiffany & Company. Although Tiffany lamps, windows and decorative accessories continued to be made through the 1920s, the heyday of production ended at the onset of World War I, when European markets closed and tastes changed.[xxxiii]

# Willet

William Willet, an artist and leader in the American Gothic Movement, founded Willet Studios studio in 1898. Working with noted architect Ralph Adams Cram, William created traditional designs that rivaled the works found in the finest European Cathedrals. In 1910, William Willet was invited to compete for the large chancel window in the Cadet's Chapel at the United States Military Academy at West Point. After winning the competition, Willet Studios was selected to design and fabricate all of the stained glass windows in this large cathedral-like building. In that the cadets desired to give the window sections as class gifts, the commission lasted 66 years and became the longest continuing stained glass commission in American history.

Richard Gross, editor of *The Stained Glass Quarterly*, believes that William Willet *"laid the foundation for a new twentieth century revival when he founded his studio in Philadelphia in 1898. He designed windows of painted, richly colored antique glass with his figures reflecting a full-figured Renaissance influence that was the taste of the times. His wife, Anne Lee Willet, who ran the studio for a time after his death, assisted him in his work."* [xxxiv]

William's son, Henry Lee Willet (1899-1983), took over the studio after his father's death. Under Henry Lee's guidance, the company expanded from a regional studio to a national studio, with completed projects in all 50 states and 14 foreign countries. Willet Studios experimented with new techniques and in the 1950s, Willet Studios was one of

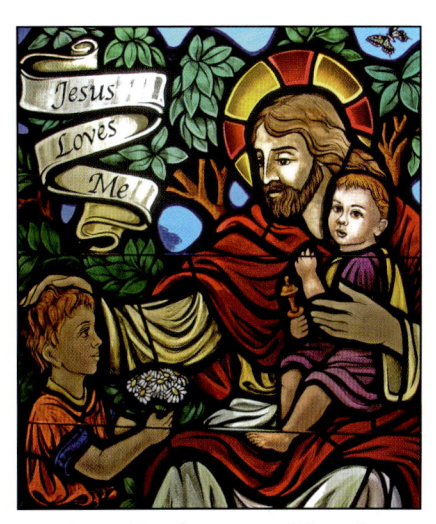

***First Presbyterian Church, Plymouth, Mich.***

the first American studios to design and fabricate faceted glass windows. Willet Studios also developed the famous sculptured gold window technique and experimented with different methods of laminating stained glass. Under Henry Lee's leadership, Willet Studios became known and respected throughout the stained glass world. He served as President of the SGAA in 1942-1943.

In 1965, E. Crosby Willet, the son of Henry Lee Willet, became the President of Willet Studios. Under his leadership, Willet windows were created for many of the major churches and cathedrals in the United States, including the National Cathedral in Washington, D.C. and Saint Mary's Cathedral in San Francisco.

In 1977, Willet Studios became a division of the Hauser Art Glass Co., Inc. Crosby Willet continued with the studio as President and Art Director of the Willet division. In 2005, the company changed its name to Willet Hauser Architectural Glass, but continues with Crosby Willet and the second generation of the Hauser family (James A. Hauser and Michael Hauser) maintaining the quality that has long been associated with the studio. To date, the studio has completed windows in over 15,000 buildings located throughout the world.[xxxv]

Selected Work: *St. Martins, Philadelphia; Covenant Presbyterian, Charlotte, NC; Druid Hills Presbyterian Church, Catholic Co-Cathedral of Christ the King, Atlanta; First Presbyterian Church, Pittsburgh; Proctor Hall and Chapel, Princeton; West Point Military Academy Chapel; Cathedral of St. John the Divine, NYC; Washington National Cathedral, DC; Grace Episcopal Cathedral, San Francisco; St. Matthew's Roman Catholic Church, Conshohocken, PA; Holy Trinity Church, Calvary Protestant Episcopal Church, St. Matthew's Catholic Church, Philadelphia; Trinity Cathedral, Cleveland; St. Paul's Roman Catholic Cathedral, Pittsburgh; Church of the Holy Spirit, Asbury Park; Greenwood Cemetery Chapel, Brooklyn; Episcopal Hospital Chapel, Washington, DC; Garrett Bible Institute Chapel, Evanston, IL.*[xxxvi]

# F. X. Zettler

Franz Xavier Zettler, Joseph Gabriel Mayer's son-in-law, originally worked in the window portion of the Mayer business, before striking out on his own in 1870. His fledgling company achieved its first success with award-winning windows displayed at the 1873 International Exhibition at Vienna. By the end of the decade, Zettler's firm had 150 employees. In 1882 the company was appointed as the *"Royal Bavarian Art Institute for Stained Glass"* by King Ludwig II (the "Mad King" who was a patron of composer Richard Wagner and builder of the fairy-tale like *Neuschwainstein Castle*).

Both the Mayer and Zettler studios perfected what became known as the "Munich Style," which was copied by more than a dozen other window makers who set up shop in the area. In this method, the religious scenes were painted on larger sheets of glass, and then fused to the glass through firing in intense heat. This allowed for a blending of colors not attainable by the old medieval style, in which any change of color in a scene required a separate piece of colored glass, which had to be cut-to-size and fitted in its own leaded framework.

In the windows of the Munich school, the leaded seams did not interrupt or intrude upon the scene portrayed, but were camouflaged by the design in a way that made them hardly noticeable. The new

**Saint Mary Cathedral, Austin, Texas**

style also allowed for extremely detailed depictions of their subjects. The scenes depicted were heavily influenced by the emotion and sentimentality of the 19th century European Romantic style of painting, and the detail and ornateness of the German Baroque style.

The use of perspective (where an object in the background of a scene is depicted smaller than an object in the foreground to give a sense of depth) was used in the latter part of the medieval age and during the Renaissance. Zettler is widely recognized as the master of this technique and is credited with being the first to use three-point perspective in stained glass windows.

Zettler windows can be found in such notable American edifices as Newark's *Sacred Heart Basilica*, Philadelphia's *National Shrine of St. Rita of Cascia, Immaculate Conception Cathedral* in Denver, and *Cathedral of St. Helena* in Montana.

When the 20th century began, the Mayer and Zettler firms were the world's leading producers of stained glass, employing nearly 500 craftsmen and artists between them.

"Professor Franz," as Zettler was known to students and admirers, died in 1916 at the age of 75. The F.X. Zettler Co. merged with its old rival, Mayer & Company in 1939.[xxxvii]

# ENDNOTES

[i] The biographies that follow were taken from other sources. Other than provide editing throughout, none of this material was written by the compilers of The Stained Glass Appraisal Guide.

[ii] Jones, Robert O (compiled by). Biographical Index of Historic American Stained Glass Makers, Stained Glass Association of America, Raytown, MO, 2002, page 19. This book was completed in conjunction with the SGAA Stained Glass School.

[iii] Jones, Biographical Index, page 19.

[iv] From the Charles J. Connick Stained Glass Foundation Web site.

[v] Jones, Biographical Index, page 26.

[vi] From "A History of the First Presbyterian Church of Birmingham," Alabama, published in 1952. It was published during the eightieth anniversary of the founding of the church, and during the pastorate of the Reverend Edward V. Ramage, D. D. It was arranged and edited by Clarence M. Kilian.

[vii] Missouri Historical Society: Emil Frei, Jr., Collection, Register by Martha Ramsey Clevenger Manuscript Processor Division of Library and Archives, June 1986.

[viii] Jones, Biographical Index, page 43.

[ix] Jones, Biographical Index, page 53.

[x] From Judson Stained Glass Web site.

[xi] Jones, Biographical Index, pages 63 and 64.

[xii] La Farge, "Window," in *Dictionary of Architecture*, vol. 3, col. 1080.

[xiii] Essay by Henry Adams, "The Mind of John La Farge" in John La Farge, Abbeville Press, New York, 1987, page 41.

[xiv] Jones, Biographical Index, page 70.

[xv] Catalogue on Figure Glass Work (New York: J. And R. Lamb, 1893), page 4. Quotes Moses King, *King's Handbook of the United States* to this effect. Used by David Adams, *J. and R. Lamb Studios, The First 75 years, 1857-1932*" in Stained Glass, Quarterly of the Stained Glass Association of America (Volume 102, Number 2, Summer 2007), page 120.

[xvi] Adams, *J. and R. Lamb Studios*, page 122.

xvii  Jones, Biographical Index, page 71.

xviii  Information from the J & R Lamb Web site.

xix  Jones, Biographical Index, pages 70-72.

xx  Jones, Biographical Index, page 74.

xxi  <u>Gabriel Loire: Les Vitraux [Stained Glass]</u>, by Charles W. and Joan C. Pratt. Pomme Press, 1997.

xxii  Adapted from the 'Mayer of Munich, Inc.' Web site.

xxiii  Jones, Biographical Index, page 85.

xxiv  Courtesy Peter Rohlf, Rohlf Stained Glass.

xxv  Jones, Biographical Index, pages 93 and 94.

xxvi  From Rohlf Studios files.

xxvii  Jones, Biographical Index, page 101.

xxviii  Bio information provided by Rohlf Studio.

xxix  From Conrad Schmitt Studios brochure.

xxx  Jones, Biographical Index, page 110.

xxxi  <u>Stained Glass</u>, by Lawrence Lee, George Selden and Francis Stephens; Crown Publishers, Inc., New York, pages 156 and 157.

xxxii  Jones, Biographical Index, page 122.

xxxiii  A major portion of the Tiffany biography was taken from the Albany Institute for History and Art website.

xxxiv  Richard Gross, "History of Stained Glass" Stained Glass Association of America Web site, page 19.

xxxv  Willet history provided by Willet Hauser Studios.

xxxvi  Jones, Biographical Index, pages 132 and 133.

xxxvii  Adopted from the Web site: F.X. Zettler & The Royal Bavarian Art Institute: Crafters of St. Martin's Windows

St. Mary's Episcopal Cathedral, Memphis, Tenn.
Studio of Len R. Howard, Kent, Conn.

# Stained Glass Association of America Members

**A & H Art & Stained Glass Co., Inc.**
P.O. Box 67
3374 Harmony Highway
Harmony, NC 28634
(704) 546-2687
ahstainglass@yadtel.net
www.ahstainedglass.com

**Advent Glass Works, Inc.**
P.O. Box 174
242 SW George Glen
Ft. White, FL 32038
(888) 528-8803
tgatagw@alltel.net
www.adventglassworks.com

**Art Glass Crafters, Inc.**
16908 York Road
Monkton, MD 21111-1033
(410) 329-6005
kimberelite@wildblue.net

**Artistic Designs Enterprises**
3873 El Paso Alto
San Marcos, CA 92069
(800) 339-6259
mtatina@ix.netcom.com
www.artisticdesign.org

**Artistic Stained Glass Studio**
607 Flaten Court
Eau Claire, WI 54703-5901
(715) 832-4110
pdgbill@charter.net

**Bera Stained Glass Studios**
760 North Twin Oaks Valley Road, #A
San Marcos, CA 92069-1775
(760) 744-9282
nicole@beraglass.com
www.beraglass.com

**Beyer Studio, Inc.**
9511 Germantown Avenue
Philadelphia, PA 19118
(215) 848-3502
mail@beyerstudio.com
www.beyerstudio.com

**Botti Studio of Architectural Arts, Inc.**
919 Grove Street
Evanston, IL 60201-4315
(800) 524-7211
botti@bottistudio.com
www.bottistudio.com

**Bovard Studio, Inc.**
2281 Highway 34 East
Fairfield, IA 52556-8560
(800) 452-7796
info@bovardstudio.com
www.bovardstudio.com

**Bullas Glass, Ltd.**
15 Joseph Street
Kitchener, ON N2G 1H9
(519) 658-0724

**Cascade Glass Art Center**
9003 151st Street NE
Redmond, WA 98052
(425) 861-8600
richard@nwartglass.com
www.cascadegac.com

**Casola Stained Glass Studio, Inc.**
11000 Metro Parkway, Suite 11
Ft. Myers, FL 33966-1210
(800) 330-4527
casolasgs@aol.com
www.churcharts.com

**Cavallini Company, Inc.**
3410 Fredricksburg Road
San Antonio, TX 78201-3847
(800) 723-8161
cavallinis@aol.com
www.cavallinistudios.com

**Church Art Glass Studio, Inc.**
12 US Highway 51 S
Clinton, KY 42031

**City Glass Specialty, Inc.**
2124 South Calhoun Street
Ft. Wayne, IN 46802
(260) 744-3301
cityglassspecialty@yahoo.com
www.cityglassspecialty.com

**Conrad Pickel Studio, Inc.**
7777 20th Street
Vero Beach, FL 32966
(772) 567-1710
info@pickelstudio.com
www.pickelstudio.com

**Conrad Schmitt Studios, Inc.**
2405 South 162nd Street
New Berlin, WI 53151
(800) 969-3033
studio@conradschmitt.com
www.conradschmitt.com

**Creative Glassworks, Inc.**
1875 Mealy Street South
Atlantic Beach, FL 32233
(888) 606-0630
staff@creativeglassworks.com
www.creativeglassworks.com

**Creative Stained Glass Studio**
5318 Evergreen Heights Drive
Evergreen, CO 80439
(303) 988-0444
myksds@aol.com
www.csgstudio.com

**Cumberland Stained Glass**
5232 East Trindle Road
Mcchanicsburg, PA 17050
(717) 691-8290
info@cumberlandstainedglass.com
www.cumberlandstainedglass.com

**DePirey International, Inc.**
143 West 29th Street - 7th floor
New York NY 10001
(212) 714 0246
info@depirey.com
www.depirey.com

**Dittrich-Lips Art Glass & Mirror, Inc.**
601 Phlox Avenue
Metairie, LA 70001

**Durhma Studios, Inc.**
330 Eagle Avenue
West Hempstead, NY 11552
(516) 481-5656
durhanstudios@verizon.net

**Ellen Mandelbaum Glass Art**
39-49 46th Street
Long Island City, Queens, NY 11104-1407

**Emmanuel Stained Glass Studios, Inc.**
410 Maple Avenue
Nashville, TN 37210
(800) 326-2228
dennis@emmanuelstudio.com
www.emmanuelstudio.com

**Fox Studios, Inc.**
5901 North College Avenue
Indianapolis, IN 46220
(317) 253-0135
cfox@foxglassstudio.com
www.foxglassstudio.com

**Franklin Art Glass Studios, Inc.**
222 East Sycamore Street
Columbus, OH 43206
(800) 848-7683
info@franklinartglass.com
www.franklinartglass.com

**Full Spectrum Stained Glass**
31323 Colon Road
Colon, MI 49040
(269) 432-2610
fssgi@aol.com
www.churchwindows.net

**Gaytee Stained Glass, Inc.**
2744 Lyndale Avenue South
Minneapolis, MN 55408
(888) 872-4550
gayteeglass@qwest.net
www.gayteestainedglass.com

**Gilbertson's Stained Glass Studio**
705 Madison Street
Lake Geneva, WI 53147-1409
(262) 248-8022
gsgs@genevaonline.com
www.stainedartglass.com

**Guarducci Stained Glass Studios, Inc.**
127 South Main Street
Warrenton, NC 27589
(252) 257-6287
guarducc@bcn.net
www.guarduccistudios.com

**Haeger Stained Glass**
10741 Ridgeview Avenue
San Jose, CA 95127
(408) 251-2019
art-glas0@pacbell.net
www.haegerstainedglass.com

**Hershey Studio**
20907 Acorn Avenue
Milton, IA 52570
(641) 675-3740
artglass@netins.net
www.hersheystudio.com

**Hiemer & Co. Stained Glass Studio**
141 Wabash Avenue
Clifton, NJ 07011
(973) 772-5081
judi@hiemco.com
www.hiemco.com

**Hunt Stained Glass Studios, Inc.**
1756 West Carson Street
Pittsburgh, PA 15219-1036
(412) 391-1796
huntsg@msn.com
www.huntstainedglass.com

**IHS Studios Inc.**
1400 FM 2093
Fredericksburg, TX 78624
(800) 259-1842
sales@ihsstudios.com
www.ihsstudios.com

**J. Piercey Studios, Inc.**
1714 Acme Street
Orlando, FL 32805
(800) 368-9226
jpstudios@aol.com
www.jpiercey.com

**Jennifer's Glass Works, Inc.**
4875 South Atlanta Road
Smyrna, GA 30080
(800) 241-3388
sales@jennifersglassworks.com
www.jennifersglassworks.com

**Jerome R. Durr Studio**
206 Marcellus Street
Syracuse, NY 13204
(800) 552-9836
jrdurr0art@aol.com
www.jeromedurr.com

**Jersey Art Stained Glass Studio**
35-37 Bridge Street
Frenchtown, NJ 08825
(908) 996-2223
mpadovan@jerseyart.com
www.jerseyart.com/

**John W. Winterich & Associates, Inc.**
9545 (M) Midwest Avenue
Cleveland, OH 44125
(800) 255-4544
john@winterichs.com
www.winterichs.com

**Kaleidoscope Stained Glass, Inc.**
1214 North Street
Lafayette, IN 47904
(765) 423-1951
kalscope@geetel.net
www.kaleidoscopeglass.com

**Karen Hendrix Studio of Stained Glass and Sacred Arts, LLC**
907 NW 20th Street
Oklahoma City, OK 73106
(800) 747-3656
khendrix2915@aol.com
www.karenhendrix.com

**Kebrle Stained Glass Studio, Inc.**
2829 Bachman Drive
Dallas, TX 75220
(214) 357-5922
kebrlestainedglass@yahoo.com

**Kinetic Arts Studio, LLC**
Suwanee, Georgia
(678) 447-7356
kelly@kineticarts.org
www.kineticarts.org

**Laws Stained Glass Studios, Inc.**
145 Ebenezer Lane
Statesville, NC 28625
(800) 820-1292
info@lawsstainedglass.com
www.lawsstainedglass.com

**Lynchburg Stained Glass Co.**
P.O. Box 4453
Lynchburg, VA 24502
(434) 525-6168
info@lynchburgstainedglass.com
www.lynchburgstainedglass.com

**Mezalick Design Studio, LLC**
4526 Griscom Street
Philadelphia, PA 19124-3640
(215) 744-5490
nidia@mezalick.com
www.mezalick.com

**Midwestern Stained Glass Studios, Inc.**
214 South Cedar
Nevada, MO 64772

**MJB Art Glass Studio**
118 Pine St.
Pine, AZ 85541-5522

**Mominee Studios, Inc.**
5001 Lincoln Avenue
Evansville, IN 47715-4113
(800) 473-1691
artbox@sigecom.net
www.momineestudios.com

**Morava Studios**
11 Harrison Street
Oak Park, IL 60304
(708) 383-9333
moravastudios@sbcglobal.net

**Moss Stained Glass, LLC**
2501 East Eighth Street
Anderson, IN 46012
(888) 833-6677
tsmith@mossglass.com
www.mossglass.com

**Oakbrook-Esser Studios, Inc.**
129 East Wisconsin Avenue
Oconomowoc, WI 53066-3033
(800) 223-5193
info@oakbrookesser.com
www.oakbrookesser.com

**Pacific Glass, LLC**
47-395 Ahaolelo Road
Kaneohe, Hawaii. 96744
(808) 262-7771
psg@lava.net
www.pacificglassllc.com

**Paul Friend Architectural Stained Glass, LLC**
1916 Old Cuthbert Road, #B-19
Cherry Hill, NJ 08034
(856) 428-9100
paul@paulfriendartglass.com
www.paulfriendartglass.com

**Pearl River Glass Studio**
142 Millsaps Avenue
Jackson, MS 39202
(800) 771-3639
pearlstudio@bellsouth.net
www.prgs.com

**Perry Stained Glass Studio**
470 Front Street North
Issaquah, WA 98027
(425) 392-1600
psgstudio@aol.com
www.perrystainedglass.com

**Phillips Stained Glass Studio, Inc.**
2310 Superior Avenue
Cleveland, OH 44114-4225
(216) 696-0008
mospanphil@yahoo.com

**Pittsburgh Stained Glass Studios**
160 Warden Street
Pittsburgh, PA 15220
(412) 921-2500

**Poremba Stained Glass Studio, Inc.**
20806 Aurora Road
Cleveland, OH 44146-1006
(216) 662-8360
fporemba@alltel.net
www.porembastudio.com

**Powell Brothers & Sons Glass Art**
4050 South Howick Street, #10E
Salt Lake City, UT 84107
(888) 484-5184
jenkyn@aros.net
www.powellbrosglassart.com

**Rambusch Decorating Company**
160 Cornelison Avenue
Jersey City, NJ 07304
(201) 333-2525
martinr@rambusch.com
www.rambusch.com

**Rasmussen Stained Glass, LLC**
9837 Cobblestone Dr.
Warrenton, VA 20186-8620

**Raynal Studios**
P.O. Box 405
Natural Bridge School Road
Natural Bridge Station, VA 24579
(800) 305-0959
raynal@rockbridge.net
www.raynalstudios.com

**Reinarts Stained Glass Studios**
73 Washington Street
Winona, MN 55987-0872
(507) 452-4465
reinarts@hbci.com
www.reinarts.com

**Renaissance Glassworks, Inc.**
3311 Washington Road
McMurray, PA 15317
(724) 969-9009
hbmertz@verizon.net

**Rohlf's Stained & Leaded Glass Studio, Inc.**
783 South Third Avenue
Mt. Vernon, NY 10550
(800) 969-4106
rohlf1@aol.com
www.rohlfstudio.com

**Shobe's Stained Glass Art Studio**
P.O. Box 1692
Huntington, WV 25717-1692

**Stained Glass Associates, Inc.**
P.O. Box 296
Knightdale, NC 27545

**Stained Glass Resources, Inc.**
15 Commercial Drive
Hampden, MA 01036
(800) 883-5052
sgr@map.com
www.stainedglassresources.com

**State of the Art, Inc.**
8705 Unicorn Drive, #B310
Knoxville, TN 37923
(888) 539-0415
sotaglass@aol.com
www.sotaglass.com

**Statesville Stained Glass, Inc.**
136 Christopher Lane
Statesville, NC 28625
(704) 872-5147
dl@statesvillestainedglass.com
www.statesvillestainedglass.com

**The Boulder Stained Glass Studios**
1920 Arapahoe Avenue
Boulder, CO 80302
(303) 449-9030
rdlbsg@comcast.net
www.bldstglst.com

**The J. & R. Lamb Studios**
862 Van Houten Avenue
Clifton, NJ 07013-1374
(877) 700-LAMB
info@lambstudios.com
www.lambstudios.com

**The Judson Studios**
200 South Avenue 66
Los Angeles, CA 90042
(800) 445-8376
info@judsonstudios.com
www.judsonstudios.com

**The Leaded Glass Studio, Inc.**
15801 East 23rd Street South
Independence, MO 64055

**The Lyn Hovey Studios, Inc.**
1476 River Street
Hyde Park, MA 02136
(617) 333-9445
officemgr@lynhoveystudio.com
www.lynhoveystudio.com

**Tooley Art Glass Studio**
2742 San Ramon Drive
Rancho Palos Verdes, CA 90275
(fabrication studio in Louisiana)
(310) 832-0418
duncan@tooleystudio.com
duncan@church-windows.com
www.church-windows.com
www.tooleystudio.com

**Tulsa Stained Glass Co.**
7976 East 41st Street
Tulsa, OK 74145
(918) 664-8604
richard@tulsastainedglass.com
www.tulsastainedglass.com

**Washington Art Glass Studio**
6618 Walker Mill Road
Capitol Heights, MD 20743
(301) 735-6292
washartglass@comcast.net
www.washingtonartglass.com

**Whitworth Stained Glass**
700 South Bridge Street
Brady, TX 76825
(800) 318-0122
jack@whitworthstainedglass.com
www.whitworthstainedglass.com

**Willet Hauser Architectural Glass, Inc.**
10 East Moreland Avenue
Philadelphia, PA 19118
(800) 533-3960
info@willethauser.com
www.willethauser.com

**Williams Stained Glass Studio**
1115 Castle Shannon Boulevard
Pittsburgh, PA 15234
(412) 344-0220
wsg@williamsstainedglass.com
www.williamsstainedglass.com

**Window Creations, LLC**
P.O. Box 485
Ottoville, OH 45876
(800) 633-4571
bstudios@bright.net
www.bstudios.net

*St. Mary's Catholic Church, Marshalltown, Iowa*

# Index

## A

All Saints Episcopal Church
   Los Angeles, Calif., 168
   Pasadena, Calif., cover, 200
All Souls Unitarian Universalist Church (Colorado Springs, Colo.), 70
Annunciation Greek Orthodox Church (Wauwatosa, Wis.), 100
Anshe Emet Synagogue (Chicago, Ill.), 8
Appraisal
   process 33–35
   report 35
   tools 31
   updating 36
Arborlawn United Methodist Church (Fort Worth, Texas), 182
Art Glass by Wells, ii
Ascalon Studios, ii

## B

Baker Memorial United Methodist Church (St. Charles, Ill.), 22
Basilica of the Sacred Heart (Notre Dame, Ind.), xii
Baylor Baptist Hospital (Plano, Texas), 11
Bellevue Baptist Church (Cordova, Tenn.), 196
Blessed Sacrament Church (Valley Stream, N.Y.), 144
Botti Studios of Architectural Arts, Inc., ii
Broadmoor United Methodist (Shreveport, La.), 142
Burnham, 200–201

## C

Carmelite Sisters' Le Mans Glass Works, xii
Cartoon, 36
   secure location 35

Casola Stained Glass, ii
Cathedral of Our Lady of Perpetual Help (Oklahoma City, Okla.), 24, 108
Cathedral of St. Helena (Helena, Mont.), 4–5, 24, 158
Cathedral of St. John the Baptist (Savannah, Ga.), 11
Cathedral of the Ozarks (Siloam Springs, Ark.), 84
Cedar Valley Community Church (Waterloo, Iowa), 66
Central Baptist Church (Winchester, Ky.), 80, 86
Christ and Holy Trinity Episcopal Church (Westport, Conn.), 94, 201
Christ Church Episcopal (Grosse Point Farms, Mich.), 114, 176, 204
Church Insurance Fine Arts Policy 35
Church of St. Frances of Rome (Bronx, N.Y.), 212
Church of the Holy Cross (Paris, Texas), iv
Church of the Incarnation Episcopal (Dallas, Texas), 17, 74, 132
Church of St. Luke (St. Paul, Minn.), 231
Congregation Rodeph Shalom (Philadelphia, Penn.), 236
Connick, 9, 38, 90, 92, 201–202
Connick Associates, 94
Conrad Pickel Studio Inc., ii
Conrad Schmitt, 61, 90
Conrad Schmitt Studios, ii, x, 13, 14, 36, 50, 96, 98, 100, 162, 164, 186, 188, 212–213
Conservators, Stained Glass, 20–21
Cottage Glass, ii
Cox & Sons, 102
Creative Glassworks, ii

## D

D'Ascenzo, 104, 106, 202–203
Dale de verre. *See Faceted Glass*

## E

Emil Frei Art Glass Co., 36
Enterprise Art, ii

## F

Faceted Glass, 61, 178–193
First Baptist Church
    Germantown, Tenn., 196
    Seymour, Texas, 88
    Wichita Falls, Texas, 180
First Congregational (Kenosha, Wis.), 164
First Lutheran Church (Nashville, Tenn.) 238
First Presbyterian Church
    Birmingham, Ala., 104, 202
    Gulfport, Miss., viii
    Hollywood, Calif., 116
    McKenzie, Tenn., 13
    Plymouth, Mich., 215
    Raleigh, N.C., 5, 10, 76
    Ridgewood, N.J., 176
    River Forest, Ill. 57
First United Methodist Church
    St. Petersburg, Fla., 134
    Colorado Springs, Colo., 21, 82
    Gulfport, Miss., x
    Marion, Iowa, 78
    McKinney, Texas, 6
Frei, Emil, 24, 58, 90, 108, 203–204

## G

Glass by Knight ii
Greendale Community Church
    (Greendale, Wis.) 14
Gruenke, Gunar x

## H

Haeger Stained Glass, ii
Heaton, 114, 204
Hiemer & Co. Stained Glass Studio, ii
Holy Rosary Parish (Bozeman, Mont.), 209
Holy Family Cathedral (Tulsa, Okla.), 234
Hope Stained Glass, ii
House of Hope Presbyterian Church
    (St. Paul, Minn.), 38, 92, 170, 201, 207
Howard, Len R. (Kent, Conn.), 219
Hucher, Eugene, xii
Hurricane Katrina, vi, viii, 49

## I

Idlewild Presbyterian Church (Memphis, Tenn.), 14
Imagine Stained Glass, ii
Immanuel Congregational Church
    (Brush, Colo.), 68
Inspecting Stained Glass, 52–54
    bluge, 52
    braces, 53
    cement, 54
    glass, 53
    lead, 52

## J

Judson, 2, 61, 90, 116, 118, 168, 178, 190, 204–205

## K

Kebrle Stained Glass Studio, Inc., ii, 223

## L

Lamb, 90, 124, 126, 206–207
Landau, Jacob 240
LaSalle Street Church (Chicago, Ill.), 30
La Farge, 61, 90, 120, 122, 205–206
    replication 63
Leaded stained glass, 61
LeCompte, 170, 207
Loire, Gabriel 192, 208
Loman Studios, ii

## M

Maitland Armstrong & Company, 2, 200
Mayer, Franz, 61, 90, 110, 112, 166, 208–209
Moody Memorial First United Methodist Church (Galveston, Texas), 192
Moss Stained Glass, LLC, ii, 223
Munich of Chicago, 128, 130, 209
Myers Park Presbyterian Church (Charlotte, N.C.), 12, 150

## N

National Presbyterian Church (Washington, D.C.), 146, 184
New Stained Glass 26–28
    budget 28
    color 27
    design style 26
    shape 27
    theme 26
Nichols Hills United Methodist Church (Oklahoma City, Okla.), 203
Northern Oklahoma College 42, 54
North Avenue Presbyterian Church (Atlanta, Ga.), 13, 18, 63, 152, 214

## O

Old Stone Church (Cleveland, Ohio), 120, 206

## P

Palm Valley Lutheran Church (Round Rock, Texas), 17
Pax Christi Catholic (Rochester, Minn.), 29
Payne, 90, 132, 134, 136, 210–211
Perry Stained Glass Studio, ii, 224
Philbrook Museum (Tulsa, Okla.), 106
Phipps, Ball, & Burnham, 138
President's Window, Iona College (New Rochelle, N.Y.), 172
Preston Art Glass Studio, ii
Preventive maintenance, 44
Protecting stained glass, 22–23, 44, 56–57

## R

Rambusch, 140, 211
Rambusch Decorating Company, 224
Rambusch Studios, 28
Rancho Bernardo Community Presbyterian Church (San Diego, Calif.), 190
Raynal Studios, ii, 224
Reform Congregation Keneseth Israel, (Philadelphia, Penn.) 240
Reinarts Stained Glass Studios, ii, 29, 36, 54, 61, 195, 224
Replacement value, 10–25
    custom > catalog, 15–16
    design > no design, 14–15
    figures > medallions > symbols, 17
    good > poor condition, 19
    multi-layers > single layer, 13–14
    national firm > local artist, 18
    older > new, 10–11
    painted/fired > stained, 12
    protected > unprotected, 22
    signed > unsigned, 23
    small > large, 10
    varied lines > straight lines, 12
Restoration, 20–21, 45–47
River Terrace Church (East Lansing, Mich.), 13
Rohlf's Stained & Leaded Glass Studio, Inc., ii, x, 20, 61, 63, 90, 122, 142, 144, 160, 172, 174, 212, 224
Rohlf, Peter x, 20, 63

## S

Sacred Heart (Indianapolis, Ind.), 50
Saint Mary Cathedral (Austin, Texas), 209, 216
Salem Stained Glass, 15, 17, 41, 61
Second Presbyterian, (Indianapolis, Ind.) 154
Shenandoah Stained Glass Studio, 54, 57
SLFirpo Design/Craft, ii
St. Aidan's (Westwood, Los Angeles, Calif.), 116
St. Aloysius Church Gonzaga College High School, (Washington, D.C.) 72

St. Ambrose Cathedral (Des Moines, Iowa), 96
St. Edmond Catholic Parish (Oak Park, Ill.) 2, 156
St. Elizabeth Ann Seton Catholic Church (New Berlin, Wis.), 162
St. Francis of Assisi Church (Donaldsonville, La.), 213
St. Francis Xavier (Enid, Okla.), 130
St. Gertrude Catholic Church (Franklin Park, Ill.), 100
St. James Church (Los Angeles, Calif.), 205
St. John's Episcopal Cathedral (Jacksonville, Fla.), 136, 140, 210
St. John's Episcopal Church (Butte, Mont.) 124, 148
St. Joseph Catholic Parish (Butte, Mont.), 128
St. Luke's United Methodist Church (Oklahoma City, Okla.), 58
St. Mark's Episcopal Church (Cheyenne, Wyo.), 102, 112
St. Mary's Catholic Church (Marshalltown, Iowa), 226
St. Mary's Episcopal Cathedral (Memphis, Tenn.), 219
St. Mary's Greek Ruthenian (New York City, N.Y.), 186
St. Michael's Catholic Church (Biloxi), 49
St. Michael the Archangel Cemetery (Palatine, Ill.), 188
St. Paul's Episcopal Church (Key West, Fla.), 138
St. Paul's National Historic Landmark (Mt. Vernon, N.Y.), 122
St. Paul Baptist Church (Paris, Texas), 10
St. Paul School (Concord, N.H.), 110, 166
St. Paul United Methodist Church (Louisville, Ky.), 22
St. Peter's by the Sea Episcopal Church (Gulfport, Miss.) v, vi
St. Peter's Episcopal Church (Charlotte, N.C.), 126, 207
St. Stephen Presbyterian (Fort Worth, Texas), 208
St. Xavier Parish (Missoula, Mont.), 5

Stained Glass Association of America, ii, 24, 63
Studios, different types of, 39–43

# T

Temple Israel (Columbus, OH), 198
The Boulder Stained Glass Studios, ii, 225
The J. & R. Lamb Studios, 225
The Judson Studios, 225
The Leaded Glass Studio, ii
Tiffany, 13, 18, 21, 61, 63, 146, 148
  replication, 63
Tiffany, Louis Comfort, 23, 90, 213–214
Tooley Art Glass Studio, ii, 225
Trinity United Methodist Church (Huntsville, Ala.), 12

# U

University Baptist Church (Fort Worth, Texas), 28, 211
University of Illinois Neumann Center, 54

# V

Velasco, Leandro, 28

# W

Weston and Leighton of Minneapolis, 31
Whitworth Stained Glass, ii, 225
Willet, 13, 90, 150, 152, 154, 176, 184, 215–216
Willet Hauser Architectural Glass, Inc., 225
Window Creations, ii

# Z

Zettler, 2, 5, 24, 61, 90, 156, 158, 216–217

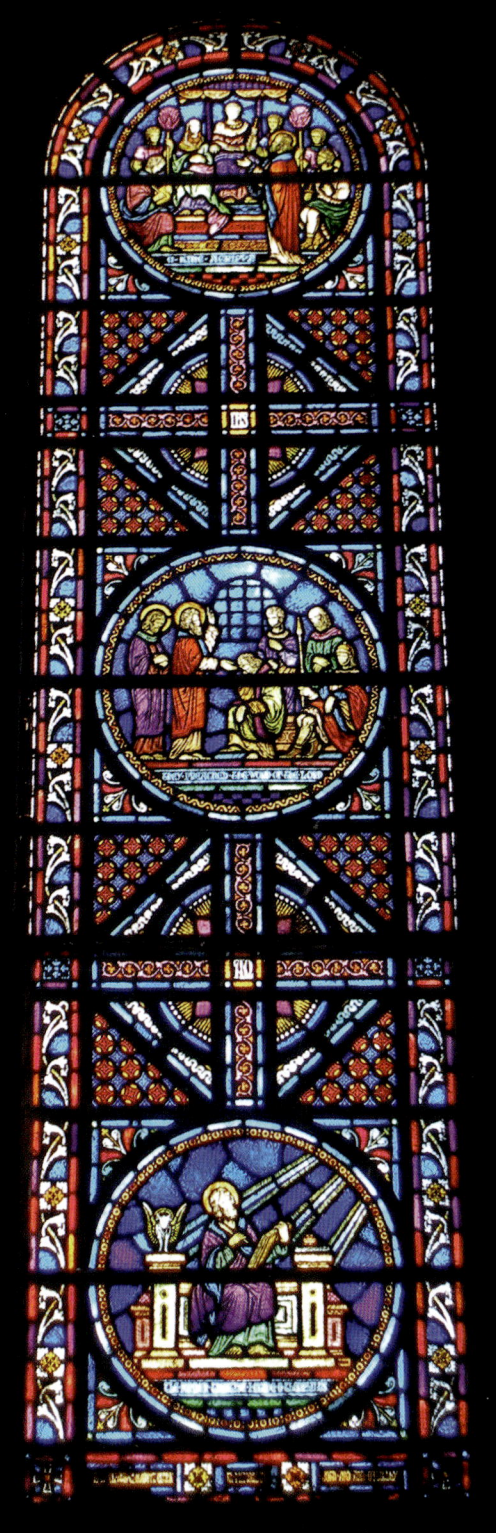

*Church of St. Luke, St. Paul, Minn.*
*Designed by Weston and Leighton of Minneapolis*

# Dr. Gary M. Gray

Dr. Gary M. Gray, stained glass consultant, has inspected and appraised stained glass in some two thousand churches and synagogues. He has conducted stained glass work in every state (among the "lower 48"), and is the author of twelve books (including *God's Story Through God's Light*) and the former editor of two national Christian magazines. He holds graduate degrees from Phillips University, Southern Methodist University and Notre Dame University. He also holds an American University Professional Certificate in Church Management and a D. Ed. from Oklahoma State University.

Early in his career, Dr. Gray was the Executive Director of the National Institute on Church Management where he taught and consulted with thousands of ministers, church administrators, and military chapel administrators on the concept of mission oriented management. The NICM was sanctioned by the National Association of Church Business Administration. Writing along with his brother, Dr. Robert N. Gray, the five-volume *Managing the Church* series served as pioneer volumes in this new and evolving profession. In 1996, Dr. Gray was named to the Church Management Hall of Fame.

Concurrent with his stained glass consultation, Dr. Gray has developed into a historian, writer and actor renowned for his brilliant and historically accurate portrayals of eight of America's greatest citizens: Presidents Washington, Jefferson, A. Johnson, Garfield, T. Roosevelt and FDR, plus General of the Army, Douglas MacArthur, and Barry Goldwater. These portrayals were all gathered together in his recent book *Mr. Presidents: Voices of Freedom, Equality and Dignity*. See MrPresidents.com for details.

Dr. Gray may be contacted at 800-821-9595 or gary.gray@sbcglobal.net. Please visit americanstainedglass.org for more information on the American Consultation on Stained Glass.

Orders for individual and bulk copies of *The 2008-2009 Stained Glass Appraisal Guide* may be made by visiting www.americanstainedglass.org or by e-mailing stainedglassappraisalguide@yahoo.com. For more information, please call (800) 762-6759.

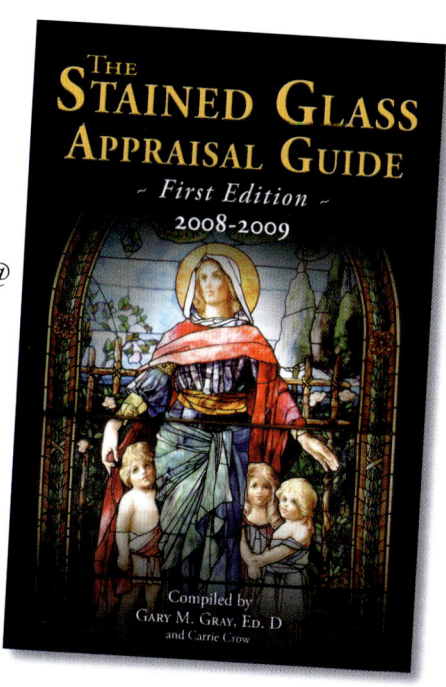

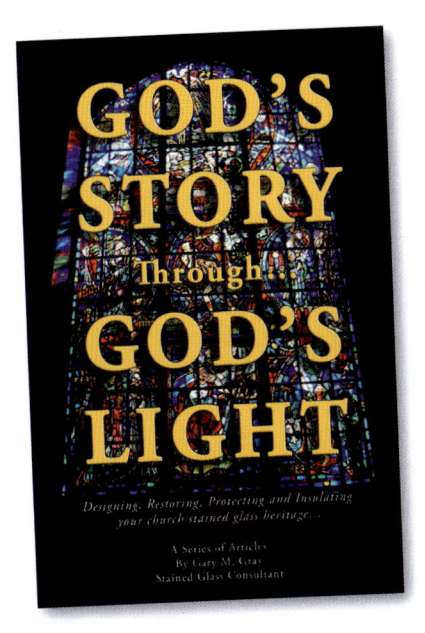

Dr. Gray's *God's Story Through God's Light* can be purchased for $10.95 (plus $2.00 shipping) or may be sent free via e-mail upon request to the stainedglassappraisalguide@yahoo.com.
ISBN: 0-595-40374.

Carrie Crow, ACSG vice president of communications and research, has worked with Dr. Gray since 2005. She holds a degree in public relations from Campbell University and a master's degree in international studies from Oklahoma State University.

# Notes

*Right: Holy Family Cathedral, Tulsa, Okla.*

# Notes

*Right: Skylight at Congregation Rodeph Shalom, Philadelphia, Penn.*

# Notes